A Reader's Guide to
Fifty American Novels

Reader's Guide Series
General Editor: Andrew Mylett

A Reader's Guide to

Fifty American Novels

by Ian Ousby

Heinemann – London
Barnes & Noble – New York

Heinemann Educational Books Ltd

LONDON EDINBURGH MELBOURNE AUCKLAND HONG KONG
SINGAPORE KUALA LUMPUR NEW DELHI IBADAN NAIROBI
JOHANNESBURG KINGSTON PORT OF SPAIN

First published 1979 by Pan Books as
An Introduction to Fifty American Novels in the Pan Literature
Guides Series
First published in this casebound edition 1979

ISBN (UK) 0 435 18744 9
ISBN (USA) 0-06-495318-1

Library of Congress Number 79-53437

Published in Great Britain by
Heinemann Educational Books Ltd
22 Bedford Square, London WC1B 3HH
Published in the U.S.A. 1979 by
Harper & Row Publishers, Inc.
Barnes & Noble Import Division

Printed and bound in Great Britain by
Richard Clay (The Chaucer Press) Ltd,
Bungay, Suffolk

Contents

Introduction

Fifty, or even thirty years ago this book would probably not have been written. If it had, it would have needed to begin on a defensive and apologetic note. In the nineteenth century American fiction produced its full share of 'classics' – Melville's *Moby Dick*, Hawthorne's *Scarlet Letter*, Twain's *Huckleberry Finn* and so forth. In the twentieth century American novelists began to receive international recognition: the award of the Nobel Prize to Sinclair Lewis in 1930 is an obvious example. Even in America itself intellectuals (let alone general readers) often approached their literature in a shame-faced or indifferent spirit. Irving Babbitt, the influential Harvard professor, was given to remarking that America was where Europe went when it died – an epigram hardly designed to encourage interest in American culture. In 1930 the Yale University Library still listed *Moby Dick* under 'Cetology' rather than 'American Literature'. Outside America the lack of respect for its fiction was even more striking. Sydney Smith's famous gibe ('In the four quarters of the globe, who reads an American book?') still echoed in English ears; and it was not uncommon to hear otherwise well-read men confess to an ignorance of Hawthorne or Melville without embarrassment.

Today, of course, the situation is very different. Most major American novels are widely available in cheaply priced editions and their study is assumed to be a natural part of the average American student's liberal education. On the scholarly level, the study of American literature has assumed the proportions of a minor industry; it has traced a familiar success story from log cabin to Guggenheim grants. Its characteristic failure, indeed, is no longer the neglect of major figures but the endless exhumation of minor ones. Some American scholars are willing to proffer, say, William Gilmore Simms (whom this book does not mention anywhere else) as an important novelist. There is not merely a substantial body of scholarship and criticism about Edgar Allan Poe; there is a regular bi-annual journal, *Poe Studies*. In time there will no doubt be a *Dos Passos Newsletter* and even a *John Barth Newsletter*.

The emergence of 'American studies' began in the 1920s. Ironically enough it received its initial impetus from a book by an Englishman: D. H. Lawrence's *Studies in Classic American Literature* (1923). Reaching out for new modes of expression in his own art, Lawrence responded eagerly to that new voice he detected in American writing:

> We like to think of the old-fashioned American classics as children's books. Just childishness, on our part. The old American art-speech contains an alien quality, which belongs to the American continent and to nowhere else. But, of course, as long as we insist on reading the books as children's tales, we miss all that.

For all the quirkiness and dogmatism of many of its judgements, *Studies in Classic American Literature* remains probably the best general introduction to its subject. It has been profoundly influential; for example, most essays on Fenimore Cooper (including my own in this volume) are essentially elaborations of Lawrence's view.

After Lawrence the interpretation of American literature passed largely into the hands of Americans and academic scholars. Since the late 1920s there has been a steady flow of classic studies of American culture and fiction: V. L. Parrington's three-volume *Main Currents in American Thought* (1927–1930), Van Wyck Brooks' multi-volume *The Makers and Finders: A History of the Writer in America* (1936–1952), Perry Miller's *The New England Mind* (1939), F. O.

Matthiessen's *American Renaissance* (1941) and Richard
Chase's *The American Novel and Its Tradition* (1957). Today
much about these books seems dated, but none is of purely
antiquarian interest. In fact, they still form the central core
of any reading list with which the serious student of American
fiction should equip himself.

They do not present a single or unanimous interpretation
of the American novel. There have been, for example, continual clashes between the proponents of the 'genteel' school
of fiction represented by Henry James and the 'frontier'
school represented by Mark Twain. But by far the most
serious divergence has centred on the rival merits of
'romance' and 'realism'. On the whole, earlier scholars like
Parrington and Brooks saw the main and characteristic
achievement of American fiction in the realist novels that
began to appear after the Civil War: novels that deal with
contemporary issues and with the individual in society.
Later critics like Matthiessen and (in more extreme fashion)
Chase placed their emphasis on writers of romance like
Hawthorne and Melville – writers whose main preoccupation is with man alone or man and nature, rather than man
and society.

For all their differences these pioneers of American
criticism were undertaking a common task. To men like
Parrington and Matthiessen the writing of literary history
was not an academic exercise but an attempt at cultural
(and sometimes even personal) self-definition. Like D. H.
Lawrence they were intrigued by that 'alien quality' which
America had introduced into world culture; their interest
lay in analysing what F. R. Leavis has called 'the Americanness of American literature'. This, of course, is both inevitable
and proper. Comparing English and American poetry
Wallace Stevens remarked: 'We live in two different physical
worlds and it is not nonsense to think that that matters.'
Even the casual reader of American fiction will quickly find
himself fascinated by the divergences from English and
European traditions of the novel.

But this zealous attempt to identify the 'American voice'

in fiction can lead to distortion. It often assumes that the New World represents a sharp and absolute break with the Old. American writers are portrayed as completely cut off from older traditions, free to start anew by themselves. In historical terms, this is simply not the case. As the early sections of this book show, earlier American novelists like Charles Brockden Brown and Fenimore Cooper began as imitators of English fiction; only later did peculiarly American characteristics emerge. Even when this happened the American writer was not necessarily alienated from the European heritage. A figure like Mark Twain, so often praised as uniquely 'American' because of his frontier attitudes and his rich folk idiom, still shows identifiable affiliations with Dickens and the European realists. Complete cultural freedom was not only impossible; it was also undesirable. In his introduction to *Pudd'nhead Wilson* F. R. Leavis gives a typically acerbic, but in this case justified, rebuke to those Americanists who regard lack of connection with Europe as a virtue: 'Such an alienation could only be an impoverishment: no serious attempt has been made to show that any sequel to disinheritance could replace the heritage lost.'

The very terms 'Americanness' and 'American voice' can also carry the misleading implication that America is a uniform and homogeneous nation. Nothing in fact could be further from the truth. America's variety is often difficult for foreigners to appreciate. The English, in particular, are almost addicted to large-scale generalizations about America; they sometimes appear to envisage the country as one vast superhighway punctuated occasionally by gas stations, race riots, golf courses and skyscrapers. A look at the map can produce salutary results. It reminds us that Boston and Seattle are further apart than Boston and Rome, and that America's southern parts are in the tropical zone while, with the acquisition of Alaska, its northern territory comes close to the Arctic circle.

Such size inevitably creates diversity. Particularly in the eighteenth and nineteenth centuries, when communications were of the most primitive sort, different communities naturally developed their own peculiar flavours. New England, Virginia, Missouri: these became the names not just of different places, but of subtly different attitudes to life. Regional divergences could be sharp enough to produce the sort of hostility shown in the Civil War. In cultural terms, the result was a literature where the inflections of regionalism were all-important. If the reader detects different notes in the work of Cooper, Hawthorne and Twain, he should remember that these are partly attributable to the fact that the first writer came from New York State, the second from Massachusetts and the third from Missouri. To call any one of these men more 'American' than the others would be mere parochialism. Faced with such variety the critic can only confess that there is no 'American voice' in fiction: there are American voices.

The growth of modern communications has inevitably destroyed much of the regional flavour of American life and culture. Yet its diversity has been guaranteed by the multifarity of ethnic groups. The Red Indian, of course, was there before the white man arrived. He was succeeded by English, Dutch and French settlers – and black slaves. Their numbers were later swelled by successive influxes of Scandinavian, Irish, Italian, Russian Jewish, German Jewish, Puerto Rican and Mexican immigrants. The 'melting pot' theory of American society, beloved by so many generations of sociologists, stressed the country's ability to assimilate different racial stocks into a unified whole. But what is most likely to impress the observer of contemporary America is the ability of various ethnic groups to retain, as much as to lose, their distinctive heritages.

Of course, many of the standard generalizations about the distinctive quality of American fiction remain true. Early American novels, the products of primitive and recently established communities, tended to concentrate on abstract issues rather than those nuances of social structure which tend to obsess the English novelist. In formal terms this led to a love of symbolism and allegory instead of a detailed

fidelity to life's surface. This habit also created a preference
for lonely, grand and unsociable heroes which has survived
into current American fiction. When later American
novelists turned towards realism, they often did so with a
gritty inelegance that can, in English eyes, seem either
engagingly frank or disconcertingly uncouth. Yet still the
most important generalization about the American novel is
that all generalizations have innumerable and important
exceptions. It is a field of study that frustrates the seeker
after easy truths, and rewards those who cherish variety and
abundance. The reader of American fiction should bear in
mind Robert Frost's warning in his poem about Christopher
Columbus:

America is hard to see.
Less partial witnesses than he
In book on book have testified
They could not see it from outside—
Or inside either for that matter.
We know the literary chatter.

A few words about the organization of this book. It is
designed to be used in two ways. It may be read as a continuous whole by the student interested in the history of
American fiction. But the individual sections can also be
treated as self-contained units by the reader in search of
information about a specific writer or work.

As with a party guest list, my inclusions and omissions
are bound to offend somebody. My criteria of selection
have been both aesthetic value and historical significance.
I have dealt in detail with Mark Twain's *Pudd'nhead Wilson*,
for example, not because it exercised a great influence on
succeeding writers or because it has attracted a great deal
of critical attention; I do so simply because it is a very good
novel. On the other hand, Charles Brockden Brown's
Wieland is analysed individually because of its historical
interest as the first American novel of any substance. These
grounds seemed to justify its inclusion over, say, Kate
Chopin's *The Awakening* – a far better novel but one of

infinitely less importance in the development of American fiction.

It is inevitable that one should feel a book to be the sum of one's own errors and of other people's good advice. In particular I should like to thank Andrew Mylett, the most patient, encouraging and knowledgeable of editors. I would also thank Arthur Sale, who first introduced me to American literature, were it not for the fact that he is so often being acknowledged in books by his ex-students. It would be foolish to try putting my debt to Heather Dubrow into words.

1 The Beginnings

By the end of the eighteenth century America boasted a history that, for its brevity, had an air of epic grandeur. To early voyagers and explorers the country had offered an exciting vision of a 'New World', an immense virgin continent. The process of gaining a foothold in the wilderness began in the early seventeenth century. In 1620 the Pilgrim Fathers arrived in Massachusetts to establish a settlement where they could enjoy freedom of worship. During the same period the Southern states – first Virginia, then Maryland, Georgia, North and South Carolina – were attracting English farmers. In the eighteenth century an influx of Dutch, German and Swedish immigrants led to the creation of the so-called 'Middle Colonies' – New York, New Jersey, Pennsylvania and Delaware. With the War of Independence (1774–1783) America ceased to be a colonial experiment and became a self-governing nation.

Yet the work of pioneering was far from complete. The American writer Henry Adams began his *History of the United States of America during the First Administration of Jefferson* (1889) with this description of the country:

> According to the census of 1800, the United States of America contained 5,308,483 persons. In the same year the British Islands contained upwards of fifteen millions; the French republic, more than twenty-seven millions. Nearly one fifth of the American people were negro slaves; the true political population consisted of four and a half million free whites, or less than one million able-bodied males, on whose shoulders fell

the burden of a continent. Even after two centuries of struggle the land was still untamed; forest covered every portion, except here and there a strip of cultivated soil; the minerals lay undisturbed in their rocky beds, and more than two thirds of the people clung to the seaboard within fifty miles of tidewater, where alone the wants of civilized life could be supplied. The centre of population rested within eighteen miles of Baltimore, north and east of Washington.

A nation so involved in establishing the rudiments of civilization could not be expected to produce much literature of its own. The earliest American writings are small in number and of largely specialist interest. In New England and Virginia settlers wrote topographical descriptions and local histories. The religious tradition of Massachusetts bred its own brand of devotional literature: the poetry of Anne Bradstreet (1612–1672) and Edward Taylor (1642–1729), and the sermons of Cotton Mather (1663–1728) and Jonathan Edwards (1703–1758). In the later part of the eighteenth century minor literati began to emerge. Benjamin Franklin (1706–1790) included the role of author in his exacting definition of the all-round man; the poet Philip Freneau (1752–1832) wrote an elegy to Red Indians and an ode to Tom Paine; Washington Irving (1783–1859) published graceful sketches and stories.

On the whole Americans borrowed their culture from Europe. They read and imitated the fashionable English novels of the day. Various candidates for the title of 'first American novel' have been advanced: Charlotte Lennox's *Life of Harriet Stuart* (1751), Thomas Atwood Digges' *Adventures of Alonzo* (1775) and William Hill Brown's *The Power of Sympathy* (1789). But these works are American in name only; they are really provincial pendants to English traditions of sentimental and picaresque fiction. As late as 1831 the French observer Alexis de Tocqueville could note of American novelists: 'They paint with the borrowed colours of foreign manners, and as they hardly ever portray the country of their birth as it actually is, they are seldom popular there . . . So the Americans have not yet, properly speaking got any literature.'

The work of Charles Brockden Brown and James Fenimore Cooper does not break with this pattern; it shows no sudden emergence of a distinctive 'American voice' in fiction. Brown began as an imitator of the English novelist William Godwin, and Cooper as a follower of Sir Walter Scott. Even at its best their work still has an air of clumsy provincial imitation. Yet both men tried to assimilate their experience of America into their writing. Moreover, they both won a degree of international recognition that had eluded their predecessors. America had at last begun to export as well as import fiction.

Charles Brockden Brown

To Charles Brockden Brown belongs the distinction of being the first professional writer in America. Born in Philadelphia in 1771 of a Quaker family, Brown was originally educated for the law, but his rebellious temperament, increasingly radical political views and love of literature made him ill-suited to the profession. He soon abandoned its practice and went to New York to embark on a literary career. His first published work was *Alcuin: A Dialogue* (1797), a treatise advocating women's rights, but Brown soon turned to fiction. His four major novels, all deeply influenced by the English school of Gothic fiction, were written at headlong speed: *Wieland or The Transformation* (1798), *Arthur Mervyn* (1799), *Ormond* (1799) and *Edgar Huntly* (1799). Three later novels – the unfinished *Memoirs of Stephen Calvert* (1800), *Clara Howard* (1801) and *Jane Talbot* (1801) – show a great decline in power, for Brown's interest was already turning to non-fiction. He even came to resent his reputation as a novelist for distracting attention from his later work as historian and political polemicist. He died of tuberculosis in 1810.

In his own age Brown was highly respected by both American and English readers. He was especially admired by the Romantic poets: Keats found *Wieland* 'a very powerful book' and Shelley recognized in Brown a kindred spirit. Yet today his importance is largely historical for, except at rare moments, his novels do not come alive for the modern reader. He has been praised – and rightly – for his realistic descriptions of city life and his insights into feminine psychology, but these occupy only a small part of his work. For the most part it consists of stilted and lurid melodrama obviously derived from Gothic novels like Mrs Radcliffe's *The Mysteries of Udolpho* (1794) and William Godwin's *Caleb Williams* (1794). It has considerable dramatic power but, perhaps owing to the speed at which Brown wrote, it frequently topples over into the ludicrous and incredible.

Nor can it be said that Brown's fiction succeeds in striking a distinctively American note. *Edgar Huntly* makes use of the American landscape and Red Indians, but usually Brown's novels travel the well-worn paths of English Gothic. America had achieved its political independence from the Old World some twenty years before Brown began writing; his work shows that the achievement of cultural independence was a slower and more complicated process.

Wieland

SUMMARY   The elder Wieland is a prosperous farmer in Mettingen, near Philadelphia; he is also a gloomy religious fanatic. One day he goes out to pray in a small 'temple' that he has constructed some distance from his house. After he enters the building a ghostly light is seen and an explosion is heard. When Wieland's wife and brother arrive at the spot they find him badly burnt and bruised. He dies soon afterwards; overcome by shock, his wife quickly follows him to the grave.

Their children, Clara and Theodore Wieland, grow up happily in the care of an aunt and make friends with Catharine Pleyel, the daughter of a neighbour. Wieland marries Catharine and returns to the family mansion, while Clara chooses to live in a separate house on the estate. The Wielands have several children of their own in addition to an adopted daughter, Louisa. A visiting English officer, Major Stuart, recognizes Louisa as his own daughter; apparently the mother had mysteriously fled from England with the child. Henry Pleyel, Catharine's brother, returns from Europe to join the group at Mettingen. He is Wieland's temperamental opposite – being light-hearted where the other follows his father in being morbidly religious – but they become firm friends.

One evening Wieland has a strange experience on his way to the temple. He is called back by his wife's voice, yet when he returns to the house he finds that Catharine has not spoken. The ghostly voice is later heard warning Pleyel that his fiancée Theresa is dead. This news is confirmed when a mailboat arrives from Europe.

One day Clara sees a stranger near her house. From a distance he looks uncouth, but when he comes closer he turns out to be striking in appearance and well-spoken. Shortly afterwards Clara is woken in the night by the sound of whispered voices coming from a closet in her bedroom: she can hear two men apparently plotting her murder. She rushes from the room in panic and collapses in the hall. Her brother and Pleyel are awakened and brought to her aid by the mysterious voice, but no sign of any intruders can be found. When she is in the temple one evening Clara again hears the mysterious voice, warning her to avoid the place. She is rescued by the timely appearance of Pleyel, who takes her home.

Pleyel explains that he has met the stranger and recognized him as Carwin, an acquaintance from Europe. When Carwin visits the Wieland household Clara finds him still impressive and mysterious. When Carwin hears about the puzzling events that have been occurring he is deeply interested. Although he admits that supernatural explanations are possible, he points out that the incidents could have been caused by trickery.

Carwin's repeated visits upset Pleyel. Clara realizes that he is in love with her and fears the newcomer as a rival; she eagerly waits for Pleyel to propose marriage. One night in her room she remembers the previous occasion when she overheard the whispered conspiracy and becomes frightened. Again she hears the mysterious voice warning her, and when she opens the closet Carwin comes out. He confesses that he had been planning to rape her but reassures her that she need no longer fear: he has been impressed by the mysterious power that apparently guards her. The next morning Pleyel confronts Clara, abusing her for having secret midnight assignations with a murderer and a thief. When she goes to seek her brother's advice about answering this calumny, Clara finds that Pleyel has almost persuaded Wieland to believe it. She returns to plead with Pleyel. He tells her of the growth of his love and his fear of Carwin's rivalry. The previous day he had learnt from the newspapers that Carwin was wanted in Dublin for theft and murder. That night he had overheard Carwin and Clara in a lovers' conversation. Her frantic denials go unheeded, and Pleyel prepares to return to Europe.

Clara receives a letter from Carwin asking for an interview that night at her house. Yet when she keeps the appointment she finds the murdered body of Catharine in the bedroom. Almost immediately she learns that Wieland's children have also been killed. She collapses with shock. During her convalescence she is tended by her mother's brother, Thomas Cambridge. To her surprise she learns that the murderer was not Carwin but Wieland, who has already been convicted and imprisoned. She reads a transcript of his speech to the court in which he explains how the voice of God commanded him to murder his wife and children. When Clara asks to see her brother she learns to her horror that he now believes that God wants him to murder her and Pleyel.

On her recovery she returns to her house despite its macabre associations. To her surprise she encounters Carwin: he protests his innocence of the tragedy that has overtaken the Wieland family. He did, he admits, practise ventriloquism and mimicry on several occasions: he counterfeited Catharine's voice, the amorous conversation between himself and Clara, and the voice that warned her of danger. Yet he insists that he was not responsible for the voice that incited Wieland to murder, and this is corroborated when Wieland himself appears, escaped from prison and intent on killing Clara. Carwin saves her life by counterfeiting the voice of God, and telling Wieland that he should not have killed his wife and children. Stricken with guilt and horror Wieland kills himself. When he hears the story Pleyel agrees with Carwin that the dead man was a victim of religious mania. Pleyel has remained in America, since he has discovered that his fiancée was not dead as reported. He marries her.

For a while Clara stays at her house, but when it burns down she agrees to go to Europe. There she sees Pleyel and, after his wife's death, marries him. She also sees Major Stuart. He has discovered the reason for his wife's flight to America: she had been seduced by the treacherous Maxwell and was ashamed to face her husband. Stuart meets Maxwell and challenges him to a duel; but the night before the encounter Stuart is stabbed to death by an unknown assassin.

CRITICAL COMMENTARY   Since there were so few precedents in his own country it was natural that Brown should have turned to English fiction for guidance, and it was equally natural that he should have fallen under the influence of the Gothic school. For at the end of the eighteenth century Gothic was the dominant mode in art, architecture and literature throughout Europe. It had been introduced into English fiction by Horace Walpole's *The Castle of Otranto* (1764) and it had recently inspired Mrs Radcliffe's *The Mysteries of Udolpho* and William Godwin's excellent *Caleb Williams*. Gothic depended on a rejection of the civilized, the tame and the ordinary in the name of the wild, the thrilling and the frightening. It took the sublimities of nature or the gloom of the medieval past as its setting; it constructed its plots out of melodramatic and unusual incidents; and its characters were often morbid and obsessed.

The stamp of all this on *Wieland* is very clear. Particularly important is the influence of Godwin and Mrs Radcliffe. From the authoress of *The Mysteries of Udolpho* Brown borrowed the idea of using the endangered heroine as a centre of interest and a source of continual suspense. In her breathless and excited manner Clara Wieland narrates a story that consists, especially in its latter stages, of successive threats to her safety and chastity. From Mrs Radcliffe, too, comes the habit of introducing apparently supernatural events that turn out to have natural explanations. The plot, in fact, stems from three such incidents: the death of the elder Wieland apparently by divine visitation but really by spontaneous combustion; the mysterious voices produced by Carwin's ventriloquism (or 'biloquism', as Brown calls it); and the religious mania that causes Wieland to murder his wife and children.

Mrs Radcliffe's work influences the novel's structure, but its tone owes much to the English radical, Godwin. Philosopher and political thinker as well as novelist, Godwin had already influenced Brown before the composition of *Wieland*; Brown's first book *Alcuin* was a defence of women's rights inspired by his thought. In *Wieland* itself Godwin's influence is apparently mainly in the handling of Carwin, probably the book's most interesting character. Like Falkland, the sympathetic murderer in *Caleb Williams*, Carwin is a hero-villain – a person about whom both reader and writer have ambivalent feelings. On the one hand, he is the closest thing to a personification of evil in the book; his malicious tricks with ventriloquism and mimicry trigger off most of the trouble that afflicts the Wieland family. On the other hand, he is an attractive and striking figure; he may be damned, but he still has a romantic charm. It was, of course, this type of person who was later to be known as the 'Byronic hero'.

Wieland has the ingredients of an entertaining (though hardly profound) novel. Yet its potential is largely vitiated by Brown's carelessness and inexperience. His prose style is of a badness that cannot be completely explained by haste ('Notwithstanding the uncouthness of his garb, his manners were not unpolished'), while the plot, sound enough in its essentials, is tortuously and even incoherently developed. Because of inadequate preparation, several crucial scenes appear sketchy and implausible. For these reasons *Wieland* remains a historical curiosity rather than a living novel in its own right, marking nonetheless the first crude and tentative appearance of American fiction. Later writers like Poe and Hawthorne were also attracted to the type of Gothic fiction that Brockden Brown wrote; but they handled it with a technical fluency and invested it with an artistic meaning that eluded their predecessor.

FURTHER READING   Editions of *Wieland* are easily obtainable, while the best collection of Brown's works is the six-volume edition published in 1887. Two biographies are available: David Lee Clark's *Charles Brockden Brown: Pioneer Voice of America* (1952) and Harry R. Warfel's *Charles Brockden Brown: American Gothic Novelist* (1949). These are the only modern full-length studies, but in the nineteenth century several American writers – E. T. Channing, Margaret Fuller and R. H. Dana – wrote useful essays on Brown's fiction.

James Fenimore Cooper

James Fenimore Cooper was born at Burlington, New Jersey in 1789 and brought up on the family estate at Cooperstown, New York. After being dismissed from Yale and spending several years as a sailor, he married and settled down as a country gentleman. His first novel, *Precaution*, written in emulation of Jane Austen, was published in 1820. But it was with a very different sort of book, *The Pioneers* (1823), that he achieved fame. *The Pioneers* introduced Cooper's two best-known creations, the scout Natty Bumppo and his Indian friend Chingachgook. They reappear in four other novels – *The Last of the Mohicans* (1826), *The Prairie* (1827), *The Pathfinder* (1840) and *The Deerslayer* (1841) – which complete the series popularly known as the 'Leatherstocking Tales'. After the success of *The Pioneers* Cooper lived in New York and then (1826–1833) travelled in Europe. On his return to America he became a progressively harsh and disillusioned critic of his country's failings. His unpopular views often involved him in bitter public controversy. His social and political attitudes are expressed in the two novels, *Homeward Bound* (1838) and *Home as Found* (1838), and in the treatise, *The American Democrat* (1838). Cooper died in 1851.

Although he wrote over thirty novels Cooper is best remembered as the author of the Leatherstocking Tales. In their own time these won Cooper an international popularity that few American writers, before or since, have achieved. In France they were idolized by Balzac, who called one of his own early novels *Les Mohicans de Paris*. In England they became fireside favourites. Writing some ten years after Cooper's death, the English novelist Wilkie Collins could still speak of him as 'the greatest artist in the domain of romantic fiction yet produced in America'.

The Leatherstocking Tales also gained Cooper his nickname – 'the American Scott'. Never a man to admit his literary debts, Cooper himself always resented the label. Yet it is certainly just, for Cooper's romances of backwoods life borrow and adapt the formulae of Scott's tales of the Highlands. From Scott, too, comes the stiff and formal prose style that continually impedes the narrative, and the pasteboard quality of the heroes and heroines.

For all his indebtedness to English fiction, Cooper also managed to introduce an authentically American note into his work. In the preface to *Edgar Huntly* Charles Brockden Brown had grandly announced:

One merit the writer may at least claim; that of calling forth the passions and engaging the sympathy of the reader, by means hitherto unemployed by preceding authors. Puerile superstition and exploded manners; Gothic castles and chimeras; are the materials usually employed for this end. The incidents of Indian hostility, and the perils of the western wilderness are far more suitable; and for a native of America to overlook these would admit of no apology.

Edgar Huntly scarcely fulfills this claim, but the Leatherstocking Tales do. Cooper described the American landscape and its inhabitants with an exactitude unprecedented in earlier fiction. He put the Red Indian on the literary map, creating a stereotype that has survived into modern Hollywood films. And in the canny woodsman Natty Bumppo he created the first truly American hero of fiction.

The Pioneers

SUMMARY   On Christmas Eve 1793, Judge Marmaduke Temple brings his only daughter, Elizabeth, back from school to the family home at Templeton in New York State. Temple, the chief local magistrate and landowner, is a wise and kindly man of Quaker stock. The only stain on his reputation is old and almost forgotten. Some years before, Edward Effingham had helped Temple's career and made him manager of the Effingham property. When the War of Independence broke out the friends were on different sides, Effingham being a Colonel in the King's army. At the end of the war, when Effingham did not return from England and was presumed dead, Temple appropriated his estates. Templeton is now a prosperous and rapidly expanding settlement, already boasting several pretentious houses, of which Temple's is the grandest. It was designed by Richard Jones, the Judge's cousin and business manager.

During the sleigh-ride home Temple, shooting at a buck, wounds Oliver Edwards. Edwards is a young hunter, new to the district, who lives with Leatherstocking (Natty

Bumppo), an elderly woodsman who keeps himself apart from the citizens of Templeton. The Judge insists on taking the young man home to have the wound treated. On the way they are joined by another party, consisting of Jones, Monsieur Le Quoi, Major Hartmann, and Mr Grant, the local clergyman. Edwards manages to avert an accident caused by Jones' reckless driving but Jones, an incorrigible boaster, is too vain to admit his error. At Temple's house the party is met by the housekeeper, Remarkable Pettibone, and Benjamin Penguillan (commonly known as Ben Pump), a former sailor now employed as the Judge's major-domo. Dr Todd is summoned but Oliver prefers the medicine of Indian John (Chingachgook). John is a Mohican Indian and a friend of Leatherstocking. Though once a brave and noble warrior, he is now sadly declined from his former grandeur.

The inhabitants of Templeton go to church to hear Mr Grant's Christmas sermon. John, a convert to Christianity, also attends. After the service he and Oliver accompany Mr Grant and his daughter, Louisa, part of the way home. The clergyman is shocked to hear Oliver expressing hostility towards Judge Temple. Later, the settlers gather in the bar of 'The Bold Dragoon'. Temple tells the company about a new law restricting hunting. This is one of his favourite projects, for he is continually reproaching his fellow countrymen for their waste of America's natural resources of timber and game.

On Christmas Day there is a turkey-shooting competition. Leatherstocking, shooting on behalf of Elizabeth, beats Billy Kirby, a local woodchopper, and wins the prize bird. Temple announces that during his recent visit to the city he has secured Richard Jones' appointment as High Sheriff and is hence in need of a new business manager. He offers the post to Oliver, who accepts, though in a churlish way.

In the spring the settlers organize a pigeon shoot under Jones' direction. It is a wasteful business, for they kill far more birds than they need. Leatherstocking denounces them, contenting himself with killing just one pigeon. The

Judge agrees with the woodsman's strictures. But the settlers go on to hold an equally irresponsible fishing party. Natty holds himself aloof, spear-fishing from a canoe made by Indian John. When Ben Pump falls in the lake Natty saves him from drowning.

Shortly afterwards the Judge receives a disturbing letter from England, which he shows to his cousin Jones. They summon a lawyer, Mr Van Der School, for advice but exclude Oliver from the consultation. On the same day, Leatherstocking and Indian John kill a buck in defiance of the new law. Later, Natty rescues Elizabeth and Louisa, who are out walking in the mountains, from two savage panthers. Hiram Doolittle, a dishonest settler who has been spying on Natty, reports the deer-killing. Reluctantly Temple orders Leatherstocking's arrest, but the woodman assaults Hiram and Billy Kirby when they attempt to execute the order. Jones leads a posse to arrest Leatherstocking. But they find that the woodsman has burnt down his hut and is willing to give himself up quietly.

Natty is acquitted of assaulting Doolittle but found guilty of threatening Kirby with his rifle. Temple sentences him to an hour in the stocks, a fine of one hundred dollars, and a month in prison. Ben Pump sides with Natty and insists on joining him in the stocks; he also assaults Doolittle and is himself imprisoned. Elizabeth visits the woodsman in prison, bringing money from her father to pay the fine. Leatherstocking refuses the money and escapes with Pump; Oliver is waiting outside the jail to help them.

The next day Elizabeth goes to the mountain to give Leatherstocking some gunpowder he has requested. John is there, dressed in full Indian costume: he inveighs bitterly against the white race for its treatment of the Indians. A forest fire breaks out. Oliver joins Elizabeth and John, and the trio is rescued by Leatherstocking. Mr Grant, whom Louisa has sent in search of Elizabeth, joins them. Indian John dies, observing Indian rather than Christian rituals. A rainstorm quenches the fire and Elizabeth and Mr Grant are able to return safely to Templeton.

Richard Jones again organizes a posse to catch Leatherstocking, and there is a fight in which Doolittle is injured.
This is interrupted by Oliver, who emerges from the cave
where Leatherstocking has been hiding, bringing an old
man with him. This is Major Effingham, the father of
Temple's friend, whom Natty has been sheltering. Oliver
explains that he himself is the Major's grandson and the
son of the man whom the Judge defrauded. Temple answers
that he had assumed all of the Effingham family to be dead,
and in reparation he gives half of his estate to Oliver.
Shortly afterwards old Major Effingham dies. Oliver and
Elizabeth marry. Natty is pardoned by the Governor of the
state but, to the regret of his friends, goes off again on his
travels through the forest.

CRITICAL COMMENTARY If the reader is to enjoy *The Pioneers*
fully he must first adjust to Cooper's relaxed and digressive
narrative style. Considered as an adventure story the novel
is irritatingly slow-moving by modern standards. Its exciting incidents are continually interrupted by lengthy
accounts of minor characters (like Major Hartmann and
Monsieur Le Quoi), or by apparently irrelevant episodes
(like the Judge's visit to Billy Kirby's maple syrup refinery).
Much of this slowness is simply the result of Cooper's
relative inexperience as a writer. *The Pioneers* is only his
third novel – by the time he came to write books like *The
Deerslayer* or *The Pathfinder* he had learnt to tell a story with
much greater economy.

Yet the slowness is partly intentional. As well as being
an adventure story, *The Pioneers* is designed (in the words
of its subtitle) as 'a descriptive tale'. Writing in the 1820s
Cooper is trying to recreate a pioneer life that already
seemed dated to his American contemporaries and was
virtually unknown to European readers. He is led continually into historical and sociological commentary – about
Indian tribal customs, early American architecture, and
the different characteristics of the French, German and

English settlers. As a historical novelist Cooper is modestly successful, though hardly inspired. He has none of the brilliance of his master, Walter Scott, but he does manage to create a rounded portrait of American settlement life.

Cooper, of course, relied heavily on his own boyhood memories of Cooperstown. Inevitably, his portrait of Templeton is at times suffused in an atmosphere of sentimental nostalgia. The early chapters, in particular, are strongly reminiscent of some of Dickens' cosy Christmas episodes in *The Pickwick Papers*. In *Studies in Classic American Literature* (1923) D. H. Lawrence confessed: 'Perhaps my taste is childish, but these scenes in *Pioneers* seem to me marvellously beautiful . . . some of the loveliest, most glamorous pictures in all literature.'

Yet Cooper also had more detachment than Lawrence allowed. Indeed, he often adopts a tone of amused condescension toward his subject: this is particularly apparent in the descriptions of Richard Jones' buildings and of the pioneers' attempts to imitate the cultured life of Europe. No doubt the life of the early settlers did seem hopelessly primitive to an American writing in the 1820s, and no doubt Cooper was anxious not to appear an uncultivated backwoodsman in the eyes of his European readers. The result, at any rate, is a rather snobbish and disdainful attitude to American life – an attitude that reappears in more extreme forms in the social criticism he wrote after his return to America in the 1830s.

There is much about his country's past that Cooper does not like. The growth of Templeton is presented not as the triumphant march of civilization but as the destruction of a natural paradise by petty and insensitive people. The settlers fell timber to build pretentious houses or to burn in wastefully large amounts in their fires. They destroy game with an extravagance that cannot be justified by economic need. Such criticisms have become familiar in later commentaries on America. The poet W. H. Auden remarked: 'In the Fifth Circle on the Mount of Purgatory,

I do not think that many Americans will be found among the Avaricious; but I suspect that the Prodigals may almost be an American colony. The great vice of Americans is not materialism but a lack of respect for matter.'

This gives a crucial role to two of the book's characters: Judge Temple and Leatherstocking (Natty Bumppo). Temple is an idealized portrait of the sort of squire that Cooper himself wished to be. The key to his attitudes is a belief in law. The extravagances and excesses of the settlers should be held in check by sensible laws – against, for example, the wanton destruction of game. And these laws should be enforced impartially. Temple, however reluctantly, acknowledges the need to punish Leatherstocking even though the hunter has saved Elizabeth Temple's life.

In the dispute about Natty's killing of the buck Cooper's intellectual alignment is with Judge Temple, but his emotional sympathy is with Leatherstocking. The hunter and his Indian friend are the last survivors of an older and nobler way of life that is being destroyed by the growth of places like Templeton. Natty does not need laws to tell him how to behave because he has a natural and instinctive code of his own. He does not waste timber building pretentious houses but lives in a simple log cabin in the woods. He may kill deer out of season but he never takes more from nature than his simple life requires.

Natty and Chingachgook are the living embodiments of the natural paradise that is giving way to the artificial vulgarities of Templeton. The book is their swan-song and it is appropriate that it should end with the Indian's death (more from sorrow than from wounds caused by the forest fire) and with the hunter's departure in search of new and unspoilt territory. For all their rude simplicity and lack of book-learning the two hunters have an honesty, bravery and natural good sense that is superior to even the intellectual refinements of Judge Temple, let alone the pettiness of men like Hiram Doolittle. In looking back at America's past Cooper finds his heroes not amongst the leaders of the society but in a dispossessed Red Indian and a woodsman who becomes first the critic and then the outlaw of the new civilization.

The Last of the Mohicans

SUMMARY In 1757, during the American wars between the French and the English, a small party leaves the English Fort Edward heading for Fort William Henry, which is being threatened by Montcalm's army. Major Duncan Heyward is taking Cora and Alice Munro to join their father, the head of the garrison at William Henry. Shortly after their departure they are joined by David Gamut, a pious but eccentric singing-master. However, the Indian guide Magua (also known as Le Renard Subtil) betrays them and leads them into territory inhabited by the hostile Maquas Indians. The group is saved by an accidental encounter with Hawk-eye (Natty Bumppo), a clever and experienced scout, and his Indian friends, Chingachgook and Uncas. Uncas, Chingachgook's son, is the last surviving Mohican chieftain.

Hawk-eye takes the party by canoe to a convenient hiding-place on an island in the river. The Maquas, led by Magua, attack and when the group's powder runs out Hawk-eye and his Indian friends go to fetch help. The rest are captured and led through the forest to an Indian encampment. Heyward tries to bribe the canny and treacherous Magua. But the Indian wants Cora for his squaw to revenge himself for a humiliating whipping he once received at Munro's hands. When Cora rebuffs him Magua incites his followers to kill the white party. At this point Hawkeye, Chingachgook, and Uncas intervene: rather than go for help they have been following the Indians and their captives. In the ensuing fight all the Maquas are killed except Magua, who runs away into the woods. Hawk-eye then leads the party through the forest to a ruined blockhouse – the scene of his first battle, he explains – where they rest. Then they continue their journey to William Henry, narrowly avoiding the hostile

Indians. Although the English fort is already surrounded by the French army, Hawk-eye is able to bring his friends safely through the enemy lines.

On arriving at the fort Heyward tells Munro that he wants to marry Alice. At first Munro is angered that Heyward has not chosen Cora. Cora, Munro's daughter by his first marriage, has West Indian slave blood in her veins and Munro is quick to take offence on her behalf. But he is soon appeased and gives his blessing, provided that Alice consents to the marriage. Meanwhile, the fort is hard pressed by the French army. Montcalm offers Munro and Heyward generous and honourable terms of surrender, which they reluctantly accept. The Indian allies of the French, however, ignore the treaty. When the English emerge from the fort they are massacred by Magua and his followers. Magua himself abducts Cora, Alice and David Gamut.

A few days later Munro, Heyward, Hawk-eye, Chingachgook and Uncas return to the fatal spot to search for the hostages. Since the retreating Indians have covered their tracks carefully Hawk-eye and his Indian friends need all their skill to follow the trail. Finally they arrive on the outskirts of a Huron camp, where they meet David Gamut, who has been forced to dress as an Indian. He explains that Munro's daughters are both safe but have been separated: Alice is with the Hurons while Cora has been taken to a nearby village of Lenni Lenape Indians, part of the Delaware tribe. Since Chingachgook and Uncas are related to the Delawares they decide to go with Hawk-eye to bargain for Cora's release. Meanwhile, Heyward enters the Huron camp disguised as an Indian. He pretends to have been sent by the French to treat the braves wounded in the recent battle.

Uncas, however, is soon captured and the Hurons, at Magua's instigation, decide to execute him the next morning. Hawk-eye arrives disguised as a bear, and he and Heyward manage to find out where Alice is being held prisoner. Magua interrupts their meeting but is overcome, and left bound hand and foot. Heyward and Alice leave but Hawk-eye insists on remaining to help Uncas. With Gamut's help he frees the Mohican brave. Uncas dons the bearskin and Hawk-eye dresses as Gamut, and together they make their way out of the camp. Gamut himself remains behind disguised as Hawk-eye, but the imposture is soon detected.

Magua goes to the Lenape tribe and, under the eyes of the Lenape chief, Tamenund, he confronts Hawk-eye and his friends. The Lenape at first sympathize with Magua but, when they learn that Uncas is a Mohican chief, they change their allegiance. Alice and the whites are freed; according to Indian law, Magua still has the right to take Cora with him. He insists on doing so, even though Hawk-eye offers himself as Magua's prisoner in her place. Uncas then leads the Lenape tribe in pursuit of Magua and his Huron braves. A long and fierce battle results. One of the retreating Hurons kills Cora, and Uncas himself is killed by Magua. Hawk-eye, proving his reputation as an expert long-distance shot, kills Magua. The whites mourn Cora, while Uncas is buried according to Indian rituals.

CRITICAL COMMENTARY In *The Pioneers*, his first novel about Natty Bumppo, Cooper showed his hero in old age – scarcely declined in his powers but already looking like a survival from a bygone era. The third Natty Bumppo book, *The Prairie*, picks up where *The Pioneers* left off. After Chingachgook's death Natty seems more the lonely outsider than ever and he dies at the end of this wistful and elegiac novel. But in the second novel of the series, *The Last of the Mohicans*, Cooper turns to Natty's youth – as he also does in the later Leatherstocking stories, *The Pathfinder* and *The Deerslayer*. The series, then, does not treat its hero's life in chronological sequence but moves backwards in time: Natty gets younger and younger.

Although the novels were immensely popular on both sides of the Atlantic, they did not entirely escape criticism. In his poem, *A Fable for Critics* (1848), James Russell Lowell turned a satirical eye to Cooper's recurrent use of Natty Bumppo:

> He has drawn you one character, though, that is new,
> One wildflower he's plucked that is wet with the dew
> Of this fresh Western world, and, the thing not to mince,
> He has done naught but copy it ill ever since.

Cooper's Indians, Lowell added, 'are just Natty Bumppo daubed over with red.' The complaint was echoed in an article by Lewis Cass, Governor of the Michigan territory: Cooper's 'Uncas and his Pawnee Hard-Heart, for they are both of the same family, have no living stereotype in our forests.' In a general Preface to the Leatherstocking Tales Cooper defended his habit of romanticizing his subject in characteristic lofty tones: 'It is the privilege of all writers of fiction . . . to present the *beau-ideal* of their characters to the reader.'

Yet it was D. H. Lawrence, in his invaluable *Studies in Classic American Literature* (1923), who showed the finest perception of Cooper's intentions. Noting the manner in which the Leatherstocking series moves backwards in time, Lawrence suggests that it shows 'a decrescendo of reality and a crescendo of beauty'. *The Pioneers* and *The Prairie* strike a recurrent note of social criticism: they show Natty progressively at odds with the civilization which he, as scout and pathfinder, has helped to create. But by turning to Natty's youth in *The Last of the Mohicans* Cooper presents a romantic and idyllic world. The settlers have not yet arrived and the forest remains a virgin territory where Natty can live and move unfettered. Where *The Pioneers* has an embittered and disillusioned air, *The Last of the Mohicans* breathes an atmosphere of almost primal innocence.

This myth of 'virgin land' – of an America unspoilt by man's encroachment – is one of the driving forces of the American literary imagination. It is America's own version of a dream that most men feel: the longing for a Golden Age or a Garden of Eden. American fiction continually turns away from ordinary society in pursuit of this dream. Its heroes turn their backs on civilized life to run away to sea, like Poe's Arthur Gordon Pym and Melville's Ishmael, or to float lazily down the Mississippi on a raft, like Mark Twain's Huck Finn.

Natty Bumppo, then, is the first embodiment of a powerful American dream. He is the first hero of a recurrent national epic. It is interesting to note how much closer he is to the traditional heroes of epic than to the customary heroes of nineteenth-century fiction. He lives a simple life in communion with nature, untouched by theoretical knowledge – 'book-learning', as he contemptuously calls it. From his knowledge of the forest he has developed almost legendary skills and powers: he is a prodigious hunter, scout and tracker, and an endlessly resourceful expert in survival. As is customary in epic, his skills are recorded in the impressive variety of names by which he is known: he is not just Natty Bumppo but 'Hawk-eye' and 'La Longue Carabine'. Again, like the epic hero, he has a favourite weapon, 'Kill-Deer', a magic talisman.

In epic the hero often has an inseparable companion, a spiritual blood-brother. Cooper's choice of Chingachgook, the Mohican Indian, for this role is especially interesting. Natty's friendship with the Indian is, of course, an expression of how deeply he has been assimilated into the natural life of the country. Although himself a white man, he feels in some ways closer to the forest's indigenous inhabitants. As Lawrence pointed out, this fraternization between the white man and the black or red man is one of the favourite motifs of American literature, and one that usually appears in conjunction with the idea of escape from normal society. In their adventures at sea Poe's Arthur Gordon Pym and Melville's Ishmael both develop deep friendships with Indians, while Twain's Huck Finn journeys down the river with Nigger Jim, the runaway slave. With the escape from the artificialities of society, so the dream goes, the artificial distinctions of race also break down.

FURTHER READING The student will have no difficulty in

finding editions of those perennial favourites amongst Cooper's work, the Leatherstocking novels. But for the lesser known (though often no less interesting) books he will need to consult one of the several nineteenth-century *Works*, of which the most easily available is the 33-volume edition published 1895–1900. The first four volumes of *The Letters and Journals of James Fenimore Cooper*, edited by J. F. Beard, have recently been published (1960 and 1965).

The best general introduction to Cooper's work is by James Grossman (1949), but much of the most rewarding commentary has come from other novelists. The publication of *The Pathfinder* occasioned a fine essay, 'Fenimore Cooper et Walter Scott', by Balzac. Mark Twain wrote a witty and merciless attack on the Leatherstocking novels, 'Fenimore Cooper's Literary Offenses'. D. H. Lawrence's discussion of Cooper in *Studies in Classic American Literature* (1923) is often factually inaccurate but is always brilliantly perceptive.

2 The American Renaissance

The title of this section is borrowed from F. O. Matthiessen's monumental study of mid nineteenth-century American literature. *American Renaissance* (1941) begins with an epigraph from the writings of Ralph Waldo Emerson, the New England philosopher and poet:

> There is a moment in the history of every nation, when, proceeding out of this brute youth, the perceptive powers reach their ripeness and have not yet become microscopic: so that man, at that instant, extends across the entire scale, and, with his feet still planted on the immense forces of night, converses by his eyes and brain with solar and stellar creation. That is the moment of adult health, the culmination of power.

The years 1850–1855 are America's 'moment of adult health'. They saw the publication of Emerson's *Representative Men* (1850), Nathaniel Hawthorne's *The Scarlet Letter* (1850) and *The House of the Seven Gables* (1851), Herman Melville's *Moby Dick* (1851) and *Pierre* (1852), Henry David Thoreau's *Walden* (1854), and Walt Whitman's *Leaves of Grass* (1855). Professor Matthiessen comments: 'You might search all the rest of American literature without being able to collect a group of books equal to these in imaginative vitality.'

Secure in the knowledge that their claim to a national culture no longer depended on having produced Brockden Brown (the American William Godwin) and Fenimore Cooper (the American Scott), Americans could now look Europeans squarely in the eye. In 1820 the English critic

Sydney Smith had asked sneeringly: 'In the four quarters of the globe, who reads an American book?' In his essay on Hawthorne, Melville could answer exuberantly: 'Believe me, my friends, that men not very much inferior to Shakespeare are this day being born on the banks of the Ohio. And the day will come when you shall say, Who reads a book by an Englishman that is a modern?'

What, then, were the characteristic qualities of American fiction during this period? Trollope provided a valuable clue when he noted that: 'The creations of American literature generally are no doubt more given to the speculative – less given to the realistic – than are those of English literature. On our side of the water we deal more with beef and ale, and less with dreams.' Victorian novelists wrote about social manners, social change and individual psychology. Their American counterparts cultivated a form that they liked to call the 'romance'.

Inevitably, so vague and abstract a term means very different things in the hands of different writers. The first emergence of American romance can be seen in the work of Edgar Allan Poe, the most important forerunner of the American Renaissance. Working in the popular magazine culture of the 1830s and 1840s, Poe managed to convert the jaded scenery of European Gothic into something new and more vital. His short stories and his one novel, *The Narrative of Arthur Gordon Pym of Nantucket* (1838), are symbolic explorations of the underside of human consciousness.

Hawthorne and Melville, the major novelists of the American Renaissance, were both deeply indebted to Poe, but their own practice of romance is significantly different. They were both New Englanders, while Poe was a Southerner brought up to despise everything Bostonian. Hawthorne and Melville mingled freely with Emerson's circle of New England Transcendentalists, and were profoundly affected by its sense of romantic optimism, its belief in the nobility of democratic man, its vigorous love of what Whitman called 'man in the open air'. Yet, for all the freshness of its landscape, New England was one of the oldest established parts of America. By the 1850s it had its own graveyards, prisons and gibbets, its own catalogue of witch trials and religious persecution. This mixture of innocence and evil provides a keynote to the work of Hawthorne and Melville. To borrow from one of their own favourite images, they felt like men re-entering the Garden of Eden only to discover that a burden of sin and guilt remained. Their mood was like that of John Donne, who, after cataloguing the beauties of Twicknam Garden, adds:

And that this place may thoroughly be thought
   True Paradise, I have the serpent brought.

Edgar Allan Poe

Edgar Allan Poe was born at Boston in 1809. On the death of his mother, an actress, in 1811 he was adopted by Mrs John Allan and brought up in her household, first in England and then in Richmond, Virginia. After a year at the newly established University of Virginia and a brief unsuccessful spell in the army Poe settled down to a career as a journalist. He worked in Baltimore, Philadelphia and New York. Despite his connections with the East Coast he always aggressively regarded himself as a Southerner, opposing the abolitionist movement and continually poking fun at the New England Transcendentalists. His personal life was largely one of disappointment, frustration and tragedy. He seems never to have recovered from the early death of his wife, Virginia, in 1842. He died in October 1849, apparently as the result of a prolonged drinking bout.

To contemporaries Poe's career seemed an example of waste and failure from which various lessons could be drawn. To early temperance advocates it was a dramatic warning of the dangers of drink; to Walt Whitman an illustration of the ill-treatment that America accorded its literary men; and to the French poet Baudelaire an emblem of demon-haunted romanticism. Yet although Poe died young after being chained to journalistic hackwork for most of his life, he managed to produce a literary *oeuvre* of surprising distinction, variety and substance. He wrote poetry, literary criticism, aesthetic theory and philosophy. But it is on his short stories – pieces like 'The Fall of the House of Usher' and 'Ligeia' – and on the novel *Arthur Gordon Pym* (1838) that his reputation really rests.

In his *Democracy in America* (1835–1840) Alexis de Tocqueville gave this account of American literary taste:

> They like facile forms of beauty, self-explanatory and immediately enjoyable; above all, they like things unexpected and new. Accustomed to the monotonous struggle of practical life, what they want is vivid, lively emotions, sudden revelations, brilliant truths, or errors able to rouse them up and plunge them, almost by violence, into the middle of the subject.

As the novelist Piers Paul Read has noted, Poe's fiction answered this need admirably. Its predominant vein was, in Poe's own phrase, 'the grotesque and arabesque': it extracted a full measure of suspense and horror from the conventional machinery of Gothic. The result, as the poet James Russell Lowell observed in *A Fable for Critics* (1848), was 'three-fifths . . . genius and two-fifths sheer fudge'. At their worst, Poe's horror stories are merely macabre thrill-seeking; at their best, they are valid vehicles for exploring the hidden hinterland of the human mind.

The Narrative of Arthur Gordon Pym of Nantucket

SUMMARY   Arthur Gordon Pym, who narrates the story, comes from a respectable Nantucket trading family. Stories told him by his friend Augustus Barnard excite an interest in travel and adventure. When Augustus and his father sail from Nantucket in the *Grampus* Pym manages to stow away on board. But he soon begins to suffer from claustrophobia and becomes alarmed when his friend does not bring supplies of food and water. At last Augustus does come, explaining that the *Grampus* has been taken over by mutineers. The loyal members of the crew have been murdered or set adrift; Augustus himself owes his life to the intervention of a half-breed, Dirk Peters.

Augustus tells Peters of Pym's presence on board and the trio plan to take over the ship. Pym disguises himself as the ghost of one of the dead crew and, in the ensuing panic, he and his colleagues are able to overcome the mutineers. Only Parker is left alive. A storm batters the ship and leaves it drifting helplessly. Desperate for food, the four wait for help. But the only ship that passes is strewn with putrefying bodies, dead of fever. On the sixth day Peters, Parker and Augustus debate cannibalism despite Pym's protests: they draw lots to select a victim. Parker loses and his corpse provides them with food for several days. Luckily Pym contrives to break into the ship's storeroom, where they find a small supply of food and water. In the fight with the mutineers Augustus had been stabbed in the arm; his wounds become infected and he dies in great agony.

Pym and Peters are at last picked up by an English trading ship, the *Jane Guy*. They head southward into the Antarctic circle. To the crew's surprise they find that, once an initial ice barrier has been passed, the weather grows warmer. The *Jane Guy* arrives at a group of islands where they are met by seemingly friendly natives, whose chief is Too-Wit. The island is an enchanting place: it has unique trees and animals and its water is a mixture of changeable purple hues. At the end of their visit the sailors go to the natives' village for a farewell feast. On the way Pym and Peters turn aside to explore a fissure in the ravine through which they are passing, and a sudden rockslide walls them up. They escape, but only to find that the rockslide was part of a deliberate ambush by the natives. The rest of the crew are dead, and Pym and Peters watch the *Jane Guy* being captured. When the ship is beached its gunpowder store explodes, causing terrible carnage.

The two friends are forced from their hiding place by lack of food. After a brief skirmish with the savages they escape to sea in a canoe, taking one of the natives, Nu-Nu, as a guide. As they travel south, the water gets warmer and the landscape becomes an eerie white. Nu-Nu is terrified. The boat is now in the grip of a strong southern current which draws the travellers towards a greyish vapour, occasionally streaked with flashes of colour. This proves to be an immense rock and, as the boat is sucked into one of its yawning chasms, Pym sees before him a large white human figure.

Pym's narrative ends here. An appended note, supposedly by the publisher, explains that the author died before completing his story. Peters survived and now lives in Illinois, but efforts to contact him have failed.

CRITICAL COMMENTARY Poe's novel is based on the idea of the journey. In this respect, of course, it takes its cue from several older traditions – most obviously the large body of literature about fabulous voyages. Ever since Homer writers have delighted in telling stories of strange lands and strange peoples. The form arises out of a love of the unlikely, of comedy and of simple tall-story telling. Poe shares all these feelings and adds one of his own: he likes trying to hoax people. He is careful to deck out his extravagant tale with as many authentic touches as possible. Pym's narrative is surrounded with elaborate editorial paraphernalia, and the story itself is spiced with a small encyclopaedia of information about ships, weather and animal life. It is as if Poe were trying to see how far he can go before his incredibilities provoke absolute disbelief from the reader. *Pym* is identifiably the work of the man who once wrote an elaborate and fictitious newspaper report of the first balloon voyage across the Atlantic. At the same time, the novel owes much to a more homely tradition: the picaresque novel. With its scapegrace hero, its fascination with the sea and its loose episodic construction, *Pym* is a close relative of Defoe's *Robinson Crusoe* and Smollett's *Roderick Random*.

Despite these precedents, Poe's interest in journeys is also distinctively American. It is present in Cooper's *The Prairie*, Melville's *Moby Dick* and Twain's *Huckleberry Finn*, while Jack Kerouac's *On the Road* shows that the tradition is still alive. The English novel usually deals with static social groups and examines their structures; it often takes rootedness or a sense of entrapment in a particular social milieu as its themes. But American fiction – perhaps because America itself for a long time lacked elaborate social structures – tends to deal with man outside society. It abounds in outdoor or runaway heroes, and in lonely quests into the unknown.

This might seem to smack of boys' adventure fiction, but there is certainly very little sense of the healthy outdoors in Poe's work. Pym travels not through wonders and enchantments, or even stirring adventures, but through a succession of graveyard horrors. Poe seems almost to revel in piling on the agony – Pym's sufferings as a stowaway, the description of the *Grampus* mutiny, the ship with fevered corpses, the cannibalism, the death of Augustus, the massacre of the crew of the *Jane Guy*, and so forth. Much of this is obviously overdone and exudes an unpleasant air of gratuitous cruelty – an effect reinforced by the grating racial parable about Too-Wit's tribe, 'the most wicked, hypocritical, vindictive, bloodthirsty, and altogether fiendish race of men upon the face of the globe'.

Nevertheless, the horrors are often convincingly chilling. Poe commands attention if only because of his intense belief in his own imaginings. Nor are his terrors merely physical. For all the stress on putrefying and dismembered corpses, the main accent is still on psychological horror. As D. H. Lawrence noted in his *Studies in Classic American Literature* (1923), Poe is 'an adventurer into vaults and cellars and horrible underground passages of the human soul'. By a process familiar in serious travel literature Pym's quests become a metaphor for an exploration of the underside of the human mind – an interior voyage. The story is about a mind getting closer and closer to the end of its tether.

For Pym the end of the tether is that final glimpse of the large human figure, 'of the perfect whiteness of the snow'. It is a neatly disquieting touch to conclude a book that has dealt so much with the horrors of darkness. But the abrupt and cryptic nature of the ending has puzzled and annoyed many readers. Certainly, it shows Poe at his most deliberately tantalizing, and the appended note, with its reference to Peters being alive but untraceable in Illinois, only confirms the suspicion that the writer has his tongue in his cheek. Yet Poe is also being serious. Throughout the novel Pym has been entirely unable to control his own fate (that is what makes the story so frightening). All he can do is record the stages of his destruction. As he plunges helplessly towards the last horror even this ability fails him: language itself breaks down before the final abyss.

FURTHER READING   There is no standard edition of Poe's work. The best is the seventeen-volume edition by James A. Harrison (1902; reprinted 1965), but this is dated and incomplete. There are, however, many readily available selections from Poe's major poetry, fiction and criticism; most of these are inexpensive paperbacks. John Ward Ostrom has compiled an excellent edition of Poe's letters (1946). The best biography is the two-volume work by Arthur Hobson Quinn (1941); most of the other accounts of Poe's life are sensationalistic and unreliable.

The recognition of Poe's work began in France: Baudelaire (who also translated Poe's stories), Mallarmé and Valéry were amongst his earliest and most passionate admirers. Interest has since spread and in this century W. H. Auden, D. H. Lawrence, Allen Tate and Richard Wilbur (amongst others) have contributed valuable essays. The most reliable longer studies are Edward H. Davidson's *Poe: A Critical Study* (1957) and the relevant section of Harry Levin's *The Power of Blackness: Poe, Melville, Hawthorne* (1958).

Nathaniel Hawthorne

Nathaniel Hawthorne was born in 1804 at Salem, Massachusetts, of an old local family whose members had included John Hathorne, one of the judges at the Salem witch trials of 1692. After a solitary childhood that left a lasting mark of sombre reserve on his character Hawthorne attended Bowdoin College. On his return to Salem he read widely and began his own first tentative literary efforts: the partly autobiographical novel, *Fanshawe* (1828), neither a commercial nor a literary success, and the short stories later collected as *Twice-Told Tales* (1837). He subsequently married Sophia Peabody and lived in Concord, Massachusetts. For a brief part of this time he was a member of the Transcendentalist community at Brook Farm. During these years he wrote a volume of tales, *Mosses from an Old Manse* (1846), the manse of the title being his house at Concord. From 1846 to 1849 he was Surveyor of Customs at Salem. After losing this job he published his best-known work, *The Scarlet Letter* (1850).

Residence at Concord had led to a close friendship with Ralph Waldo Emerson, the philosopher and poet. A later stay at Lenox, Massachusetts, brought him into contact with Melville. Whilst living in Lenox he published two more novels, *The House of the Seven Gables* (1851) and *The Blithedale Romance* (1852). In later life he went to Europe, first working as Consul at Liverpool and then living in Italy, the scene and inspiration of his last completed novel, *The Marble Faun* (1860). He died at Concord in 1864.

Hawthorne's significance is simply expressed: he was the first unquestionably major writer whom America produced. Cooper had introduced a distinctively American voice into fiction, but his novels are often formless and inarticulate. Poe's stories contain many flashes of brilliance, yet these remain merely flashes and are often marred by affectation and carelessness. Hawthorne, however, was the finest literary embodiment of the New England traditions in which he was so deeply imbued. He inherited characteristic Puritan preoccupations – with sin, with guilt and with secrecy – and became at once their chronicler and their critic. His best work is carefully and tightly organized, blending elements of realism, allegory and symbolism into a form that he himself likes to call 'romance'. Hawthorne's major achievements are the four novels – *The Scarlet Letter*, *The House of the Seven Gables*, *The Blithedale Romance* and *The Marble Faun* – yet his short stories should not be neglected. Amongst the best are: 'The May-Pole of Merry Mount', 'Endicott and the Red Cross', 'The Birthmark', 'Young Goodman Brown', 'Rappaccini's Daughter', 'The Artist of the Beautiful', 'Ethan Brand', and 'My Kinsman, Major Molineux'.

The Scarlet Letter

SUMMARY In an introductory sketch, 'The Custom House', Hawthorne gives a fictionalized account of his three years' experience as Surveyor of Customs at Salem, once a busy port but now largely disused. The Custom House itself is staffed by elderly, somnolent workers and an air of drowsy comfort prevails. In a deserted upstairs room Hawthorne discovers a piece of gold-embroidered scarlet cloth in the shape of the letter A. With it there is a manuscript, by Jonathan Pue, a former Surveyor at Salem, recounting the life of Hester Prynne. With the election of a Republican administration Hawthorne, a Democrat appointee, loses his job. This is no great blow to him for he had already been growing anxious to resume his literary career. A free man again, he takes Pue's narrative as the starting-point for his romance.

Hester Prynne, impulsive and passionate, is convicted of adultery by her fellow citizens in a small seventeenth-century New England town. In accordance with the stern Puritan laws she is made to stand on the public scaffold with her illegitimate child and then to wear the letter A emblazoned on her dress. During her public humiliation she is lectured by Governor Bellingham and Reverend John Wilson. The local clergyman, Reverend Arthur Dimmesdale, highly respected for his piety, exhorts her to reveal the name of her lover but Hester refuses. In the crowd is Hester's husband, a reserved and scholarly man, who has just arrived to join her after several years amongst the Indians. Husband and wife recognize each other but make no sign of acknowledgement. Later the husband – who has taken the name of Roger Chillingworth – visits Hester and her child in prison. He asks for the name of her partner in adultery and, when she refuses, expresses a confident intention of finding out for himself. He forces her to agree to keep his real identity secret.

After her release Hester takes a cottage on the outskirts of town and becomes a needlewoman; her work is soon widely in demand. She brings up her daughter Pearl, dressing her in elaborate clothes in striking contrast to her own drab attire. Pearl is a strange, elf-like child with a lawless energy. Sometimes Hester even wonders if her child is possessed by an evil spirit. The townspeople share the suspicion and there is a move to have Pearl taken from Hester's charge. On her visit to Governor Bellingham Hester's request to keep Pearl is earnestly supported by Dimmesdale, who chances to be present. The Governor agrees.

Dimmesdale has become progressively emaciated, and has developed a nervous habit of holding his hand over his heart. Chillingworth, who now enjoys a considerable local reputation as a man of science, shows a special interest in him. He becomes the clergyman's medical adviser, and the two lodge together. A sinister intimacy develops, with Chillingworth probing the source of Dimmesdale's sorrow. On the night of Governor Winthrop's death Dimmesdale, impelled by some secret care, goes to the scaffold where Hester had stood. He is met there by Hester and Pearl, who are returning from the Governor's deathbed. A flash of meteoric light reveals Chillingworth standing in the shadows watching them. To Dimmesdale the light appears to form the letter A; but the local sexton thinks that this stands for 'Angel' and is an omen connected with the Governor's death.

By brave submission to her fate Hester has won the respect of the community. She is hard-working, charitable and, in times of illness, a self-appointed Sister of Mercy. Indeed some people say that the A on her dress stands for 'Able'. One day she meets Chillingworth in the forest and remonstrates with him about the way he is covertly torturing Dimmesdale. In a second interview in the forest she warns the clergyman against Chillingworth. In this scene the fact that Dimmesdale had been Hester's lover is openly stated for the first time. They briefly recover confidence in their love and plan to go away together; Hester even discards her scarlet A, but Pearl insists that it be put back. Dimmesdale returns alone to the town, planning to make his forthcoming Election Day sermon the occasion of his departure.

Invigorated by this decision, he preaches an especially eloquent address. At its end he is again debilitated and obviously on the verge of death. Despite Chillingworth's attempts to intervene, he publicly acknowledges Hester and Pearl for the first time. As he dies, he bares his bosom to the crowd. Most people claim to have seen the letter A branded on it. Others deny this, or that the clergyman made any specific confession of guilt; they say that Dimmesdale chose to make his death an instructive parable by dying in the arms of a fallen woman.

Chillingworth dies a year later, leaving his fortune to Pearl. Pearl goes abroad with her mother and marries a European aristocrat. Hester returns to the town and spends the rest of her life doing charitable work. When she dies the letter A is used as a heraldic device on her tombstone.

CRITICAL COMMENTARY Hawthorne was always a modest and self-doubting man; he had, as his contemporary James Russell Lowell remarked, a 'genius so shrinking and rare / That you hardly at first see the strength that is there.' Hawthorne prefaced *The Scarlet Letter* with an apologetic autobiographical sketch, and he was astonished at the enthusiasm with which his publisher James T. Fields accepted the completed manuscript. In America the novel's reception was predominantly favourable. There were, of course, moralists who complained of Hawthorne's treatment of adultery; one critic asked, 'Is the French era actually begun in our literature?' But on the whole Americans greeted the book as a major step in the development of a national literature. In his excellent study of Hawthorne (1879), Henry James described the pride that Americans felt about *The Scarlet Letter*: 'something might at last be sent to Europe as exquisite in quality as anything that had been received.'

Since *The Scarlet Letter* is probably Hawthorne's most assured achievement it is instructive to examine the ways it helps to define that concept of romance so vital to both Hawthorne's own art and the American novel. In this respect the introductory sketch of 'The Custom House' is especially important – far more than the artless little biographical essay it might seem at first sight. By using this section to describe ordinary people and ordinary work Hawthorne gives a glimpse of that area of life with which the realistic novel usually concerns itself. Here is the territory of a Balzac or, in terms of American literature, a Howells or a Frank Norris. Hawthorne concedes that normal life can be a subject for art but resolutely takes a different course himself. 'A better book than I shall ever write was there,' he comments as he bids goodbye to the Custom House.

Hawthorne takes his inspiration from an antique remnant of cloth found in an upstairs room rather than from his office or his colleagues. But if he turns back to the past it is not in the spirit of a literal chronicler. His claim of Hester's historical existence is entirely unfounded; and anyway, in the introduction itself he warns that he has freely embellished her story. For romance is pre-eminently the genre where the writer can work his material according to the dictates of his imagination rather than the exigencies of fact. He can introduce symbolic elements: the scarlet A itself, or the juxtaposition of the prim Puritan town and the dark forest where Indians live, witches practise their rites and illicit lovers meet. And he can hint at the supernatural, as when he recounts the story of the Indian's arrow bouncing off the A on Hester's breast.

Romance turns back to history and it incorporates fantastic and improbable events; but it does not cultivate these for their own sake. It aims at a heightened vision of reality. In his novel *The Confidence Man* (1857) Melville proclaimed: 'It is with fiction as with religion; it should present another world, and yet one to which we feel the tie.' This is immediately felt in the narrative style that Hawthorne adopts in *The Scarlet Letter*. The book derives much of its effect of compression and intensity from the way it moves through a series of static scenes or tableaux, rather as some medieval paintings do. Indeed, the idea of the tableau is introduced in the first scene when Hawthorne remarks that a Catholic would find the sight of Hester and Pearl on the scaffold reminiscent of a portrait of Madonna and Child. To this original picture are added first the nocturnal scene in which Dimmesdale is joined on the scaffold by Hester and Pearl, and then the climactic scene in which the trio stand there in the light of day. Similarly, the forest is used as a setting for contrasting tableaux – Hester's successive interviews with Chillingworth and Dimmesdale. Through such groupings the dynamics of the story are presented.

A similar stylization is apparent in Hawthorne's treatment of his characters. Henry James noted: 'The people strike me not as characters, but as representatives, very picturesquely arranged, of a single state of mind.' Hester is the woman with the scarlet letter on her bosom, while Dimmesdale, with his hand held continually over his heart, is the living embodiment of a guilty conscience. Chillingworth, the villain of the story, is a compound of several stereotypes familiar in folk literature; he is part devil, part medieval alchemist and part malicious scientist. Often the names of the characters ('Pearl', 'Dimmesdale', 'Chillingworth') enforce these allegorical hints.

Yet the total effect, at least in the case of the major characters, is not to give a reductionist view of human psychology. Although Hawthorne's characters may lack an air of individuality, they inhabit real and complex dilemmas. Indeed, Hawthorne's musings on the various meanings of the letter A is an implicit warning against making snap judgements of people. To the Puritans A means 'Adulteress' and that is all that need be said about Hester. But as the story progresses the letter takes on other and unexpected meanings: 'Able', for example, or 'Angel'. Hester's adultery is obviously a central fact of her character but it is not its sum total. She can reveal new qualities and can change by painful degrees, until what was originally designed as a brand of shame becomes almost a mark of honour.

Clearly, Hawthorne's attitude to his material is far from simply moralistic. Although preoccupied by the Puritan view of life he is also deeply critical of it. His main emphasis is not on sin, a theological phenomenon, but on guilt and secretiveness, psychological phenomena. Because of this, his sympathy for Dimmesdale's dilemma is at least as profound as his feeling for Hester. Hester has been found out and can keep nothing secret; indeed, the book hints that the letter gives her insight into other people's secrets. But Dimmesdale can and does keep much of himself hidden from the public gaze. Hawthorne's portrait of the twistings and windings of a guilty conscience is finely observed and vividly rendered. It is noteworthy that even at the end Dimmesdale cannot make an unambiguous avowal of his guilt: to some observers he still seems a saintly man who chooses a symbolic mode of death. Fittingly, the nearest thing to a moral that Hawthorne can extract from his complex study is a plea for openness and self-revelation: 'Be true! Be true! Be true! Show freely to the world, if not your worst, yet some trait whereby the worst may be inferred!' That last strange qualifying clause is perhaps an indication of how deep were the author's own impulses to secretiveness and reserve.

The House of the Seven Gables

SUMMARY The land on which the House of the Seven Gables stands originally belonged to an early New England settler, Matthew Maule. A neighbour, the stern Colonel Pyncheon, laid claim to the land but Maule resisted. Soon afterwards Maule was executed for witchcraft; Colonel Pyncheon was his chief accuser. Maule, believing that Pyncheon had acted out of personal enmity, cursed him from the scaffold: 'God will give him blood to drink!' With Maule out of the way Pyncheon was able to buy the land and build a fine house; the architect was Thomas Maule, the dead man's son. On the day of the house-opening, however, Colonel Pyncheon was found mysteriously dead in his study.

Over the centuries the Maules have apparently died out; the Pyncheons have been visited by ill-fortune. Some thirty years before the narrative begins the head of the family was murdered. His nephew, Clifford Pyncheon, was found guilty and sentenced to life imprisonment. Judge Pyncheon, another nephew, inherited the family fortune but Clifford's sister, Hepzibah, retained a life interest in the house.

Hepzibah lives alone except for a young lodger, Holgrave, a daguerreotypist. To relieve her poverty Hepzibah opens a small general shop on the ground floor of the house; but her apparently formidable manner – she is really timid and good-natured – discourages customers. With the arrival of Phoebe, Hepzibah's young cousin, the house becomes more cheerful and the shop begins to thrive. Phoebe is impressed by the young daguerreotypist despite herself, for she had been prejudiced against him in advance by Hepzibah's account of his radicalism.

After a bustle of mysterious preparation by Hepzibah, Clifford returns to the house. He is a tired, delicate man with an air of childlike innocence. At this time Phoebe also encounters Judge Pyncheon and finds him repugnant, for all his smiling benevolence. When the Judge tries to enter the house Hepzibah stops him, and Clifford is scared.

Essentially sybaritic, Clifford finds the ugly Hepzibah irritating and prefers Phoebe's company. She sings and reads to him in the garden. In fact, the garden is a great source of pleasure to Clifford, in whom a taste for beauty reasserts itself after years of suffering. Together with Holgrave and Uncle Venner, an old pauper from the town, the Pyncheons enjoy Sunday garden parties. At other times Clifford watches the life of the street from an upstairs window. He has not yet left the grounds of the house; once he resolves to go to church but his courage deserts him.

Phoebe has become less innocently cheerful and more maturely thoughtful. Holgrave tells her about his chequered and picaresque past: he has worked at many varied jobs and travelled widely in Europe. Despite her liking for him she is made uneasy by his lack of reverence for the past and by his detached attitude to the people around him. Holgrave reads her a story he has written about her family's past: it tells how Matthew Maule, grandson of the executed man and son of the builder of the house, gained a destructive hypnotic control over Alice Pyncheon. Holgrave possesses hypnotic powers himself and, by his reading of the story, unintentionally mesmerizes Phoebe. Unlike the Maule of the tale, however, he immediately releases his victim from the spell.

After Phoebe's departure the house and its inhabitants relapse into their customary gloom. Judge Pyncheon arrives demanding to see Clifford and threatening to put him in an asylum unless he agrees to the interview. Clifford, the Judge claims, has stolen and secreted money belonging to the murdered uncle. Hepzibah tries vainly to keep the Judge out but is forced to give way. After an agony of indecision she goes to fetch Clifford from his room; he is not there and, on her return to the parlour, she finds him standing over the Judge's dead body. Brother and sister run away from the house. Hepzibah is scared by the bustle of the outside world she has so long avoided, but Clifford finds a heady sense of exhilaration and freedom. On the train that he and Hepzibah board at random he embarrasses his fellow-passengers by launching into a panegyric in favour of rootlessness and nomadism. But the next morning he and his sister return exhausted to the family house. In their absence Phoebe has returned, and she and Holgrave have discovered the Judge's corpse. Drawn together by the emergency, they have confessed their love for each other.

Medical opinion decides that the Judge died not by Clifford's hand but from a type of seizure hereditary to the Pyncheons. In retrospect it becomes clear that this is how the Judge's uncle had also died. Holgrave uses mesmerism to ascertain the full facts of the supposed murder: the uncle had discovered the young Judge Pyncheon going through his private papers in search of money and had died of a seizure. Judge Pyncheon had deliberately arranged the evidence to incriminate Clifford. One more revelation completes the dénouement: Holgrave confesses that he is a descendant of the Maule family. At the end of the novel, Hepzibah and Clifford, together with Holgrave, Phoebe and Uncle Venner, leave the House of the Seven Gables to live in the country seat they have inherited at the death of Judge Pyncheon.

CRITICAL COMMENTARY Like *The Scarlet Letter*, *The House of the Seven Gables* shows Hawthorne's preoccupation with the past, particularly the Puritan heritage of New England, but it speaks more directly to this theme than its predecessor. It uses motifs common in Gothic and melodramatic fiction – the haunted house, the inherited curse, the decaying aristocratic family and the mysterious murder – to examine how much an awareness of the past is useful and how much it is a crippling burden. Like *The Scarlet Letter* it also poses the question: how can a sense of guilt created by one's personal or inherited past be exorcized?

At the beginning of the novel the House of the Seven Gables seems simply to represent the oppressive power of past history over the present. Originally founded on crime, the house is now stifling its inhabitants. In this context Hepzibah's decision to set up a general shop is a brave effort to break free – to reject the genteel traditions of the Pyncheon family in the name of common sense and economic need. But Hepzibah's nervousness and her initial failure as a shopkeeper show the difficulties of such an attempt.

Subsequent events, however, quickly complicate the reader's view of the past. The most obvious of these is the return of Clifford. In one sense Clifford has no past and this, it appears, can be a disadvantage. It is appropriate that his prison years should never be described or even directly referred to, for they represent a gap in his life. During the years when most people are gaining maturity Clifford merely has a blank in his experience. The result is that he is both a child and an old man but not a mature adult.

Lacking ordinary experience, he is detached from ordinary life. After his release he stays secluded in the family mansion so that it becomes a metaphorical extension of his literal prison. He is a nervous watcher of life from the windows of the house, quickly moved to childish pleasure but equally susceptible to childish fear.

In another sense Clifford is a victim of the past: his life has been ruined by an unjust accusation of murder. With the death of Judge Pyncheon near the end of the book he feels that the spell has been broken and that he is free at last. He flees the house and expatiates on the advantages of rootlessness. But his actions and his words are clearly hysterical. Hepzibah, who travels with him, realizes that the house and its history are not physical entities but psychological forces that cannot be so easily evaded: each time she looks out of the train window she seems to see the house keeping pace with her journey. Clifford's freedom is short-lived and he and Hepzibah are drawn ineluctably back to the house.

Holgrave, the daguerreotypist who lodges with Hepzibah, resembles Clifford. He too is given to viewing life as if it were an aesthetic spectacle, to celebrating the idea of rootlessness and to hating the past. But he has to learn a lesson similar to the one implied by Clifford's return to the house after his abortive attempt at escape. Although Holgrave may jeer at the past he is unable to escape its influence. As he confesses at the end of the book, he is a Maule returning in fascination to the spot where his ancestor suffered. And, as his role in solving the Pyncheon murder mystery makes clear, the past must be properly understood before the present can be freed from its grip. The past cannot be simply disregarded.

Phoebe's role suggests that an awareness of the past – with a concomitant sense of guilt and evil – is a necessary part of adult life, however painful that may be. At the beginning she is the epitome of freshness and innocence, a healthy contrast to the other surviving members of the Pyncheon family. She has an enviable air of freedom and cheerfulness that rubs off on others, brightening the lives of Hepzibah and

Clifford and even making the house itself seem cosy. Yet Hawthorne insists that the gradual subduing of her carefree manner is an inevitable part of growing up. Before Phoebe can admit her love and be united with Holgrave – before she can become fully adult – she must confront the horror of the past in its most brutal form: the body of Judge Pyncheon. This process hints at the idea of the 'Fortunate Fall' – a common theme in Hawthorne's fiction. Perhaps, this theory suggests, Man should welcome Adam's Fall as the means by which he became completely human.

Most critics have agreed that Hawthorne's grasp of these ideas is sophisticated and that he embodies them successfully in concrete situations. Yet they have also found the novel's conclusion disappointing: the miraculously happy ending seems like an evasion of complexities that the book itself has raised. In his pioneering study of Hawthorne (1879), Henry James summed up a reaction to the novel that has been echoed many times since. *The House of the Seven Gables* is 'a rich, delightful, imaginative work, larger and more various than its companions . . . but it is not so rounded and complete as *The Scarlet Letter*.'

The Blithedale Romance

SUMMARY   Miles Coverdale, a poet and the narrator of the story, joins the would-be Utopian community of Blithedale in New England. Blithedale is based on socialist ideals of sharing and on the desire to return to a simple natural life. There Coverdale meets Zenobia, a champion of women's rights and the community's guiding light. 'Zenobia' is not her real name but the *nom de plume* for her magazine articles; her friends have adopted it in private life because it suits her proud and sensuous nature. The company is joined by Hollingsworth, a philanthropist dedicated to reforming criminals by an appeal to their higher instincts. Hollingsworth brings with him the shy and nervous Priscilla, an unexpected addition to the community. Zenobia does not immediately welcome Priscilla – though she later becomes attached to her – while Priscilla adores Zenobia from the start. Later, a letter arrives from one of the city's missionaries commending Priscilla to the care of the people at Blithedale, and hinting that the girl has only just escaped, or may indeed still be threatened by, some unspecified danger.

The next day Coverdale is ill of a fever contracted during the cold and wintry journey to Blithedale. He is tended by Hollingsworth with cheerful sympathy and Christian kindness. Priscilla, meanwhile, has become fresh and animated through her exposure to country life, though she still suffers from occasional bouts of listlessness and nervousness. Despite their personal idiosyncrasies, the members of the community begin to work together as a team, changing their original city clothes for the simple homespun of the labourer and learning about farming from Silas Foster, the hired manager. Inevitably, their rural neighbours are scornful and declare that the Blithedale socialists know nothing about agriculture. Coverdale quickly becomes disillusioned with farm work. He finds in it none of the spiritual significance he had expected: merely tiring and irksome toil.

Coverdale is fascinated by Zenobia, Hollingsworth and Priscilla, who form a distinct trio from which he feels partly excluded, being relegated to the role of observer. Both of the women are obviously attracted to Hollingsworth. Despite his initial respect and affection for the philanthropist, Coverdale quickly becomes suspicious. Hollingsworth, he feels, is too obsessed with his cranky plans for reforming criminals to be wholeheartedly dedicated to the goals of Blithedale. Moreover, Hollingsworth's obsession makes him less than a full human being.

The farm is visited by Mr Moodie, a shy and shabby middle-aged man, who had tried to buttonhole Coverdale just before the poet's departure from Blithedale. Moodie inquires after Priscilla and shows a furtive interest in Zenobia, but does not speak to either of them. Shortly afterwards there is another visitor, Professor Westervelt, a handsome but sinister figure. Coverdale inadvertently overhears the stranger talking to Zenobia: Westervelt is apparently telling her something disturbing about Priscilla. After Westervelt has gone Zenobia tells the story of 'The Veiled Lady' to the group. The veiled lady is a famous contemporary mesmerist and seer who always wears a veil during her public appearances; nobody knows her real identity. She fled – much as Priscilla has done – to a pastoral community like Blithedale for refuge. But the magician in charge of her followed. He asked another woman in the community to throw a veil over the lady to again bring her under his spell. At the end of the story Zenobia playfully throws some gauze over Priscilla, who faints.

The members of the community are in the habit of gathering each Sunday at Eliot's pulpit, a natural rock formation near the river. On one of these occasions, when Zenobia has surprisingly failed to challenge Hollingsworth's contemptuous rejection of women's rights, Coverdale suddenly realizes that Zenobia is in love with the philanthropist. This disquiets him since he suspects that Hollingsworth wants to convert Blithedale to his own ends by making it a centre for the reformation of criminals. He would use Zenobia's money – she is a rich heiress – for this purpose. Hollingsworth and Coverdale quarrel.

Coverdale leaves Blithedale and stays at a hotel in the nearby city. To his surprise he sees Zenobia and Priscilla at the window of a house opposite. When he calls at the house he finds that it is Zenobia's apartment, a luxurious contrast to the simplicities of the Blithedale farm. Westervelt is also there, and Zenobia receives Coverdale coldly. Still curious, he seeks out Mr Moodie in a local bar and hears from him the story of 'Fauntleroy' (obviously Moodie himself). Twenty-five years before, Fauntleroy, a rich man of expensive tastes, committed an unspecified crime in order to retain his wealth. When the crime was discovered he ran away, leaving his daughter Zenobia behind him. After living in furtive obscurity for a while Fauntleroy married again and had a second daughter, Priscilla. Priscilla developed extra-sensory powers and fell under the influence of the sinister Professor Westervelt. A few weeks after hearing

Moodie's story Coverdale attends a public appearance of the Veiled Lady (whom he now, of course, knows to be Priscilla). She is introduced by Westervelt but the performance is interrupted by Hollingsworth. The philanthropist manages to free Priscilla from the Professor's mesmeric influence and take her away.

Coverdale returns to Blithedale, now a changed and saddened place. He interrupts Hollingsworth, Zenobia and Priscilla at a tense moment. To Zenobia's anger and disappointment Hollingsworth has announced that he loves Priscilla and intends to go away with her. Zenobia drowns herself in the river near Eliot's pulpit. Afterwards Hollingsworth and Priscilla lead a secluded life and he never begins his cherished project for the reformation of criminals. At the end of the story Coverdale confesses to the reader that he himself had been in love with Priscilla.

CRITICAL COMMENTARY As Hawthorne himself explains in his preface, *The Blithedale Romance* has a more directly autobiographical origin than any of his other novels. Blithedale is modelled on the Transcendentalist community at Brook Farm, where Hawthorne himself stayed for several months. Like Blithedale, Brook Farm was an experiment in Utopian living based on progressive political ideals; its members flirted with embryonic forms of socialism, with women's rights, and with a radical rejection of urban life. One of its leading lights, the feminist Margaret Fuller, obviously provided Hawthorne with the inspiration for his heroine, Zenobia.

The novel's background is important and gives it a special interest, but it should not be over-stressed. For *The Blithedale Romance* is clearly not a fictionalized historical record, let alone a *roman à clef*: such uses of fiction are entirely alien to Hawthorne's art. Indeed, many aspects of the Blithedale community are handled only sketchily. Its political ideals are spelt out in the briefest terms and its members, apart from Hollingsworth, Zenobia, Priscilla and Coverdale, hardly mentioned. Nor are these central figures at all representative of the community: Coverdale is something of a professional cynic, Hollingsworth a prison reformer, and Priscilla a refugee from danger.

Blithedale interests Hawthorne because it represents a new version of a theme that pervades his work: the attempt to return to a Utopian world, an Eden of pre-lapsarian innocence or an Arcadia of pastoral simplicity. This theme crops up in *The House of the Seven Gables*, where the Pyncheon garden is continually compared to the Garden of Eden, and is handled at some length in *The Marble Faun*, where Donatello's ancestral home recalls the world of classical pastoral. As these parallels bear witness, the attempt to return to Utopia is always shown to be based on dangerous delusion. *The Blithedale Romance*, like so much of Hawthorne's work, asserts the irrevocability of man's connection with sin and guilt. For better or for worse, Hawthorne's characters are trapped in a world of bitter experience that precludes any escape into innocence. In this respect, Priscilla's situation is emblematic: Blithedale, though it seems a refuge, is really powerless to protect her from the dangers represented by the sinister Professor Westervelt.

From the start, then, the members of the Blithedale community bring with them qualities that erode their idealistic goals. Coverdale comes in a spirit of flippant cynicism, while Hollingsworth is still dangerously obsessed with his ideas for the reformation of criminals. Zenobia, despite her air of apparent modesty and the deliberate simplicity of her dress, still has more than a touch of pride and sensuality; this is neatly epitomized by the exotic flower she customarily wears in her hair. Passion, in fact, proves the most dramatically destructive force. Hollingsworth quickly becomes the centre of an uneasy sexual triangle that finally destroys Zenobia and blasts his own and Priscilla's life.

The presence of these themes indicates how central *The Blithedale Romance* is to Hawthorne's preoccupations. Yet it cannot be said that the book is entirely successful, for it lacks the formal assurance and neatness of his best work. The characters of Zenobia and Hollingsworth never come to life properly; they seem more like suggestive rough drafts than fully rounded portraits. The plot is developed hesitantly and with an excess of mystery-making (particularly about Priscilla's past), while the final dénouement – the revelation that Priscilla and Zenobia are both Moodie's daughters – seems contrived.

Yet in one respect the novel is entirely successful and this alone would justify its inclusion amongst Hawthorne's major works. Rather than being simply the passive medium through which the action is viewed, Miles Coverdale is a superbly realized creation in his own right. He is, in fact, probably the best embodiment of a type of person that haunted Hawthorne's imagination: the cold, reserved man who is dangerously detached from his fellow human beings. Coverdale, indeed, spends much of his time spying upon the other characters. Rather than dealing with his own emotions – his concealed, if not repressed, love for Priscilla – he eavesdrops on other people during their moments of emotion. On one such occasion, when he has been watching Zenobia from the window of his hotel room, he has a sudden perception of his own inadequacies: 'That cold tendency, between instinct and intellect, which made me pry with a speculative interest into people's passions and impulses, appeared to have gone far towards unhumanizing my heart.' This dehumanization of the heart fascinated Hawthorne because he feared that it was an occupational hazard of the artist. Concerned to probe people's characters and to find an aesthetic design in the living reality around him, the artist could become a coldly detached observer rather than a fully human and sympathetic participant in life.

The Marble Faun

SUMMARY Miriam, Hilda and Kenyon, touring the art gallery of the Capitol in Rome with their Italian friend, Donatello the Count of Monte Beni, notice his resemblance to Praxiteles' statue of the Faun. Indeed, Donatello, with his innocent and genial nature, also seems very like the faun in character. His three friends are all artists living in Rome. Kenyon is a sculptor and Hilda an inspired copyist of paintings by the old masters. She is pure and ethereal, living at the top of a tower where she tends doves and (though she is not a Catholic) guards the ever-burning lamp at a shrine to the Virgin.

Nobody knows anything about Miriam's past, except that it is shrouded in slightly sinister mystery. This has recently been intensified by an incident during the four friends' visit to the gloomy catacombs of St Calixtus. After being temporarily separated from the rest of the party, Miriam returned with a sinister but picturesque stranger. Their guide suggests that the stranger is the so-called Spectre of the Catacombs, the ghost of a man who had spied on the early Christians and had been condemned to wander around the subterranean corridors until someone volunteers to lead him out into the daylight. The stranger follows Miriam out of the catacombs and haunts her; she uses him several times as a model for some of her drawings. Miriam becomes melancholy and secretive. Visiting Hilda one day she entrusts her friend with a mysterious package, to be delivered to an address in Rome in four months' time.

Donatello is in love with Miriam, though this is not reciprocated. One day, however, he persuades her to walk with him in the woods near Rome, enchanting her with his gay and unaffected manner. They join a party of peasant dancers and Miriam briefly forgets her troubles. But her model reappears and her melancholy returns; she stays behind to talk with him. Kenyon, seeing Miriam return to Rome in the model's company, realizes that she is in the stranger's power in some mysterious way. However, his offers to help are refused.

The four friends go together to a gathering of artists, where Hilda finds a sketch by Guido of the Archangel Michael triumphing over Satan. Donatello fancies there is a resemblance between Guido's Devil and the mysterious model but Miriam strenuously denies this. Afterwards the party walk through the darkened streets of Rome, visiting

its historic sites. The model dogs their footsteps and approaches Miriam and Donatello when they stay behind
together at the Tarpeian rock. Donatello throws the model
to his death from the rock. Hilda, who has returned in
search of Miriam, is a silent and inadvertent witness to the
murder.

After tramping the streets of Rome for the night the
guilty couple join Kenyon next morning at a local church.
They see the body of a monk laid out on a bier: it is Miriam's
model. It bleeds when Miriam looks at it, as corpses are
fabled to do in the presence of their murderers. Donatello
and Miriam agree to part. Later, when Miriam visits Hilda
she is rebuffed. The cold and pure Hilda, shocked by the
crime she witnessed, now feels distaste for her former friend.

The following summer Kenyon visits Donatello at his
ancestral home in the Tuscan hills but finds his host a
changed man. Rather than leading his former gay pastoral
life, Donatello now seems sombre, reserved and thoughtful.
This new gravity, however, has brought with it a corresponding development of intellectual and moral power.
Kenyon discovers that Miriam is also staying at Monte Beni,
though without Donatello knowing. He arranges for her and
Donatello to meet on a given day in Perugia, a nearby town.
The meeting results in the couple's reunion.

In the meantime Hilda has remained in Rome burdened
by the knowledge of Donatello's crime. Her artistic talents
have deserted her and she begins to frequent Catholic
churches, despite the fact that she comes from a solidly
Puritan New England family. On one occasion she goes so
far as to receive confession, telling the priest about the
murder of the model. Kenyon, who is in love with Hilda,
returns to Rome to try to help her. She, however, feels only
friendship and affection for him. Hilda decides to deliver the
mysterious package that Miriam had entrusted to her, but
she does not return from this errand.

After several days of frantic searching Kenyon at last
meets Miriam and Donatello, who assure him that Hilda is
safe and will soon return. Miriam also explains some of the

mysteries of her past. She comes from an ancient Italian family, but disassociated herself from her relatives after she had been unjustly accused of a crime. The model was a madman involved in the crime. At the Roman carnival two days later Kenyon sees Hilda again, though she offers no explanation for her disappearance. During the carnival the police arrest Donatello and Miriam.

In a concluding note Hawthorne offers some explanation of the plot's obscurities. The package that Hilda delivered was a communication from Miriam to her family. Since both the family and the Roman police were seeking Miriam in connection with the model's murder, they detained Hilda in the hope that she could tell them about her friend's whereabouts. Subsequently, Miriam is released but Donatello imprisoned.

CRITICAL COMMENTARY There was a gap of eight years between *The Blithedale Romance* and the publication of Hawthorne's next (and last complete) novel, *The Marble Faun*. The author spent this period away from the New England that had inspired his earlier work, living first in England and then in Italy. His daily experiences and reflections during these years are recorded in his *Notebooks*, but the novel itself is by far the most important expression of his reactions to European culture. For Italy dominates *The Marble Faun* as powerfully as New England had dominated *The Scarlet Letter*. The book abounds in set-pieces of description dealing with the Italian landscape, social customs and the monuments of the Roman past. Many of these descriptions, of course, are too long (Hawthorne concedes as much in his preface) and impede the movement of the narrative.

Yet Italy is important as far more than a picturesque backdrop or a source of interesting local colour. Where earlier American novels had dealt almost exclusively with American settings, *The Marble Faun* is the first novel to concern itself with America's efforts to come to terms with the Old World. We see, for example, Hilda being attracted to Catholicism despite her Puritan upbringing, and the resolutely commonsensical Kenyon being seduced by the agelessly pastoral atmosphere of Donatello's home at Monte Beni. By touching on these subjects Hawthorne is venturing into a territory that later American novelists eagerly explored. Henry James, himself an expatriate for most of his adult life, was to make such 'transatlantic' themes peculiarly his own.

In James' own age the American interest in Italy had become so intense that *The Marble Faun*, now the most neglected of Hawthorne's major novels, was probably the most popular. As James himself testified in his study of Hawthorne (1879), *The Marble Faun* was regarded as a fictional supplement to Baedeker's guide: 'It is part of the intellectual equipment of the Anglo-Saxon visitor to Rome, and is read by every English-speaking traveller who arrives there, who has been there, or who expects to go.'

Above all, Italy to Hawthorne means art – the statues and ruins of the classical age and the paintings of the Renaissance. The book is so abundant in artistic references that at times it threatens to become a handbook to Western painting. Yet these allusions are used with a serious purpose, for the characters are often defined by parallels with works of art. Thus, for example, Donatello is compared to the innocent faun of Praxiteles' statue and the stranger in the catacombs to the Devil in Guido's painting. Kenyon's own statue of Cleopatra hints at a streak of sensuality in his nature that relates him to Miriam and distinguishes him from the coldly chaste Hilda. The contrast between Hilda and Miriam is further highlighted by their differing reactions to Guido's portrait of Beatrice Cenci.

In his preface Hawthorne seeks to explain the attraction that Italy has for the writer of romances. The American landscape, because of its very newness, has few of those associations in which romancers delight: it has 'no shadow, no antiquity, no mystery, no picturesque and gloomy wrong, nor anything but a commonplace prosperity, in broad and simple daylight'. Yet this does not mean that Hawthorne uses his European setting for mere picturesqueness. In his eyes Italian culture is so streaked with myth and its present realities so overshadowed by the grandeur of the past that the artist is freed from the demands of painstaking fidelity to ordinary life and the laws of probability. In *The Marble Faun* Hawthorne moves further towards a type of romance that consists almost entirely of allegory and owes little to realism. The tendency of his characters to become emblematic types, already noted in connection with *The Scarlet Letter*, becomes more pronounced. Hilda, for example, represents what Milton called 'a cloistered virtue': she is kind and gentle, but with a purity that shrinks from any contact with the world, the flesh and the devil. So, in her treatment of Miriam after the model's murder, she seems needlessly harsh and priggish. Similarly, Donatello is far from being a typical modern Italian nobleman. He is the embodiment of a pagan innocence that is neither good nor bad, but simply pleasure-loving, thoughtless and carefree. His change after the murder is a type of man's development after the Fall into a less instinctively happy but more intellectually and morally refined being.

Indeed, the book's 'thoughtful moral' that Hawthorne tantalizingly alludes to in his preface appears to be this idea of the 'Fortunate Fall', already mentioned in the discussion of *The House of the Seven Gables*. As Kenyon observes, Donatello's sinful act has benefited him as much as it has corrupted him: '"Is sin, then, – which we deem such a dreadful blackness in the universe, – is it, like sorrow, merely an element of human education, through which we struggle to a higher and purer state than we could otherwise have attained? Did Adam fall, that we might ultimately rise to a far loftier paradise than his?"'

Even if the reader is willing to accept the conventions of allegory, *The Marble Faun* must still be adjudged a fertile experiment rather than an unqualified success. As in his earlier novels Hawthorne has great difficulty devising an appropriate ending. He originally finished the story with the arrest of Miriam and Donatello during the Roman carnival, but the bafflement of early readers persuaded him to add a further section unravelling some of the plot's obscurities. Even this did not satisfy his critics, for Hawthorne's concluding note raises as many problems as it solves. He still could not decide whether his novel should end on a note of resonant mystery or with one of those neat dénouements so beloved by nineteenth-century readers. The result of his indecision is an irritating mixture of deliberate obscurity and half-hearted explanation that does much to spoil the effect of the book's earlier successes.

FURTHER READING There is no completely satisfactory edition of Hawthorne's works, a problem all too common with American writers. The best is the twelve-volume Riverside edition of the *Complete Works* (1883), edited by George P. Lathrop. In 1962 the Ohio University Press began its *Centenary Edition of the Works of Nathaniel Hawthorne*; when completed this will no doubt become standard. The most comprehensive account of Hawthorne's life is still George E. Woodberry's *Nathaniel Hawthorne* (1902). Of more recent biographical studies those by Newton Arvin (1929) and Randall Stewart (1948) are probably the best. Randall Stewart has also published useful editions of the *American Notebooks* (1932) and the *English Notebooks* (1941).

In the nineteenth century Hawthorne was the subject of a perceptive review by Edgar Allan Poe and an illuminating short book by Henry James (1879). In this century there has been an avalanche of general and specialist studies from which it is difficult as well as invidious to select a short list of titles. However, R. H. Fogle's *Hawthorne's Fiction: The Light in the Dark* (1952), H. H. Waggoner's *Nathaniel Hawthorne: A Critical Study* (1955), and Frederick Crews' *The Sins of the Fathers; Hawthorne's Psychological Themes* (1966) offer useful starting-points for the interested reader.

Herman Melville

Melville was born in New York in 1819, of English and Dutch ancestry. After leaving school at the age of fifteen and doing various clerical jobs he enlisted, in 1839, as cabin-boy on a voyage to Liverpool. Thus began five years at sea, including an eighteen-month voyage on a whaling ship and a stay with the Typee natives in the Marquesas. In 1844 he returned to America and started a career as a novelist. His early books – *Typee* (1846), *Omoo* (1847), *Mardi* (1849), *Redburn* (1849) and *White-Jacket* (1850) – draw heavily on his experiences as a sailor.

Melville married in 1847 and moved in 1850 to Massachusetts, where he lived for thirteen years. Nathaniel Hawthorne was a neighbour and close friend. With *Moby Dick* (1851) Melville reached the high-point of his art. His early books had sold well but the philosophical complexities of his later works made them commercial failures. With the publication of *Pierre* (1852), *Israel Potter* (1855), *The Piazza Tales* (1856) and *The Confidence Man* (1857) his popularity steadily waned. He finally abandoned writing, except for the novella, *Billy Budd*, completed just before his death. In 1863 he moved to New York where he lived in obscurity, working as a Customs Inspector. By the time he died in 1891 he was a completely forgotten figure.

Posterity has rectified this injustice. From the 1920s onwards there has been a steady revival of interest in Melville's work. His position as one of the masters of nineteenth-century fiction is now completely secure and his best book, *Moby Dick*, is widely recognized as one of the greatest novels in any language. As that novel would suggest, the strength of Melville's achievement lies in his mastery of a variety of literary skills. He is a first-rate adventure novelist, though he is rarely simply an adventure novelist. American fiction is perpetually fascinated by man's relation to nature and in this area Melville is supreme. In his work outdoor action is used as a springboard into complex speculation about the natural environment. Does it contain evil, or is that found only in man? If not evil, is nature amoral and so indifferent to man's suffering?

Moby Dick achieves an ideal combination of adventure

and metaphysics and is a more obviously serious work than the novels that preceded it. But in Melville's later fiction the metaphysics predominate and the result is an increasing obscurity, as well as a note of bitterness. Despite this decline in power, *The Confidence Man* is noteworthy as a spirited satire, while *Billy Budd* is a lucid treatment of Melville's perpetual theme, the 'mystery of iniquity'.

Typee

SUMMARY The hero (who also narrates the story) has spent six months at sea in the whaling ship *Dolly* and is beginning to long for the sight of land. The ship is bound on a lazy idyllic voyage for the Marquesas, a group of unspoilt South Sea islands. It arrives at Nukuheva – the best-known of these islands – just after the French have asserted dominion. Friendly natives swim out to greet the vessel. There are three groups of inhabitants on the islands: the natives of Nukuheva bay, the Happars and the Typees. 'Typee' means 'cannibal', though *all* the natives on the island are reputed to eat human flesh.

The hero is enchanted by the island's verdant and peaceful scenery and, when he sees the French admiral Du Petit Thouars, receiving tribute from the King of Tior, he reflects on the superiority of so-called barbarism over civilization. Already discontented with long spells at sea and with the bad and tyrannical conditions on board the ship, he decides to desert. He plans to stay in the mountains of the island, where he would not be found by the natives until the *Dolly* had gone. He persuades another member of the crew, Toby, a gentleman who will not talk about his past or his origins, to join him.

They carry out their escape successfully – but in a heavy rainstorm that damages their supplies of food. After an uncomfortable night in the open they awake weak with hunger. They see a beautiful and verdant valley beneath them, but hesitate to descend for fear that it is the home of the savage Typee tribe. They set out in the hope of finding another, untenanted valley, but the journey is arduous and involves much difficult rock-climbing. To make matters worse, the hero develops an intermittent fever. After a second uncomfortable night Toby insists that they return to the first valley, trusting that it is inhabited by the friendly Happars rather than the Typees. Toby's confidence heartens his friend and makes him better able to endure the difficult journey.

On their arrival in the valley they soon meet two young natives, who seem shy but friendly. Their entry into the native village causes great excitement. They are introduced to chief Mehevi and realize to their alarm that they are amongst Typees; but the natives are not actively hostile. The hero gives his name as Tom, which the Typees quickly corrupt to Tommo. The next morning they are visited by a succession of inquisitive natives. Tommo's leg is badly swollen after his climbing and he has to suffer the clumsy ministrations of the tribe's doctor. The two white men are lodged in a comfortable bamboo and coconut house (called a 'pi-pi'), with a servant, Kory-Kory, his elderly and eccentric father, Marheyo, and hard-working mother, Tinor. The household also includes several youths and some young girls, of whom Tommo's favourite is Fayaway.

After a public bath (which causes him much embarrassment) Tommo and his friend are taken by Mehevi to visit the taboo groves – where rites of worship and cannibal feasts are held – and the 'Ti', a large open building that seems to be Mehevi's palace. At the 'Ti' they eat, smoke and fall asleep. When they wake they find the natives assembled and a fire lit, and fear that they are about to become victims of cannibalism. But Mehevi simply offers them some cooked meat – which turns out to be pork.

Tommo's leg gets worse and, although he needs medical attention, the natives are reluctant to let the white men go. But they agree to let Toby fetch medical supplies. On his first attempt Toby is attacked by Happars and returns wounded. Shortly afterwards, hearing that boats have pulled into the harbour, Toby insists on going down to meet them; he does not return. At first Tommo does not worry and continues to enjoy the indolent Typee way of life. But he becomes depressed when Toby does not return after several days. When he hears a report of a boat again landing he tries to go down to the beach, but the Typees stop him. At last he realizes that he is a captive in the valley.

He becomes attached to Fayaway and boats with her on the lake; for this she requires a special exemption from the Typee taboo against women entering boats. One day Marnoo, a fine-looking stranger, arrives in the village. He is a 'taboo' native, allowed to move freely between the various hostile tribes. Marnoo, who speaks English, agrees to plead with the chief for Tommo's release but Mehevi violently refuses the request.

Tommo becomes reconciled to his fate, joining in the life of the Typees and observing their customs. He attends a religious feast, whose exact significance he cannot determine. Indeed, Typee religion puzzles him in many ways and he can find out little about it except that it revolves around the worship of a god called Moa Artua. He is sure, though, that the Typees are not the slaves of savage superstition that earlier travellers had made them out to be. He is struck by the health and physical beauty of the natives and is sure that they are of a different race from the inhabitants of Nukuheva bay. Typee society, he notes, is egalitarian and with few laws except the idea of 'taboo'. The Typees adorn themselves with tattoos and are irritatingly persistent in their suggestion that Tommo himself should have his face tattooed.

After a fierce battle with the Happars, the Typees hold a nocturnal feast from which Tommo is firmly excluded. Visiting its site next day he is revolted to find traces of cannibal rites. Marnoo comes again and Tommo again asks for help in escaping from the valley. Reluctantly Marnoo says that he will help if Tommo can make his own way to nearby Pueerarka. Strange boats arrive in the harbour and Tommo insists on going down to see what is happening. He finds Karakoee, a native crewmate from the *Dolly*, bargaining for Tommo's freedom. The Typees are extremely reluctant to let their prisoner go but Tommo, seizing his opportunity, jumps into the boat and is carried safely away.

A sequel to the story deals with the fate of Toby. When he went to the beach on the day of his disappearance Toby met Jimmy, an old roving sailor from Nukuheva. Jimmy persuaded Toby to leave, promising to return to fetch Tommo. On reaching Nukuheva Toby signed up on a ship and anxiously awaited his friend's arrival. But Jimmy betrayed him and Toby's ship sailed before anything further could be done. Toby and Tommo each assumed the other to be dead until they met by accident many years later.

CRITICAL COMMENTARY Published in 1846, *Typee* was Melville's first novel. It was based on his adventures in 1842 when he jumped ship in the Marquesas and spent a month living with the Typees. The book's factual basis was emphasized by the title under which it was originally published in England: *Melville's Marquesas Islands*. Unlike much of Melville's later and more complex work it was a commercial success and its popularity was aided by an unexpected piece of publicity. After the appearance of the first edition it was discovered that Melville's companion, Richard Tobias Greene – the 'Toby' of the novel – was not dead as the author had assumed. Melville quickly added a sequel to later editions recounting how Toby had escaped from the Typees. In only one respect did the book fail to please popular taste. Its many frank references to nudity and sexuality offended nineteenth-century notions of decency and were either omitted or toned down in subsequent editions.

Typee thus has in an extreme form an appeal common in Melville's work: it aims to tell the reader interesting facts. This desire to gain information is one of the deepest (and most underrated) appeals that fiction has for the reader. Melville incorporated in *Moby Dick* an exhaustive encyclopaedia of whaling lore and in *Typee* he set out to describe the life of primitive South Sea islanders. He explains the flora and fauna of the valley, the habits of the natives, their concept of law (the mysterious 'taboo'), and he ponders on their puzzling religious rites. Much of his interest is obviously polemical: he is concerned to correct the prejudiced and misleading accounts of the Typees given by earlier writers and to attack the Western influence on South Sea life. He is also something of a scholar. He probes the mysteries of Typee religion carefully and comes only to tentative conclusions, just as in *Moby Dick* Ishmael is a whimsical pedant on the subject of whaling.

Despite all this, *Typee* is not primarily a work of anthropology or travel literature. It is made art by something more than the fictive embellishments that Melville adds to his own real-life adventures. For he finds in Typee life the embodiment of a dream that haunted the imagination of American novelists throughout the nineteenth century – the dream of a blissfully innocent pastoral world, a second Eden. Melville's hero runs away from a ship that, with its bad conditions and its tyrannical administration, epitomizes the worst of civilized life. As he travels through the lush and verdant landscape of the island he is introduced to a way of life that is the antithesis of Western civilization. The young couple, almost naked, whom he and Toby meet obviously recall Adam and Eve, and the village to which the young couple lead them seems free from the stresses and artificialities of modern life. The Typees are physically beautiful, relaxed in their sexual mores, rarely ill and slow to age. They work little (in striking contrast to the world of nineteenth-century industrialism and its 'gospel of work'), for the land provides for their wants without elaborate cultivation. Tommo and Toby quickly settle down to an almost enchanted existence: they eat, smoke, sleep, bathe, play games and boat on the lake.

Typee valley, however, is not entirely idyllic. The book shows Melville's attraction to innocent pastoralism, but also his ultimate rejection of it. He is obviously disturbed by much about the natives: their idleness has a lack of intellectuality that irritates him, and their apparent innocence is sometimes a mask for deceptiveness. Despite their protestations they are cannibals, and they are also determined to keep the hero a captive in the valley. Clearly, if this is Eden, it is an Eden which the serpent has already entered. Penetrating back to nature in its simplest form, the hero discovers that the seed of evil has already been sown. This simultaneous attraction to, and suspicion of, natural life is one of the deepest tensions of Melville's art: it becomes a central theme in his greatest work, *Moby Dick*.

Moby Dick

SUMMARY Bored by life on dry land, Ishmael decides to enlist as a whaler. In New Bedford he lodges at 'The Spouter Inn', run by Peter Coffin. Because the place is crowded he agrees to share a room and bed with a harpooner. The harpooner turns out to be a tattooed savage from the South Seas, and Ishmael is at first terrified of him. But Queequeg is friendly and polite and the two soon strike up a friendship. The next morning Ishmael attends a sermon by Father Mapple, a favourite preacher amongst whaling men, who takes the story of Jonah as his text. Ishmael and Queequeg take the ferry to Nantucket, the traditional centre of New England whaling.

At Ishmael's suggestion they sign up on the *Pequod*, an old, grotesquely carved but serviceable ship. As they board they are buttonholed by Elijah, an old sailor, who warns them against Ahab, the captain of the *Pequod*. The owner, Peleg, pilots the ship out of the harbour while Ahab remains below decks in his cabin, unseen by the crew. The *Pequod*'s chief mate is Starbuck, an earnest Nantucket Quaker whose attitude to whaling is purely businesslike. Stubb is the second mate – a fearless, happy-go-lucky fellow, perpetually smoking his pipe. The third mate, Flask, is pugnacious and humorous. Of the three harpooners, Queequeg works in Starbuck's boat, Tashtego, a Red Indian, with Stubb, and Dagoo, an African, with Flask.

Only when the ship is at sea does Ishmael first see Ahab. He is an impressive, brooding figure, with an artificial leg made from whalebone and a white streak down one side of his body, like a lightning-mark. When the *Pequod* reaches warmer waters Ahab addresses the assembled crew. He nails a gold Spanish doubloon to the mast – a prize for the first man to sight Moby Dick, the famous white whale. Moby Dick is an almost legendary creature, incalculably old and supposedly malevolent. It was he who took off Ahab's leg and Ahab has become obsessed with the idea of revenge. This offends Starbuck's business sense; besides, he argues, the whale acted only out of blind instinct in wounding Ahab. But the Captain inflames the crew with his rhetoric and the harpoons are ritually dedicated to killing Moby Dick. Ishmael, too, is swayed, though he later comes to doubt Ahab's sanity.

One day, when Ishmael and Queequeg are on deck together weaving a mat, Tashtego sights a school of sperm whales. The boats are lowered and at the last minute Ahab himself appears to lead a boat of his own; its crew are a group of natives, led by Fedallah, whose presence on board has been kept a secret from the rest of the crew. Because of a squall the chase has to be called off. For several nights afterwards the crew see a ghostly whale-spout in the distance. They also mistake a giant white squid for Moby Dick. Ishmael sights a whale, which Stubb kills. The corpse is moored to the side of the ship and stripped of its blubber. The head is preserved and the rest of the body cast loose for the sharks to devour.

The *Pequod* meets the *Jeroboam* which has a contagious epidemic on board. Its chief mate has been killed in an encounter with Moby Dick. The crew of the *Pequod* drain the valuable spermaceti from the head of the sperm whale they have killed. During this difficult operation Tashtego nearly drowns but is saved by Queequeg. During the pursuit of another whale they only narrowly beat another ship, the *Jungfrau* (or *Virgin*), to the kill. But the whale they harpoon is so heavy that it almost capsizes the ship and has to be cast loose. In the Java Sea they come upon a herd of whales but manage to kill only one. One of the wounded whales is picked up by the *Rose-Bud*; in answer to the inevitable query from Ahab the captain of the *Rose-Bud* replies that he has not sighted the white whale. Pip, the *Pequod*'s Negro cabin-boy, is killed when he falls from one of the whaling boats. Under Stubb's supervision the ship starts up its try-works – large vats used to boil down whale blubber.

The *Pequod* crosses paths with the *Samuel Enderby* of London. Although its captain, Boomer, has lost an arm to Moby Dick he does not bear the white whale any special grudge. Indeed, he tries to dissuade Ahab from his vengeful quest. Returning to his own ship from the *Samuel Enderby*, Ahab damages his artificial leg, which the ship's carpenter-blacksmith replaces. Queequeg suffers from a fever and has his coffin made. Even when he recovers he still keeps the coffin by him.

When the ship enters the Pacific Ahab has his harpoon sharpened in readiness for the encounter with Moby Dick that he still desperately seeks. They pass the *Bachelor* on its way back to Nantucket after a successful voyage, but Ahab parleys only long enough to learn that there is no news of the white whale. Starbuck, disturbed by his captain's monomania, debates mutiny but suppresses the impulse. Lightning inverts the ship's compasses and Ahab has to make a makeshift substitute. The ominous atmosphere is increased when one of the crew falls from the mast-head into the sea.

A passing whaler, the *Rachel*, reports meeting Moby Dick. Indeed, the whale has sunk a boat containing the captain's son. Rather than help look for survivors Ahab presses on with his chase. Another ship, the *Delight*, has had a boat smashed by Moby Dick. At last the *Pequod* sights the white whale. The chase lasts three days. On the first day Ahab's whale boat is destroyed. On the second, the whale again defeats his hunters and Ahab's artificial leg is broken. On the last day of the confrontation Moby Dick actually sinks the *Pequod* and Ahab, holding on to a harpoon rope, is dragged off in the wake of the enraged whale. Only Ishmael survives. He floats on Queequeg's coffin and is picked up by the *Rachel*.

CRITICAL COMMENTARY When *Moby Dick* was first published in 1851 its critical reception ranged from indifference to hostility. Even those reviewers who had appreciated Melville's previous books dismissed his new novel in contemptuous and derisive terms. The American *Literary World* called it an 'intellectual chowder', while the English *New Monthly Magazine* called its style 'maniacal – mad as a March hare'. Hawthorne, to whom *Moby Dick* is actually dedicated, was amongst the very few early readers to discern its importance. 'What a book Melville has written!' he wrote to a friend. 'It gives me an idea of much greater power than his preceding ones.'

Posterity, of course, has endorsed Hawthorne's judgement. Today *Moby Dick* is widely regarded as the summit not only of Melville's art but of American nineteenth-century fiction. In his *Studies in Classic American Literature* (1923) D. H. Lawrence exclaimed simply: 'It is a great book.' In *The American Novel and Its Tradition* (1957) Richard Chase can refer to the novel as 'the grandest expression of the American imagination', with the air of a man echoing a truism rather than arguing a case.

Yet the genesis of *Moby Dick* was modest enough. In earlier works Melville had used his own youthful experiences as a sailor as the basis for his stories. No doubt he originally conceived *Moby Dick* in the same vein. It was to be an adventure story using the personal knowledge of whaling that he had acquired during his voyages on the *Acushnet* and the *Charles and Henry* in the 1840s. But as he proceeded, the novel grew in sophistication and complexity. Melville drew on his formidable expertise about the history of whaling, his reading of the Bible and Shakespeare (especially *King Lear*) and his own habit of speculation about the natural universe. The result is a book at once amazingly diverse and brilliantly unified.

How, then, did Melville convert an apparently simple adventure story into so rich and complex an achievement? Much of the answer lies in his use of allegory and symbolism, those favourite devices of American nineteenth-century fiction. The actual details of the tale develop suggestive overtones which Ishmael, the most garrulous of narrators, is quick to point out. This can be seen in its simplest form in the way many of the characters are named. Ahab, the *Pequod*'s captain, bears the same name as the vengeful and wicked King in the Old Testament, while the old sailor who warns the crew against Ahab is called Elijah. Ishmael himself is named, appropriately enough, after a Biblical outcast and pariah. Even the ships bear significant names. The *Pequod*, a doomed craft, has been christened after an extinct tribe of Massachusetts Indians. The *Rachel*, like the Rachel of the Old Testament, is sorrowing at the loss of a child.

One notes also that the details of the narrative are surrounded with ominous hints. Ishmael begins his journey at an inn run by a man called Peter Coffin and he ends floating on Queequeg's coffin. The crew mistake a giant white squid for Moby Dick – and squids are a sure sign of bad luck according to nautical superstition. The first man to stand lookout for the white whale falls from the mast-head to his death.

In fact, throughout the book Melville is in the habit of finding allegorical or symbolic meaning in the simplest and most concrete of facts. Ishmael, for example, is impressed by the ship's prow that Father Mapple uses as his pulpit, and immediately sees this as a deliberate allegory about the similarity between clergymen and ship's captains. In his eyes, the monkey-rope connecting the sailors during the stripping of the whale's blubber is not merely a practical safety mechanism; it is also an allegory of man's dependence on the goodwill of his fellows. The other characters share Ishmael's habit of mind and, when several of them find different meanings in the same object, a complex symbol begins to emerge. This is seen at its most obvious in the chapter entitled 'The Doubloon', where various members of the crew examine in turn the coin that Ahab has nailed to the mast as a reward for sighting the white whale. Predictably enough, Ahab interprets the design on the coin as a reflection of his own glory, and Starbuck sees it as a gloomy religious warning. To Stubb the design is a whimsical picture of man's inevitable progress from the cradle to the grave, while the down-to-earth Flask immediately sees the coin in terms of its financial value and the number of cigars it would buy.

Moby Dick is treated in the same way as the doubloon; Melville is concerned to show that the white whale means different things to different people. The crew of the *Pequod* is a microcosm of American society itself – it contains representatives of most social and ethnic groups – and out of their various reactions to the chase Melville constructs a complicated statement about the American view of nature. Starbuck is an earnest Nantucket Quaker and in his eyes whaling is simply a business; he is interested in earning a living, not in pursuing romantic quests. Inevitably, he disapproves of Ahab's policy, and at one point even debates mutiny against the Captain. If nature exists for Starbuck merely to be exploited, it exists for Ishmael to be enjoyed as a refuge. He becomes a whaler to get away from society. At the beginning of the book he talks about his growing depression and his discontent with life on land; at least to begin with, his motives for joining the cruise are purely escapist.

To Ahab the pursuit of the white whale is all-important. Moby Dick has wounded him (Melville discreetly hints that Ahab did not merely lose his leg, but was also castrated), and his determination to get his revenge becomes an obsession. The whale, he insists, struck him out of malice, not blind instinct; indeed, it represents all the evil in the natural universe. Ahab's quest is an attempt to penetrate to the heart of nature's mystery – to confront God himself if necessary, but certainly to go beyond the normal limits of human knowledge. The practical and God-fearing Starbuck can see only lunacy and blasphemy in such an endeavour. But, as Melville insists, it also shows that magnificent and fatal pride which one sees in the heroes of Greek and Renaissance tragedy. Captain Ahab is a latter-day Faust or King Lear.

Although Melville is impressed by Ahab's defiance of the universe, he ultimately disapproves of it, as the description of Ishmael's reactions is designed to make clear. To begin with, Ishmael is converted by Ahab's inflammatory rhetoric; he cheers his Captain enthusiastically with the rest of the crew. But as the voyage progresses, he becomes more and more detached. While Ahab conducts his frenetic pursuit of Moby Dick, Ishmael settles for a different sort of quest. He undertakes long scholarly inquiries about whales and whaling lore, and particularly about Moby Dick itself. The narrator becomes a parody of the pedantic scholar, endlessly piling up evidence; one such chapter is entitled, 'Of Whales in Paint; in Teeth; in Wood; in Sheet-Iron; in Stone; in Mountains; in Stars'. Ishmael does not see the humour of this, but Melville certainly does. Yet at the same time, Ishmael's quest is at once more intelligent and safer than Ahab's. Appropriately enough, Ishmael is the only survivor of the final confrontation with Moby Dick.

It is still, however, the tragedy of Ahab that dominates the book and gives it its peculiar grandeur. Beginning with a personal experience of whaling and a simple enough story of adventure at sea, Melville constructed a novel that is as complicated in its technique as it is daring in its speculation. For *Moby Dick* is part drama, part adventure story, part philosophical inquiry, part scientific study and part epic poem. It is a leviathan of a book.

Billy Budd

SUMMARY During the Napoleonic Wars a young sailor named Billy (or Baby) Budd is pressed from the crew of the merchant ship *The Rights-of-Man* into the service of HMS *Indomitable*. As he explains to Lieutenant Ratcliffe, Captain Graveling is sorry to lose Billy since he had been a peace-maker in an otherwise inharmonious crew. Billy is an extremely handsome young man, merry and artless in his manner. He is entirely innocent and unselfconscious; his only imperfection is a tendency to stutter when upset or angry. He quickly adjusts to his new position and becomes a favourite on the *Indomitable*.

Recent mutinies at Spithead and the Nore have roused fears of disaffection throughout the navy. Yet the *Indomitable* is apparently a happy ship. Its captain is Edward Vere, commonly known as Starry Vere. He is a brave sailor and firm disciplinarian, but his tendency to dreaminess and intellectuality makes him unpopular with his fellow-officers. The Master-at-Arms is John Claggart, a man in his mid-thirties who entered the navy only recently. He is more educated and genteel than his humble post would suggest. Nobody knows anything about his background or birth – there is even some doubt as to whether he is actually English.

Billy is punctilious in the performance of his duties, so he is surprised when he is reprimanded for carelessness with his kit. He consults the Dansker, an old veteran, who says that Claggart has a secret hatred of Billy. Billy does not believe this, but in fact Claggart does dislike the handsome young sailor. Squeak, the Master-at-Arms' underling, has been fomenting trouble and bringing back bad reports of Billy to feed Claggart's antagonism. One night the young sailor is approached by another member of the crew with the suggestion that he join a projected mutiny. Stuttering almost uncontrollably, Billy rejects the idea. He does not inform the officers but confides in the Dansker, who suggests that Claggart was in some way behind the incident.

Claggart seeks an interview with Vere and alleges that Billy is involved in a mutinous conspiracy. Vere, who has been favourably impressed by the little he has seen of Billy, receives the accusation with suspicion. Billy is summoned secretly to the Captain's cabin. Confronted with his accuser, he begins to stutter too violently to answer coherently. In frustration he lashes out at Claggart and kills him.

Vere summons a drumhead court of three officers, although he could have put Billy in irons and referred the matter to the Admiralty instead. Billy denies the accusation of mutiny. He explains that when his stutter prevented him from answering Claggart he simply struck out in blind rage. He can suggest no reason why Claggart should have hated him. Vere urges his fellow-officers to concentrate not on Claggart's character but on Billy's action. When they hesitate about a verdict, Vere advises them to set aside their compassion and carry out the letter of martial law. Billy is sentenced to death. During the night the chaplain visits him and finds him serene but uninterested in religious consolation. He is executed the next morning, dying with the words, 'God bless Captain Vere!' on his lips. Shortly afterwards Vere is killed in battle and murmurs Billy's name as he dies. Among the crew Billy becomes a legend: the spar from which he was hanged is preserved as a relic and a song, 'Billy in the Darbies', is written about him.

CRITICAL COMMENTARY After the commercial (and to some extent, literary) failure of his later novels Melville virtually abandoned writing. But he did return to fiction once; the manuscript of *Billy Budd* was left among his papers at the time of his death in 1891. It was apparently completed and revised, but in a sufficiently bad condition to pose many problems for its editors. There is still some doubt, for example, as to whether the story's full title should be *Billy Budd, Sailor* or *Billy Budd, Foretopman*. It was not published until 1924, when its appearance helped to draw attention to Melville's largely forgotten work. Now it is widely recognized as one of his finest books. Where most of Melville's later work is embittered and obscure, *Billy Budd* is lucid and graceful – a quietly assured masterpiece.

Like most of Melville's best work it deals with the sea. His own early experiences as a sailor provided continual fuel for his imagination and he always found the ship's deck the best setting for working out his human dramas. In spite of the elaborate care with which the nautical and historical background is created, *Billy Budd* is clearly not intended as a realistic work. It is neither sea-story nor historical novel in the accepted senses of those terms. Melville, like many American novelists of his age, turned naturally to symbolism and allegory, and this, his last work, shows this tendency in an extreme form.

Most obviously, the story is charged with allusions to the political upheavals of the era in which it is set. Billy himself represents, however unwittingly, something of that spirit of 'newness' and radicalism which had been expressed in the French and American Revolutions. He comes from *The Rights-of-Man*, named after Tom Paine's influential radical manifesto, to a ship that represents the Old World and the old order of things. HMS *Indomitable* is a rigidly hierarchical community whose lowest members are little better than slaves. The Captain's name – the Honorable Edward Fairfax Vere – is a small essay in aristocratic lineage, while Claggart, with his deceptively polite and unassuming manner, is a walking perversion of gentility.

These elements, however, are subordinated to a deeper – in fact, a fundamental – allegory. The clash between Billy and Claggart is presented as a confrontation of absolute good and absolute evil. The carefree and innocent Billy is (as the narrative repeatedly insists) an Adam before the Fall. By his death he becomes a Christ-figure. His hanging is accompanied by apparently supernatural phenomena – like the absence of the usual muscular spasm in the corpse. He dies, like Christ, forgiving those who kill him. And after his death, the crew cherish mementoes of him like sacred relics.

The villain, Claggart, is a more difficult character to understand. Indeed, Melville devotes two chapters (11 and 13) to analysing Claggart's motives – or rather, to explaining why his motives can never be satisfactorily analysed. As most readers have noted, there is a strong homo-erotic element in the Master-at-Arms' attitude to Billy. The young foretop-man's physical beauty is stressed (he is the 'Handsome Sailor' of the ship) and Melville drops several hints that Claggart is a homosexual. The Master-at-Arms' character shows 'a depravity according to nature' and he is 'a nut not to be cracked by the tap of a lady's fan'. Yet it would be reductionist to explain Claggart's hatred of Billy simply as the result of repressed homosexuality. For Melville is attempting something much more complex than this in his portrait of the Master-at-Arms: Claggart is a figure of elemental evil. His conduct stems from the inherent desire of evil to destroy good. It is an impressive portrait, probably the best thing in a very fine book. Rarely have such abstract notions been so convincingly embodied in an individual character.

FURTHER READING   There are now too many rather than too few editions of Melville's masterpiece, *Moby Dick*. Harold Beaver's Penguin English Library edition (1973) is thorough, reasonably priced and readily available. The most sophisticated edition is by Luther S. Mansfield and Howard P. Vincent (1962). However, there is no satisfactory collection of Melville's complete works and the sixteen-volume edition (1922–1924), though dated, is still the standard.

With the revival of interest in Melville there has been a profusion of critical and biographical studies. Indeed, as a critic recently remarked, the writing of books on *Moby Dick* has now replaced whaling as a traditional New England industry. The best general works are by Richard Chase (1949), Newton Arvin (1950) and Jay Leyda (two volumes, 1951). Charles Olson's *Call Me Ishmael* (1947) and Howard Vincent's *The Trying-Out of Moby Dick* (1949) both give fascinating accounts of the many literary influences on *Moby Dick*.

3 The Rise of Realism

Between the work of Hawthorne and Melville, the major novelists of the 1850s, and the work of Twain, James and Howells, the major novelists of the last quarter of the century, falls the shadow of the American Civil War (1861–1865). In his famous Gettysburg address Abraham Lincoln described the conflict in terms of epic simplicity:

> Fourscore and twenty years ago our fathers set forth on this continent a new nation, conceived in liberty and dedicated to the proposition that all men are created equal. Now we are engaged in a great civil war, testing whether this nation, or any nation so conceived and so dedicated can long endure.

In the event, the war showed that the nation could endure – but only in a permanently changed and, in some respects, a deeply scarred form.

The result of the Civil War was not just the triumph of the abolitionists over the slave-owners. It was also the triumph of the industrial North over the agrarian South. Despite the much-vaunted programme of 'Reconstruction' the Southern states long remained ravaged and dispirited territory; the war left a legacy of bitterness that has not yet disappeared from American politics. In the North, on the other hand, the aftermath of war brought financial boom. The North's prosperity was increased by rapid mechanization and industrialization, its population swelled by new influxes of foreign immigrants. To contemporary observers cities like Boston, New York, Philadelphia and Chicago presented a double image. On the surface there was elegance, security and comfort; but underneath there was all the seething discontent which accompanies the growth of any modern industrial society.

Mark Twain was born in Florida, Missouri in 1835; William Dean Howells in Martin's Ferry, Ohio in 1837; Henry James in New York in 1843. Coming to maturity during the years of the Civil War, all three men also viewed its aftermath through Northern eyes: Twain settled in Connecticut, Howells lived in Boston and New York, while James' American home was in Cambridge, Massachusetts. Inevitably the political and social changes of these years left an ineradicable mark on their writing. A new spirit entered American fiction. Where Hawthorne and Melville had referred to themselves as 'romancers', the three later writers proudly called themselves 'realists'.

Their choice of this term did not imply violent rebellion against the work of their predecessors. James wrote a long and sympathetic study of Hawthorne, while Twain described the Mississippi river as lyrically as Melville had described the sea. Yet where earlier writers had turned towards the world of nature and had emphasized the abstract universality of their themes, the realists were determined to produce novels which stood in a direct and topical relation to the society in which they lived. For Twain this meant the evolution of a distinctively American idiom, a style of writing that reflected the way Americans actually talked. For Howells this meant the exploration of contemporary social issues, like divorce or the rise of the self-made businessman. For James it meant the sensitive investigation of social manners and the nuances of individual psychology.

This increasing interest in 'man in society' rather than 'man in the open air' brought American fiction closer to European traditions. It is significant, then, to note how the lives of the American realists show their deep personal interest in Europe. Cooper had toured England and France on the proceeds of his Natty Bumppo novels and Hawthorne had been Consul in England and Italy. But from the 1870s onwards the American habit of travelling reached almost epidemic proportions. James was an expatriate for most of his adult life, while Twain spent much of the 1890s on European lecture tours. (By comparison, Howells' residence in Boston and New York came to seem a stubbornly patriotic gesture.) Twain continually contrasts the 'feudalism' of the Old World with the democracy of the New, and James takes Anglo-American relations as one of his major themes. The American realists were engaged in discovering the complexities of their own country; but they were also engaged in an equally complex re-discovery of Europe.

Mark Twain

'Mark Twain' was the pseudonym of Samuel Langhorne Clemens. He was born in 1835 at Florida, Missouri, and brought up in Hannibal, Missouri. His father, a Virginian, was a restless man who lived in continual hope of making a quick fortune. Twain himself seems to have inherited something of this attitude, for he led a determinedly chequered and adventurous youth, working variously as a printer, journalist, miner and steamboat pilot on the Mississippi river. The success of a short story, 'The Celebrated Jumping Frog of Calaveras County' (1865), and the encouragement of Artemus Ward, the popular humorist, determined him on a literary career. In 1870 he married and settled in Hartford, Connecticut.

During these years he published several books of satire and travel: *The Innocents Abroad* (1869), *Roughing It* (1872), *The Gilded Age* (with Charles Dudley Warner, 1873), *The Adventures of Tom Sawyer* (1876), *A Tramp Abroad* (1880), *The Prince and the Pauper* (1882), and *Life on the Mississippi* (1883). He established a reputation as an earthy humorist in the tradition of Artemus Ward; on one of his early lecture tours he was billed as 'The Wild Humorist of the Pacific Slope'. This seems to have corresponded to his personality in private life: he was a boisterous and witty man, a lover of billiards, cigars, tall stories and bawdy jokes. He had, as his close friend Howells testified in *My Mark Twain* (1910), a character of 'wild and splendid generosity'. Small wonder, then, that his relations with the genteel and respectable world of Connecticut were always complicated and uneasy. But it was this tension that informed his greatest book, *The Adventures of Huckleberry Finn* (1885), a marvellously unsentimental reminiscence of the small South-western community in which he had been brought up.

Soon after the publication of *A Connecticut Yankee in King Arthur's Court* (1889), financial troubles interrupted his writing and forced him into those inevitable lecture tours that nineteenth-century writers used as an extra source of income. As Warner Berthoff notes in his *The Ferment of Realism* (1965), the success of these tours made Twain 'the first in a still lengthening succession of American writers whose careers seem to pass altogether out of the sphere of literature into that of salesmanship and publicity'.

Yet in later life Twain still found time for serious writing. *The Tragedy of Pudd'nhead Wilson* (1894), his finest novel apart from *Huckleberry Finn*, introduces a note of mordant satire that was to sound increasingly loud in his work. *The Man That Corrupted Hadleyburg* (1900), *What Is Man?* (1906) and the posthumously published *The Mysterious Stranger* (1916) exude an air of savage despair. Mark Twain died in 1910.

Twain is a difficult writer to assess, if only because the reader is left with the impression of an immense talent that never found completely satisfactory expression. He was, as *Tom Sawyer* shows, a superb children's novelist; and he was, as his contemporaries recognized, a shrewd and salty humorist. But he was far more than an entertainer and professional funny man. *Huckleberry Finn* and *Pudd'nhead Wilson* show him to have been a serious novelist, exploring a vein of realism that breaks away from the earlier traditions of symbolism and allegory. Where Hawthorne and Melville had been attracted to history, romance and antiquity, Twain turns to present realities with a resolutely commonsensical eye. Like his finest creation, Huck Finn, he stands for a peculiarly American type of shrewdness. He is nobody's fool, rejoicing in his ability to detect cant, injustice, false gentility and sentimentality. America has produced few satirists but in Twain it found one who can stand amongst the best of any language.

The Adventures of Tom Sawyer

SUMMARY Aunt Polly has a hard time trying to bring up her orphaned nephew, Tom Sawyer, for he is a highly spirited boy, charming and skilled at avoiding punishment. One summer evening, after a day spent playing truant from school to go swimming, Tom meets a new boy in the town. The stranger is well-dressed in a stylish, urban way – as well-dressed as Tom himself is shabby. They fight and Tom wins. He chases his opponent home – so finding out where he lives – but is warned off by the boy's mother. When Tom finally gets home Aunt Polly is appalled at the state of his clothes.

On Saturday morning Tom has to whitewash the fence, but manages to persuade his friends to help him finish the irksome job quickly. That afternoon he sees a new girl in Jeff Thatcher's garden and shows off in front of her; she gives him a flower. When he returns later that evening to try to see her again, he is chased off by a maidservant. Sunday is a difficult day for Tom. First he has to learn some verses from the Bible and then attend Sunday school. Here he again sees the new girl and learns that she is Jeff Thatcher's niece. To impress her he trades Bible-reading tickets with his classmates and claims the Bible that is awarded to students who have memorized 2,000 verses. The Bible is presented by Judge Thatcher, the girl's father; unfortunately the Judge also asks Tom some questions that expose his ignorance of the Scriptures.

On Monday Tom tries to avoid school by feigning illness but Aunt Polly is not deceived. At school he comes across Huckleberry (Huck) Finn, son of the town drunkard. All the local parents disapprove of Huck and all the other boys envy him his freedom. The two boys talk so long that Tom is late for his first lesson. At last he gets a chance to meet Becky Thatcher properly, but after school they quarrel and Tom goes off alone into the woods. After luxuriating in melancholy for a while, he dreams of being a pirate. His friend Joe Harper arrives and they play at being Robin Hood together.

That night, when he is supposed to be asleep, Tom leaves the house and joins Huck Finn. The two go off to the local graveyard to perform a magic ritual for getting rid of warts. They see Doctor Robinson, together with Muff Potter and Injun Joe, robbing a grave. The three conspirators argue and fight: Potter is knocked unconscious and Injun Joe stabs the Doctor to death. Horrified, the two boys run away unseen. When Potter comes round Joe persuades him that he killed the Doctor. Huck and Tom return to the darkened village in an agony of terror lest Joe should realize that they witnessed the crime. They solemnly swear to each other to keep the matter secret. The next day the town is buzzing with the news of Robinson's murder. Muff Potter is caught in the graveyard and Injun Joe gives evidence against him. Huck and Tom are amazed but still do not offer themselves as witnesses.

Tom is upset by the murder and depressed by Becky's absence from school – so much so that Aunt Polly insists on dosing him with patent medicine. In retaliation Tom pours her favourite 'pain-killer' through a crack in the living room floor and gives some of it to the cat. Snubbed by Becky, Tom decides to run away and become a pirate; he persuades Joe Harper and Huck Finn to come with him. They go to Jackson's Island, where they enjoy themselves fishing and swimming. Yet they soon begin to feel homesick – a feeling that is intensified when they see the inhabitants of St Petersburg searching the river under the impression that the boys have drowned. That night Tom creeps home secretly and overhears Aunt Polly and Mrs Harper lamenting the supposed deaths of their boys. He steals a boat and makes his way back to the island. By this time Huck and Joe are so homesick that Tom has great difficulty persuading them to remain. That evening Huck teaches the other two to smoke a pipe, but it makes them sick. In St Petersburg the people have given up the search and, on the following Sunday, hold a memorial service for the boys. Tom, Huck and Joe arrive in the middle of the service. Tom describes the scene he witnessed between Aunt Polly and Mrs Harper, pretending that he saw it in a dream. The town marvels at his extra-sensory gifts until Joe Harper spoils the deception.

Tom is reconciled with Becky by offering to take the punishment for one of her offences at school. But she goes away during the holidays and Tom gets bored. Things become more interesting when Muff Potter is brought to trial for the murder of Doctor Robinson. Huck and Tom again agree to keep their secret for fear that Injun Joe would come after them if they spoke out. Yet they both feel guilty about not helping Potter and bring him presents in prison. At the last moment Tom yields to his conscience and gives evidence. It causes a sensation: Potter is acquitted and Injun Joe disappears immediately. Huck and Tom are the heroes of the hour, but live in fear of Joe's return.

To distract themselves, they decide to search for buried treasure at the 'haunted house' – a sinister, deserted building on the outside of town. While they are there Injun Joe (now disguised) and a fellow criminal come in. The boys hide and see the men taking money from their hiding-place in the house. They follow Joe to his room in a local hotel. Tom gives up the search temporarily to go on a picnic with Becky. Huck stays on guard and sees Joe and his comrade leaving the hotel. He follows them to the Widow Douglas' house, gathering from the conversation that Joe wants to revenge himself on the old woman for the way her husband had treated him. Huck runs off to a neighbours to give the alarm and the criminals are chased away.

During their picnic Tom and Becky wander too far into a nearby network of caves and get lost. Blundering around in the darkened tunnels they see Injun Joe; fortunately he does not see them. When Tom and Becky finally make their way out, Judge Thatcher has the entrance blocked to prevent such accidents happening again. As soon as he hears of this Tom insists on going to look for Injun Joe; but the criminal is found dead near the cave's entrance. Huck and Tom return later and, after some searching, discover the robbers' treasure. Huck, now a rich man because of his share of this treasure, is adopted by the Widow Douglas. He remains uneasy about civilized life, however, and it is only with difficulty that Tom dissuades him from returning to his former vagrant ways.

CRITICAL COMMENTARY It is not difficult to see why *The Adventures of Tom Sawyer* has been, since its publication in 1876, one of the most popular of all novels about children. As he wrote, Twain drew on his own childhood memories of Hannibal, Missouri, and he managed to create with superb exactitude the feeling of life in a small town on the banks of the Mississippi. Amidst all the praise of Twain as a wit or a psychologist it is easy to forget how good is his sense of the natural environment:

> After the dinner all the gang turned out to hunt for turtle eggs on the bar. They went about poking sticks into the sand, and when they found a soft place they went down on their knees and dug with their hands. Sometimes they would take fifty or sixty eggs out of one hole. They were perfectly round white things a trifle smaller than an English walnut. They had a famous fried-egg feast that night, and another on Friday morning.

At the centre of the book's success is Twain's appreciation of children. In a century whose literature commonly used children as an excuse for sentimental gushing or moralistic hectoring, Twain is almost unique. His portrait of Tom is virtually untouched by sentimentality or censoriousness and simply charms the reader by the continual truth of its observation. Tom is the living embodiment of an anarchic love of freedom and fun that Twain, the respectable adult writer, more than half envied. His character is divided between a businesslike common sense and an incurable streak of romanticism. The business sense is apparent when, for example, Tom manages to persuade his friends to help him paint the fence or when he claims to have 'dreamt' the scene between Mrs Harper and Aunt Polly in order to impress the townspeople. On the other hand, Tom is deeply moved by the romantic books he loves to read, for they portray alternatives to the boring rhythm of life in a small provincial town. Tom develops an elaborate storehouse of knowledge about pirates, robbers and so forth: he becomes an inveterate teller of tall and extravagant stories in which he himself partly believes.

On occasion, Tom's love of romancing is used to fine effect. One such moment occurs after he and Huck have witnessed the murder of Dr Robinson in the graveyard. The crime is one of the few moments in the story (like the death of Injun Joe in the cave) when adult reality intrudes and predominates over childish games. The children are naturally terrified and their reaction is to turn to their romantic and superstitious rituals for comfort. They draw up an elaborate (and unintentionally comic) agreement signed with their own blood: 'Huck Finn and Tom Sawyer swears that they will keep mum about this and they wish they may drop down dead in their tracks if they ever tell and rot.' Twain's psychological insight here is both sound and subtle. As elsewhere in the book, he shows the sort of understanding of children's minds that one associates with Dickens.

For all this, however, *Tom Sawyer* is in general a simple enough book – far less sophisticated than its successor, *The Adventures of Huckleberry Finn*. Its structure is episodic, a fault which occurs throughout Twain's fiction: the action consists of a string of separate incidents rather than the development of a continuous plot. Moreover, the book is resolutely sunny and good-tempered, and in this it is very unlike Twain's later work. Although he is never coy or sentimental in his view of Tom, Twain does look determinedly at the happy side of childhood. Significantly, the novel omits several of the subjects that *Huckleberry Finn* deliberately dwells on: the difficulties posed for Huck by his drunken father, for example, and the hardships suffered by the slaves in St Petersburg. However, it would be churlish to end on a note of criticism. *Tom Sawyer* may belong to a limited genre in a way that *Huckleberry Finn* does not, but within its limits it could hardly be bettered.

The Adventures of Huckleberry Finn

SUMMARY   Huckleberry (Huck) Finn, the adopted son of the Widow Douglas, is bored by civilized life. One night he climbs out of the house to meet his friend Tom Sawyer; they decide to form a gang of robbers. Soon afterwards the townspeople find a body in the river and assume it to be Huck's father, a drunken layabout. But Huck himself is not convinced and still half expects his father to return to tyrannize him one day. He gets annoyed with Tom's gang: its games are far too tame for his taste.

That winter Huck's father appears, anxious to get his hands on his son's money. (See *The Adventures of Tom Sawyer*.) He forces Huck to leave the town and live with him in a cabin near the woods. Huck himself is glad to get away from conventional life but resents his father's cruelty. He decides to escape. He fakes his own drowning and hides on nearby Jackson's Island. Next morning he watches the townspeople firing cannons over the water to bring the body to the surface. At first he meets nobody, but one day he comes across the ashes of a recent fire. Returning to the spot that night he finds a local slave, Nigger Jim, who has run away from his owner, Miss Watson. Huck and Jim make friends, although the boy has residual doubts about fraternizing with an escaped slave. One day a two-storey house floats by the island; it has a dead man in it, but Jim will not let Huck take a close look. Huck goes reconnoitring in the neighbourhood, disguised as a girl. He calls at a house near the edge of town and hears an account of his own murder and Jim's disappearance.

Knowing that the townspeople plan to search Jackson's

Island, Jim and Huck set off at night by raft. They make their way along the Mississippi, avoiding people and buying or stealing their food at night. They encounter a wrecked steamer, the *Walter Scott*. When they board it in search of provisions they find that it has been taken over by a group of murderous conspirators. Their raft floats away and they have to steal the men's dinghy. Yet Huck has qualms about leaving even murderers on a sinking vessel and he manages to arrange their rescue.

Thinking that they are getting near Cairo, and hence out of slave territory, Jim becomes excited. This disturbs Huck's latent guilt about helping a runaway to escape. He resolves to slip away and betray Jim; but when the time comes, he cannot bring himself to do it. A steamboat hits the raft. Although Huck makes his way safely to shore he can find no sign of Jim.

He now discovers that they have been going south instead of north, so that he is now deep in slave country. He takes refuge with the Grangerfords, whose son Buck is of Huck's own age and temperament. Colonel Grangerford is a Southern gentleman of the old school, who has for many years been conducting a feud with his neighbours, the Shepherdsons. One day a Grangerford slave finds a pretext for taking Huck to a nearby swamp, where Nigger Jim turns out to be hiding. Sophia Grangerford elopes with the son of the Shepherdson family and the fighting breaks out again with renewed ferocity. Most of the Grangerford family, including Buck, are killed. Huck takes to the river again with Nigger Jim.

They float peacefully along the Mississippi together. One day two fugitives from an angry mob seek sanctuary on the raft. They are both travelling confidence men; the younger says that he is Duke of Bridgewater and the elder, not to be outdone, that he is the exiled King of France. Huck is not deceived. The King takes Huck to a revivalist meeting, where he tells the congregation that he is a reformed pirate, gives a lurid account of his conversion and takes a collection. The Duke and the King also give various theatrical performances but the audience are so dissatisfied that the swindlers narrowly escape mob violence.

In the next town the Duke and King pose as the brothers of a recently dead man, Peter Wilks, claiming that they have just arrived from England. Huck, forced to act as their servant, has qualms of conscience and decides to frustrate the fraud. The Duke and King have already got six thousand dollars which rightfully belong to Mary Jane, Wilks' niece. Huck steals the money back and hides it in the coffin for safekeeping. After the funeral the King auctions off Wilks' slaves and advertises the house for sale. Huck explains the facts of the matter to Mary Jane, but before they can act the real brothers of the dead man arrive. There is an awkward confrontation in which each set of claimants vaunt their credentials. Huck runs off to the raft, but the Duke and King quickly follow, angry at him for deserting them. After a while the two men resume their old tricks – giving temperance lectures, elocution lessons and so forth. Most of these fail and, desperate for money, they turn Nigger Jim in and pocket the reward. After a struggle with his conscience Huck decides to go and rescue Jim.

Arriving at Silas Phelps' farm, where he knows Nigger Jim to be kept, Huck is mistaken for a nephew whom Aunt Sally is expecting. He plays along with the error and realizes that the nephew is Tom Sawyer. When Tom arrives he agrees not to spoil the game: Huck will remain 'Tom' while Tom will pose as 'Sid'. To Huck's surprise Tom eagerly agrees to help free Jim, but characteristically insists that they use romantic and impractical methods borrowed from books. He even alerts the whole neighbourhood to Jim's impending escape by sending an anonymous letter of warning. A posse of local farmers is organized and, though the conspirators escape, Tom is wounded in the leg. When Jim is recaptured Tom at last reveals that the slave has really been a free man all along: his owner Miss Watson has died and given her slaves their freedom in her will. At the end of the book, Aunt Sally has ambitions of civilizing Huck. But Huck has other ideas: he plans to go off on his travels again.

CRITICAL COMMENTARY Mark Twain originally conceived *The Adventures of Huckleberry Finn* simply enough, as the successor to his very popular children's book, *Tom Sawyer*. He used the same location, St Petersburg, and again drew on his own boyhood memories of Hannibal, Missouri. Huck, Tom's friend in the earlier book, is promoted to the status of hero.

Inevitably, early readers saw the novel as another *Tom Sawyer*. It was praised for its humour, but more frequently damned for its bad grammar, its coarseness and its lack of 'seriousness'. Only a few contemporary critics (like the novelist William Dean Howells) saw it as a serious work in its own right. Today, however, *Huckleberry Finn* is widely regarded as a classic. Indeed, Ernest Hemingway has paid the book the most ecstatic of tributes: 'It's the best book we've had. All American writing comes from that. There was nothing before. There has been nothing as good since.'

The most obvious change from the earlier book is a shift of narrative viewpoint. The story of *Tom Sawyer* was told in the third person, but Huck recounts his own story. His narrative is a superb rendering of dialect speech and idiom. From the first confident paragraph it really does sound like a young Missouri boy talking to the reader: 'You don't know about me, without you have read a book by the name of *The Adventures of Tom Sawyer*, but that ain't no matter. That book was made by Mr Mark Twain, and he told the truth, mainly. There was things which he stretched, but mainly he told the truth.' Yet the book is not based on a feat of mere ventriloquism. Despite appearances, the novel is not restricted to the sensibility and vision of a fourteen-year-old child of limited vocabulary. Where *Huckleberry Finn* most obviously surpasses *Tom Sawyer* is in its development of a complex and subtle view of the events it describes.

To begin with, the choice of Huck as a hero is significant. Where Tom is the conventional high-spirited child – bad but always lovable – Huck is much more the genuine outlaw. He is dirty, near-illiterate, indifferent to the religious teachings of his elders and eternally itching to 'light out for the

Territory' – to break away from the restraints of civilization. Unlike Tom, he has little conventional romance about him. Indeed, he is contemptuous of Tom's exotic games – the pretence that the Sunday school picnic is 'A-rabs and Elephants' or the belief in the elaborate ways of releasing Nigger Jim at the end of the book. Huck talks a bluntly practical language, continually using terms like 'profit' and 'advantage'. Where Tom is an impractical romantic, Huck is a canny empiricist.

This streak of practicality is apparent in Huck's (and Twain's) wholly unsentimental attitude to the river. Although Huck, like so many heroes of American fiction, yearns to escape to a more natural form of life, nature itself is not over-romanticized. The river is simply the place where Huck feels most free and can most fully exercise those practical skills in which he delights. As Huck and Nigger Jim travel down the Mississippi together their raft comes to seem an island of peace and freedom. Already the alternative to his father's or the Widow Douglas' tyranny, it also becomes the place where Huck escapes the prejudices that St Petersburg has given him. Huck's battle with his conscience about helping Nigger Jim, and his growing opposition to slavery, are amongst the most moving parts of the book. Obviously Twain is concerned to make a polemical point, but the reader never feels that didacticism gets the better of artistic instinct. Huck still speaks entirely in character and his reactions are faithful to those of a young boy in his situation.

Tom Sawyer, it was noted, virtually omitted the dark side of life: it was glimpsed only briefly, in the murder of Doctor Robinson and in the description of Injun Joe's inhumation in the cave. One of the signs of *Huckleberry Finn*'s greater maturity is the much larger role such episodes play: the floating house with the body of Huck's father in it, the sinking *Walter Scott* with its crew of robbers, the bloody Grangerford–Shepherdson feud and the progressively nasty swindles practised by the Duke and the King. The river itself is by no means free from evil, but the land is shown as a stronghold of cruelty and prejudice in a way that makes the reader sympathize with Huck's desire to escape.

Structure and plotting were never Twain's *forte*, and most readers have agreed that the ending of the novel is a disappointment. With the reappearance of Tom Sawyer the confident stream of invention that has carried the action forward falters. Tom's silly antics when freeing Nigger Jim are obviously criticized (they are so clearly inferior to Huck's quiet practicality), but they are still overworked and seem to trivialize the narrative. Moreover, the magical way that Jim gets his freedom is too good to be true. It shirks the serious questions about slavery that the book itself has raised. At the same time, however, it is difficult to see how Twain could have been expected to end the novel. For in its celebration of escape and travel *Huckleberry Finn* is too restless a book for any easy stopping-point to be imagined.

A Connecticut Yankee in King Arthur's Court

SUMMARY During a guided tour of Warwick Castle Twain meets a fellow American who seems strangely familiar with the medieval world. That evening the man visits Twain in his hotel room with a strange story to tell. He is, he explains, a Yankee from Connecticut – shrewd, hard, unsentimental stock – and worked in the arms business. One day he was knocked out in a fight at the factory and, when he recovered consciousness, found himself in Arthurian England in the year 528.

Sir Kay appears and escorts the Yankee to Camelot. He quickly makes friends with a servant, Clarence, and learns that he is Sir Kay's prisoner. He is taken to the Great Hall where the Knights of the Round Table are celebrating and boasting of their deeds at arms. He thinks Arthur and his knights engagingly naïve but is shocked by their coarseness and their inhumane treatment of the servants. Merlin tells how King Arthur got his sword Excalibur from the Lady of the Lake, but the other knights are so familiar with the story that they fall asleep. Sir Kay exhibits the Yankee to the company and gives a ridiculously exaggerated account of his capture. The Yankee is condemned to die the next day.

With typical Yankee practicality he sets about devising a way of escaping this fate. Since he had noticed that the knights were all in awe of Merlin, he claims to be a magician himself. His historical knowledge tells him that an eclipse is due to occur at the time of his execution and so he 'prophesies' this eclipse. Duly impressed, the King pardons the Yankee and makes him chief minister. The Yankee has Merlin imprisoned and, to satisfy the public clamour for another miracle, announces that he will blow up the rival magician's tower. He accomplishes this with gunpowder and completes his ascendancy over Merlin. Now one of the most powerful men at court – he is popularly nicknamed 'The Boss' – he sets out to modernize the country. A patent office, schools, newspapers, military academies, factories and a telephone system are established, but all on a secret basis to avoid alarming people.

At Arthur's insistence the Yankee undertakes a quest, guided by Alisande. After an uncomfortable journey he captures several knights, using the smoke from his pipe to make them believe him to be a dragon. They come to Morgan Le Fay's castle. He is appalled by her cruelty and uses his influence as 'The Boss' to make her empty her dungeons. Finally they reach what Sandy (as he has nicknamed Alisande) calls the 'ogre's castle': it is a pigsty guarded by swineherds. She insists that he release the swine and treat them courteously, for she thinks they are enchanted princesses. On their way back they fall in with a party of pilgrims bound for the Well of Holiness. The well, however, has dried up. The Yankee repairs it, presenting the result to the people as another of his miracles. The King visits him to confer about Army appointments and to cure the King's evil (a skin disease) by his touch. The first issue of the court newspaper, edited by Clarence, is published: it astonishes and puzzles the knights, most of whom cannot read.

King Arthur and the Yankee travel through the kingdom disguised as poor people. Predictably, the King is bad at imitating a peasant, for, try as he will, be cannot curb his haughty and aristocratic manners. Everything the Yankee learns about the condition of the poor confirms his hatred of feudalism. But although Arthur is humane and sympathetic, he is still limited by the prejudices of his class. The Yankee makes friends with Marco, a goldsmith; he entertains Marco and his friends to dinner, impressing them with his wealth. He also tries to correct their primitive notions about society, economics and the law. The King behaves tactlessly and provokes a fight. A mob pursues them and they are rescued by a passing group of gentlemen. The gentlemen, however, do not realize their noble status and sell them as slaves. They undergo terrible sufferings and the King becomes an ardent abolitionist. The Yankee escapes from the slave gang one night but, on his return to fetch Arthur, finds that the other slaves have attacked and killed the slave-master. The whole gang, including Arthur, have been sentenced to death. The Yankee phones Clarence and arranges for Lancelot and his knights to come to the rescue. The help arrives only just in time, for the Yankee and the King are already being made to mount the scaffold.

The Yankee is challenged to fight by Sir Sagramour, whom Merlin helps with his spells. The Yankee eschews medieval means of combat: he first brings Sagramour off his horse with a lassoo and then, when the knight insists that the fight should continue, shoots him with a Colt revolver. The victory consolidates the Yankee's position and allows him to make his factories and his plans for social change public. Within three years he has democratized and mechanized Arthurian England. Only two unfulfilled ambitions remain: the disestablishment of the Catholic Church and the introduction of universal suffrage. He is now married to Sandy, by whom he has a daughter.

At the height of the Yankee's power, disaster strikes. The love affair between Lancelot and Guinevere is discovered by Arthur and the country is torn by civil war. Finally the King is slain in battle by Mordred. The Church asserts its power and tries to reverse the Yankee's reforms, but he proves a difficult man to beat. He and Clarence retreat with their followers to Merlin's Cave and issue a proclamation that, since Arthur is dead, England should be made a Republic. The knights attack but the Yankee, using all the resources of modern technology, slaughters them. It is a Pyrrhic victory. The Yankee's followers are fenced in by a wall of rotting bodies which begin to stifle them with poisonous fumes. The Yankee himself is wounded and falls victim to a spell of Merlin's that puts him into a permanent sleep.

In a concluding note the author describes how he visited the Yankee in his hotel room later that night. The man is asleep but his murmurings make it clear that he is unhappy at being transported back to the nineteenth century, and that he misses his wife Alisande. He dies in his sleep.

CRITICAL COMMENTARY Like most of Mark Twain's work, *A Connecticut Yankee in King Arthur's Court* is witty and high-spirited. Twain's sense of humour, like Dickens', is based on an exuberant appreciation of language: he has a marvellously precise ear for how people speak and write. He catches the Yankee's idiom as surely as he had caught Huck Finn's Southwestern dialect. As the Yankee enters the Hall of the Round Table he notes casually that 'on the walls hung some huge tapestries which were probably taxed as works of art'. Describing his followers in the final battle with the knights, he says: 'These people knew me and had confidence in my word. They would clear out without waiting to part their hair . . .' Twain also delights in literary parody. The newspaper which the Yankee starts at Arthur's court is used as an excuse to imitate the style of American frontier journalism:

Expedition No. 3 will start adout the first of netmgnthon a search f8r Sir Sagramour le Desirous. It is in comand of the renowned Knight of the Red Lawns, assissted by Sir Persant of Inde, who is competegt, intelligent, courteous, and in every way a bri*c*k, and furtHER assisted by Sir Palamides the Saracen, who is no huckleberry himself. This is no pic-nic, these boys *m*ean busine&s.

The style of Sir Thomas Malory, author of the famous

Morte d'Arthur, is parodied with equal exactitude:

> So these two knights came together with great random that Sir
> Uwaine smote Sir Marhaus that his spear brast in pieces on his
> shield, and Sir Marhaus smote him so sore that horse and man he
> bare to the earth, and hurt Sir Uwaine on the left side.

Nothing dates faster than comedy and the danger with most 'comic classics' is that they need too much explaining to the modern reader to be genuinely funny. The danger with Twain's work, on the contrary, is that the superficial comedy remains so fresh that it can distract attention from the more serious satiric intent. Twain's friend Howells sensed that in *A Connecticut Yankee* – 'our arch-humorist imparts more of his personal quality than in anything else he has done.' In fact, the book is the fullest expression of some of Twain's most deeply held attitudes. It shows his dislike of the past and of romance, and his respect for American shrewdness and practicality.

To understand this fully we need to remember how prevalent was a nostalgia for the Middle Ages – and particularly for Arthurian England – in the nineteenth century. Turning away from the industrialism and commercialism of their own age, many of Twain's contemporaries viewed the Middle Ages as an ideal society. Gothic art and architecture were revived and imitated, and chivalric romances provided many writers (Tennyson, for example) with their favourite subjects. In Twain's eyes this was merely dangerous sentimentality, and in *A Connecticut Yankee* he confronts the issue directly. Rather than seeming a paradise on earth, Arthur's court is made to appear a haven of stupidity. Using the Yankee as his mouthpiece, Twain launches into a full-scale attack on the Middle Ages. It was a time of superstition that enslaved men's minds and bodies. An unjust social system made revered idols of silly noblemen and princes, while condemning the lower classes to indignity, hardship and suffering. Religious superstitions prevented man from exercising his full ingenuity; scientific thought was stifled and man lived in ignorance, discomfort and disease that could have been prevented by a little common sense.

Viewed in this light, the novel is an expression of democratic liberalism in the full flood of its confidence. It is a hymn to progress. Twain looks back on the past not with nostalgia but with amused condescension: the ordinary nineteenth-century Yankee is a far more admirable figure than any of Arthur's knights. Yet the satire is not entirely one-sided. Although Twain often uses the Yankee as a mouthpiece for his own views, he is also aware of his hero's limitations. Yankee shrewdness and practicality lead to an aesthetic blindness, for example; when the hero first sees medieval tapestries he dismisses them as a tax deduction. The Yankee is prudish in a typically Victorian way, easily and stupidly embarrassed by the freedom with which the knights tell bawdy stories. Moreover, the hero becomes attached to Arthurian society despite himself. He falls in love with Alisande, and even admits that King Arthur has a natural nobility and dignity.

The main criticism of the Yankee occurs in the last third of the book, for it is here that Twain's satirical vision darkens. The earlier good humour and high spirits give way to a progressively despairing vision. Even when the author is in agreement with the Yankee, the target of attack is not simply the folly of a long-distant age. The extended slavery episode, for example, is more relevant to Twain's own age and country than to Arthurian England. And, in the battle with the knights that ends the book, the Yankee himself emerges as the bringer of evil rather than progress. For all his talk of education and freedom his most concrete achievement is to introduce mechanized means of slaughter. Yankee inventiveness leads to more and better ways of killing people. The massacre of the knights – with its almost uncanny prefigurement of twentieth-century technological warfare – gives the book's ending a peculiarly bitter taste. In this respect, it echoes the way that Twain's own views developed as he grew older: his earlier high spirits yield to a Swiftian disillusion with humanity.

The Tragedy of Pudd'nhead Wilson

SUMMARY In 1830 Dawson's Landing, Missouri, is a small prosperous town, growing rapidly. Its chief citizen, Judge York Leicester Driscoll, is a Southern gentleman of the old school. He is childless but his brother, Percy Northumberland Driscoll, has an heir: Percy's wife gives birth to a boy on the same day as one of her slaves, Roxana. Though a slave, Roxy is only one-sixteenth black. After the death of Percy's wife, Roxy has to look after both baby boys. At about this time, David Wilson, a lawyer, arrives in town from the East Coast. He is friendly and pleasant, but his ironic humour is misunderstood by the locals and quickly earns him the nickname 'Pudd'nhead'. He takes a house next to the Judge but, because of his reputation for stupidity, few clients come. In his abundant leisure he studies the science of fingerprinting. He takes the prints of most of his neighbours, including Roxy's baby, Valet de Chambre ('Chambers'), and Percy's son, Thomas à Becket (Tom) Driscoll.

Roxy broods on the different fates awaiting the two boys in her charge: her son will become a slave while Tom Driscoll will be brought up as a gentleman. She changes the children around, and their similarity of appearance allows the deception to pass unnoticed. But she quickly becomes the dupe of her own deception, reverencing and spoiling the new 'Tom' (really Chambers). He grows up a badly behaved child, treating his nurse brutally. Sometimes Roxy is so angry with him that she almost confesses her fraud, and hesitates only because she fears nobody will believe her unsupported word.

Percy Driscoll dies. His will frees Roxy and commits Chambers to the care of the Judge's family. But it also reveals that Driscoll was in debt: Tom, his heir, is a pauper and is saved only when Judge Driscoll adopts him. In the Judge's family the young man is spoilt even further. A brief spell at Yale improves his manners but also teaches him to drink and gamble.

Two Italians, Luigi and Angelo Capello, identical twins, come to live in Dawson's Landing. They are a great curiosity in the community and quickly make friends with Pudd'nhead Wilson. Meanwhile, Roxy goes to see Tom but he receives her harshly and refuses her request for money. She insinuates that she knows discreditable things about him and he, thinking she has heard of his many gambling debts, capitulates. When they meet secretly later the same day, Roxy explains how she changed the children over. Tom, realizing that he is really a Negro, breaks down and agrees to pay her half of his monthly allowance. He also confesses that, desperate for money to pay his gambling debts, he has been stealing from houses in the town. Recently, he has robbed the Capellos of a valuable knife.

Tom Driscoll and the Italians go together to a rum meeting (the town is in the process of debating the temperance issue), where Tom insults Luigi and a fight breaks out. Tom sues the Italian for assault and wins, but Judge Driscoll, a firm believer in the duelling code, is outraged by the young man's resort to law. When Tom himself refuses to do it, the Judge challenges Luigi to a duel. Tom hears of the result later that night when he is visiting Roxy: Luigi was slightly wounded and the Judge unhurt. Roxy upbraids her son for his cowardice in refusing to fight.

The Capello brothers are now popular in the town, and Tom sets about spreading slander and dissension. Since nobody has claimed the advertised reward for the Capellos' stolen knife, he insinuates that the knife never existed or was never stolen: the Italians invented the affair to gain attention and prestige. The young man also works his way back into the Judge's good graces. But as he is returning to St Louis to pay his debts, his satchel of stolen goods is stolen, leaving him penniless. Roxy, now the loving mother, offers to let herself be sold back into slavery to pay Tom's debts: her only condition is that she go to a good master, not one of the harsh ones 'down the river'. Tom accepts the offer but sells her down the river to the owner of a cotton plantation.

It is election time in Dawson's Landing. Wilson, an

increasingly popular figure, is elected but the Capello brothers, running for the council, are defeated. The slanders put about by Tom, and repeated in good faith by Judge Driscoll, have had their effect. Because of the public slurs on his character, Luigi challenges the Judge to another duel; the Judge, still believing Tom's slanders, refuses to meet the Italian on the field of honour. Roxy escapes from slavery and returns to Tom in St Louis, demanding that he confess the affair to the Judge and ask for the money to buy her out of slavery again. Tom pretends to agree but privately resolves to steal the money from the Judge. During the robbery he is surprised and stabs the old man with the Capellos' stolen knife.

Inevitably, the townspeople of Dawson's Landing believe the Italians to be the murderers and, after being threatened with lynching, they are arrested. Pudd'nhead Wilson, engaged as their lawyer, examines the knife and notices that the fingerprints on it are not those of either of the brothers. He finally identifies them as Tom's. Going over his files he notices how the fingerprints of Tom as a man and as a young baby do not correspond: he realizes that Roxy must have changed over the children in her charge. He produces this evidence in court and produces a sensation. The Capellos are acquitted and Tom, now known to be Roxy's son, is arrested. He makes a full confession to the murder and is sentenced to life imprisonment. But the creditors of the late Percy Driscoll's estate protest that Tom's value as a slave should have been counted amongst its assets; Tom, they argue, is rightfully their property. The Governor of the state agrees and Tom is released from prison, but only to be seized by the creditors and sold down the river as a slave.

CRITICAL COMMENTARY In its own time *Pudd'nhead Wilson* was the most neglected of Twain's novels, but it has recently become the subject of an extensive critical dispute. Critics with as little in common as F. R. Leavis and Leslie Fiedler have hailed the book as a masterpiece. Dr Leavis has praised its 'mature, balanced and impersonal view of humanity', while Mr Fiedler (after calling it the 'most extraordinary book in American literature') pays tribute to its uncompromising presentation of harsh truths. In contrast, Richard Chase (in *The American Novel and Its Tradition* [1957]) has suggested that the novel's admirers are responding to what Twain intended rather than what Twain actually accomplished: *Pudd'nhead Wilson* is a work into which 'the breath of life has entered only here and there'. Aligning himself with Mr Chase, Larzer Ziff (in *The American 1890s* [1967]) suggests that Twain's mastery is 'evident [only] in flashes'.

Yet, as Mr Chase concedes, *Pudd'nhead Wilson* has a haunting and memorable quality despite its technical aberrations. The novel stands at the end of Mark Twain's strange spiritual pilgrimage from youthful high spirits towards a painfully honest view of human frailty. Its tone is savagely satirical, but the novel's cynicism has nothing to do with the coining of clever epigrams and its bitterness does not preclude a deep compassion for the characters.

Throughout his life Twain was fascinated and troubled by slavery. He himself was brought up in the Southwest before the Civil War and so saw the practice at first hand. Predictably, it crops up in his writings. *A Connecticut Yankee*, for example, has an outburst against slavery while *Huckleberry Finn* has the moving portrait of the runaway Nigger Jim. Yet even *Huckleberry Finn*, fine novel though it is, pulls its punches: the happy ending is contrived and nothing about it is more artificial than the way Jim miraculously gains his freedom. In *Pudd'nhead Wilson* Twain returns to the subject, but with a new honesty and directness. His view of the slaves avoids not merely the racism of a writer like Poe but also the sickly sentimentality of Harriet Beecher Stowe's famous *Uncle Tom's Cabin*. To find parallels for Twain's handling of the issue one has to turn to modern American literature – to William Faulkner's *Absalom, Absalom!* or to William Styron's *The Confessions of Nat Turner*.

At the heart of this achievement is Twain's portrait of Roxy, the slave who is only one-sixteenth black but nevertheless wholly trapped in the slave psychology and way of life. Roxy is a moving but hardly attractive figure: she cheats, lies and blackmails her way through most of the book. But her dishonesties are presented without any prim moralizing, as inevitable responses to the pressures under which she lives. Her relationship with 'Tom Driscoll', in particular, is finely rendered and the scenes between mother and son attain a tragic intensity. The portrait of Tom, again, is all the finer for its absolute lack of sentimentality and overt moralizing. Nothing of the young man's meanness is shirked and yet, as with Roxy, the reader is not invited to form shallow moral judgements.

The plot stems from Roxy's change-over of the two baby boys. This idea of the changeling is one of the oldest and most familiar in literature, particularly melodramatic literature. Twain himself had already used it in an earlier novel, *The Prince and the Pauper*. Its attraction for the writer is obvious enough: it creates an air of pleasant mystery-making and allows for a happy dénouement in which the rightful heir is acknowledged and the pretender discredited. But Twain uses it in *Pudd'nhead Wilson* with a very different purpose. The change-over of Tom and Chambers makes an important social point: the difference between the fine gentleman and the slave is one of conditioning and education, not birth. And the dénouement is anything but happy. When the real Tom Driscoll is restored to his fortune he is profoundly ill at ease in white society. Nor is the punishment of Roxy's son something at which the reader can rejoice. It is merely the book's final bitter irony: 'As soon as the Governor understood the case, he pardoned Tom at once, and the creditors sold him down the river.'

The title character, Pudd'nhead Wilson, does not play a major part in the action until the end of the book, but he is important throughout as a centre of values. He is the character with whom the reader can most easily identify. Significantly, he is an outsider. He arrives at Dawson's Landing from the East Coast and his ironic humour quickly earns him an unmerited reputation for stupidity; he becomes a rather isolated figure. Standing apart from the town, with its prejudices in favour of slavery and duelling, Wilson is a sort of choric commentator on the action. His ironic remarks exude an air of quiet good sense. This role is emphasized by the excerpts from 'Pudd'nhead Wilson's Calendar' that head each chapter. Many of these excerpts, of course, are the sort of *bon mot* that earned Twain his reputation as a wit:

> When I reflect upon the number of disagreeable people who I know have gone to a better world, I am moved to lead a different life.

> We know all about the habits of the ant, we know all about the habits of the bee, but we know nothing at all about the habits of the oyster. It seems almost certain that we have been choosing the wrong time for studying the oyster.

Yet many of Wilson's remarks express that despair with humanity which Twain himself had come to feel: 'Why is it that we rejoice at a birth and grieve at a funeral? It is because we are not the person involved.'

The book's ending gives Wilson a special role to play, more active than that of quiet observer: it is he who solves the mystery of the Judge's murder. Twain had long been fascinated by the shrewd and inventive Yankee, and Wilson, with his love of fingerprinting and logical deduction, is another version of the type. But it is a version with a difference. At the time Twain was writing, the detective story was becoming increasingly popular – the first Sherlock Holmes stories had already appeared – and he manages to introduce this element into his novel. In addition to his other roles, Pudd'nhead Wilson is memorable as one of the earliest and best handled detectives in American fiction.

FURTHER READING The standard edition of Twain's works is by Albert Bigelow Paine (thirty-seven volumes; 1922–1925). Most of the major novels are available in a variety of reasonably priced editions. Paine also wrote the authorized biography of Twain (three volumes; 1912); this has been partly superseded by J. DeLancey Ferguson's *Mark Twain:*

Man and Legend (1943) and Justin Kaplan's *Mr Clemens and Mark Twain* (1967). Of the several volumes of letters, the *Mark Twain–Howells Letters*, edited by William M. Gibson and Henry Nash Smith (two volumes; 1960), is probably the most interesting.

Amongst the older generation of Twain's critics two names are outstanding: Bernard de Voto (*Mark Twain in Eruption*, 1940; *Mark Twain at Work*, 1942) and Van Wyck Brooks (*The Ordeal of Mark Twain*, 1920). Since their time Twain studies have proliferated. T. S. Eliot and Lionel Trilling have written valuable introductions to *Huckleberry Finn*, while F. R. Leavis has introduced *Pudd'nhead Wilson*. The most balanced full-length study is Henry Nash Smith's, *Mark Twain: The Development of a Writer* (1962).

Henry James

Both America and England have good grounds for claiming Henry James as their own. Born in New York City in 1843, he enjoyed an education as cosmopolitan as that of the characters in many of his novels. By the time he came of age he had lived in Newport, Rhode Island, spent several years in Europe, and studied at Harvard Law School. He always retained a special affection for Cambridge, Massachusetts – his brother, the philosopher and psychologist William James, was a Harvard professor – but by the mid-1860s he already regarded himself as an expatriate. During these years he began his literary career, writing short stories, reviews and critical articles. A year spent in Paris in 1875 brought him into contact with Flaubert and Turgenev, novelists who took their place beside Hawthorne and George Eliot as major influences on his own work.

His career as a novelist began shortly after he took up residence in London. Neither *Roderick Hudson* (1876) nor the steady stream of novels and short stories that quickly followed can be classed as immature works, for James' fiction was notable from the start for its precision and certainty of purpose. With *The American* (1877), *The Europeans* (1878), *Daisy Miller* (1879), *Washington Square* (1881) and *The Portrait of a Lady* (1881), his identity as a writer steadily emerged. He was a novelist of manners, concerned with the minutiae of social behaviour both for comic purposes and for the light they shed on individual character; his particular territory was the meeting between Europeans and Americans.

The Portrait of a Lady, in many ways his most satisfying book, marked one of the climaxes of James' career. For several years after its publication he turned away from his beloved 'international' theme and to some extent away from the novel itself, pursuing an abortive career as a dramatist. The most important works of this period are: *The Bostonians* (1886), *The Aspern Papers* (1888), *The Spoils of Poynton* (1897), *What Maisie Knew* (1897), *The Turn of the Screw* (1898) and *The Awkward Age* (1899). The three novels, *The Wings of the Dove* (1902), *The Ambassadors* (1903) and *The Golden Bowl* (1904), represent his 'late phase' and are usually seen as a magisterial climax to his career. They are distinguished by a return to the 'international' theme, a heightened concern for the subtleties of literary form and of individual psychology, and an extremely complex prose style. After 1904 his literary output slackened. He died at Rye, Sussex, in 1916, the year after he had officially become an English citizen.

There used to be a tendency amongst American critics to upbraid James for not having stayed at home and contributed more to the development of literature in America. But on the whole, his reputation has risen steadily since the turn of the century; there has been none of that sudden disillusion that commonly follows on the death of a great writer. Simply expressed, James' achievement was to win a new respect for the novel by freeing it entirely from the commercialism and vulgarity that mar even the best nineteenth-century fiction. From George Eliot and Hawthorne he inherited the belief that literature, without aiming to be moralistic, should be passionately concerned with moral values. From the example of Flaubert and Turgenev he derived an abiding interest in precise artistic form. The result is a type of fiction that specializes in the subtleties and nuances of adult relationships. No other novelist of his age proved so deeply influential: he not only affected later novelists, but also changed readers' and critics' conceptions of fiction. Today, the adjective 'Jamesian' – and it is significant how often it is invoked in discussions of fiction – is a synonym for all that is subtle, mature and urbane.

Daisy Miller

SUMMARY Winterbourne, a young American resident in Geneva, visits Vevey. In the garden of the 'Trois Couronnes' he is accosted by Randolph, an aggressive young American boy, who is joined by his sister, the pretty Daisy Miller. Struck by her beauty, Winterbourne engages her in conversation. He speculates about her character: she is delicate but energetic, and completely without irony. He decides that she is a flirt. She explains that she comes from Schenectady, New York State – her father is a successful businessman – and is travelling with her mother and brother. The family plans to winter in Rome. She talks freely about her 'gentleman friends' – so freely that Winterbourne is puzzled. When he offers to take her to see the nearby Castle of Chillon she eagerly accepts, without suggesting that she bring a chaperone.

Winterbourne had planned to introduce the Millers to his aunt, Mrs Costello, but she declares them to be too common to be worthy of acquaintance. From his aunt he learns that the freedom of Daisy's manner is not, as he had supposed, characteristic of American girls of her generation. Daisy and Winterbourne make the trip to Chillon together. She eagerly explores the castle, chattering unaffectedly. When she hears that he is going back to Geneva the next day she insists that he join her in Rome that winter. He is able to explain that he had already been planning to visit his aunt there.

When Winterbourne arrives in Rome he learns from

Mrs Costello that the freedom of Daisy's manner with her 'gentleman friends' is already the subject of scandalous gossip. He soon meets her at the house of a mutual friend, Mrs Walker. Although her mother and brother are already bored with Rome, Daisy is still fascinated. Winterbourne escorts her when she leaves the party to meet an Italian friend, Signor Giovanelli. Giovanelli turns out to be elegant but definitely not a gentleman. Mrs Walker is even more shocked than Winterbourne, but her attempts to get Daisy to behave with greater decorum fail completely: the young American girl deeply resents any attempts at interference with her life.

To her hostess' dismay Daisy brings Signor Giovanelli to a party given by Mrs Walker a few days later. Winterbourne speaks to her privately, explaining that her familiarity with Giovanelli will shock Americans and be misinterpreted by Italians. At the end of the evening Mrs Walker cuts Daisy and vows to have nothing more to do with her. Winterbourne takes to visiting Daisy at her hotel and, though he always finds Giovanelli there, is always made welcome; obviously, he is not intruding on any secret romance. However, the other Americans in Rome follow Mrs Walker's lead and Daisy is gradually ostracized. When Winterbourne points this out to her, she refuses to believe him.

One night he accidentally encounters Daisy and Giovanelli alone in the Coliseum. This seems the final evidence of Daisy's looseness and he tells her as much. Soon afterwards she falls ill of a fever and dies. Winterbourne meets Giovanelli at the funeral in the Protestant cemetery. The Italian speaks of Daisy's 'innocence' and claims that he never dared hope she would marry him. Winterbourne goes back to Geneva to study and begins paying court to an older foreign woman.

CRITICAL COMMENTARY   Daisy Miller herself may have shocked both Europeans and Americans, but the story in which she appeared delighted them. Published in 1879, three years after James had become permanently resident in London, *Daisy Miller* was quickly pirated in Boston and New York and became a fashionable craze (there was even a 'Daisy Miller' style of hat). Its success was as enduring as it was immediate, and today it remains probably the most popular of James' early works.

Daisy Miller is one of James' most succinct and graceful treatments of his favourite 'international' theme. American by birth and cosmopolitan by education, he inevitably turned his attention to the confrontation between the Old and the New World. Indeed, with the increased traffic across the Atlantic in both directions, this was becoming a topical subject for the novelist to write about. James viewed it with a sensitive but ironic eye. In *Daisy Miller* he showed how the frank and self-confident behaviour of a young American girl from Schenectady offends the delicate social senses of various Europeans and Europeanized Americans. As the critic Leon Edel has pointed out, James' handling of the story can seem equally flattering to both Europeans and Americans.

Europeans reading the story can see it as a satire on Americans abroad. The Miller family – with the absentee father, aggressive son, quiescent mother and flirtatious daughter – are marvellous specimens of the American tourist. Daisy herself epitomizes a brash philistinism. At Rome she dismisses the works of art in as little time as possible before getting down to enjoying what she mistakenly believes to be 'Roman society' as represented by the dubious Signor Giovanelli. To the modern reader, of course, her sexual conduct seems innocent enough, however much it may have shocked the Victorians. Yet at the same time, it is difficult not to find Daisy's blithe belief in the absolute rightness of the way things are done in Schenectady comic and provincial.

Nevertheless, Daisy is a character with whom readers – and her compatriots – can easily sympathize. In the nineteenth century social convention weighed heavily on all members of polite society, but particularly on women. Their behaviour, especially with men, was rigidly circumscribed.

Inevitably, the fiction of the age abounds in heroines who delight in kicking over the traces – characters like Becky Sharp in Thackeray's *Vanity Fair* or Hester Prynne in *The Scarlet Letter*. No doubt readers secretly envied such women and sympathized with their rebellion. Daisy Miller obviously belongs to this breed and, for all her naïvety and philistinism, epitomizes a type of New Woman – a daring and unconventional representative of her sex. To some extent, of course, Daisy is also intended to be typical of her nation. 'She's an American girl,' Randolph explains to Winterbourne as Daisy first appears, and the introduction proves apt. With her 'combination of audacity and innocence', as James calls it, she epitomizes something of that free spirit which was expected of the New World. The way she flouts those codes that restricted the life of young girls shows a zest for experience that reappears in a more sophisticated form with James' most successful heroine, Isabel Archer of *The Portrait of a Lady*. It is a vibrant contrast to the sterile sense of propriety that governs the life of Mrs Walker, for example, or even Winterbourne.

When James chose to subtitle his story 'A Study' he meant that it was a study of a national type. So, at least, the story was read; the term 'Daisy Millerism' became a synonym for a trend amongst American women, applauded or deplored according to one's taste: the trend towards greater freedom and independence and a less exacting sense of propriety. Yet the subtitle surely has another meaning. The hero Winterbourne is a 'student' in the metaphorical as well as the literal senses. In fact, he is a specimen of what is commonly called 'the Jamesian observer': a detached and rather passive figure, often the narrator of the tale, who watches the other characters with persistent curiosity. Winterbourne is all of this, for he becomes a 'student' of Daisy Miller's character, continually asking himself whether she is innocent and if he approves of her. The final impression left by such figures – as James himself well knew – is one of ineffectiveness. Winterbourne is charmed by Daisy Miller, but he never defends her against criticism; he is doubtful about her, but can never make up his mind to side with her detractors.

Washington Square

SUMMARY   Dr Austin Sloper, a successful physician, lives in respectable Washington Square in New York. He is a widower and the education of his daughter Catherine has been in the hands of his sister, Mrs Penniman (Aunt Lavinia). The Doctor himself is witty and ironical, and finds Catherine disappointingly ordinary: she is neither bright nor dull, pretty nor ugly.

Mrs Almond, the Doctor's other sister, holds a party to celebrate the engagement of her daughter Marian to a young stockbroker, Arthur Townsend. Catherine meets Arthur's handsome young cousin, Morris Townsend, who pays flattering attention to her. Soon afterwards Morris and Arthur call at the Sloper residence. Arthur talks to Catherine, but she finds the stolid young businessman a poor substitute for his cousin. He explains that Morris has recently returned from abroad and is seeking a post in business. Lavinia is convinced that Morris is courting Catherine.

Townsend calls again to see Catherine and bewitches her by accounts of his European travels. Doctor Sloper decides to make some discreet inquiries; but Mrs Almond knows little about Morris except that he has a respectable widowed sister, Mrs Montgomery. Morris is invited to dinner at the house in Washington Square. He conducts himself with his usual polished assurance but fails to charm the Doctor. Catherine frankly tells Morris that her father's disapproval would weigh heavily with her.

Morris continues to visit Catherine, who receives him with grateful adoration: she has led too sheltered a life not to be enchanted by his fulsome compliments. The Doctor remonstrates with Lavinia but she has also been won over to the young man's side; her sentimental nature is easily touched by his graphic account of his youthful misfortunes. At last Morris proposes marriage. However, his interview with the Doctor quickly develops into a quarrel. Sloper tries to prevent the engagement: although he cannot stop Catherine inheriting a large fortune from her dead mother, he can strike her out of his own will.

Doctor Sloper, however, is uneasy in the role of repressive father and visits Mrs Montgomery to learn more about Morris. She is reluctant to talk, but it does emerge that, despite her poverty, her brother has depended on her for money. Rather to the Doctor's surprise, Catherine endures his behaviour in submissive silence. Mrs Penniman, excited by the situation, meets Morris secretly and urges him to elope with Catherine. He is impatient with her, for he is far from being as indifferent to Catherine's fortune as he pretends. Catherine herself, anxious not to defy her father's wishes, is annoyed at her aunt's interference.

At last Catherine does communicate with Morris, asking him to meet her privately. When he urges her to marry him privately, she consents. The Doctor steps in and takes Catherine to Europe, hoping that she will forget about her lover. They stay away for a year but she is still devoted to Morris when she returns. Meanwhile Mrs Penniman has been entertaining Morris frequently at the Slopers' house in Washington Square.

Morris has finally found a business post. He tells Catherine that he wants to speak to Doctor Sloper but she dissuades him. He then decides to break off the affair with Catherine, but cannot bring himself to tell her openly. He simply leaves New York without explanation and does not answer her letters. At last he does write from Philadelphia terminating the engagement.

Doctor Sloper never discovers the truth about this parting. He believes that it is really a 'blind': after he is dead and Catherine has inherited his fortune, Morris will reappear. This thought comes to obsess him over the years. Catherine has settled down to becoming an old maid, refusing several offers of marriage. She is embittered equally by Morris' desertion and her father's cruelty.

When Doctor Sloper dies, it is discovered that he has left

Catherine very little of his money. Soon afterwards Morris returns to New York. He is now fat and balding, and has led an unsuccessful, restless life. Mrs Penniman brings him to the house in Washington Square but Catherine receives him coldly. She is unmoved by his plea that she has misunderstood him and firmly refuses to see him again.

CRITICAL COMMENTARY Published in 1881, *Washington Square* is one of Henry James' early works. It was written shortly after he had come to live in London and, apart from *The Bostonians* (1886), it is the last of his novels to use a wholly American setting and cast of characters. Europe, the setting and theme of most of James' later fiction, is here only glimpsed: it is the source of some of those clouds of glory that Morris Townsend appears to trail to Catherine Sloper's bewitched gaze, and it is the convenient refuge to which Dr Sloper whisks his daughter when he wants to free her from Townsend's influence.

Washington Square is short – it is scarcely half the length of *The Portrait of a Lady* or *The Ambassadors* – but it is by no means a slight novel. Indeed, it is the ideal introductory book for the reader who does not know James' fiction, particularly if he is somewhat in awe of James' reputation for seriousness and complexity. For the book has several of the author's characteristic preoccupations. James always prefers to deal with the lives of the affluent middle and upper middle classes – eschewing that definition of realism which associates it with squalor and poverty – and here he chooses the fashionable world of Washington Square, the New York equivalent of the older Georgian squares of London. Moreover, the novel – like so much of James' fiction – is a *Bildungsroman*. It describes a young girl's development from vulnerable innocence to embittered experience. Catherine Sloper begins by being completely under her father's influence and sufficiently naïve to be readily deceived by the smooth manners of Morris Townsend; she ends freed from both her father's and Morris' influence, but at the price of pain and loneliness. And in common with much of James' work, the novel concerns itself with the limitations of the individual's viewpoint on the action: its characters are like a group of blundering detectives, continually probing and continually misconstruing each other's motives and characters. Out of such confusions much of the book's comedy arises. Catherine and her father are forever misinterpreting each other's actions, while both in their different ways misunderstand Morris Townsend. Only Mrs Penniman proceeds with blithe disregard of the subtleties of the situations in which she finds herself.

Yet although *Washington Square* is fairly representative of James' interests as a novelist, it lacks that close-textured complexity of his later fiction. What first strikes the reader, in fact, is the book's relaxed high spirits. It has a verve, a grace and a wit that immediately recall one of James' own favourite writers: Jane Austen. This, for example, is how Mrs Penniman, Dr Sloper's sister and Catherine's persistent misadviser, is introduced: 'He preferred Mrs Almond to his sister Lavinia, who had married a poor clergyman, of a sickly constitution and a flowery style of eloquence, and then, at the age of thirty-three, had been left a widow, without children, without fortune – with nothing but the memory of Mr Penniman's flowers of speech, a certain vague aroma of which hovered about her own conversation.' Aunt Lavinia, in fact, is one of the best things in the book; with her misplaced and disastrous preference for melodrama and sentimentality, she is a completely satisfying comic creation.

Mrs Penniman's melodramatic fantasies are relevant to an understanding of James' basic purpose in *Washington Square*. In her first novel, *Northanger Abbey*, Jane Austen parodied and rejected another literary form in order to clarify her own attitude to life and to art. She poked fun at Gothic fiction, finding its attitudes both silly and dangerous, and substituted her own resolutely commonsensical view of the world. James does something very similar in *Washington Square*. The central situation of the book – the heroine being barred from marrying a charming young man by her father's disapproval – is a cliché of romantic fiction. But James mocks some of the obvious melodramatic devices associated with the form. He also reverses a common assumption of romance: in his novel it is the older, not the younger generation who is proved right. Usually the young people defy and triumph over their parents, but in *Washington Square* Catherine is brought with sadness and bitterness to accept Dr Sloper's evaluation of Morris as a fortune-hunter.

This does not mean, however, that Dr Sloper is the novel's hero or that the reader is encouraged to sympathize with him. To begin with, of course, the Doctor does seem an attractive figure. He has an intelligence and wit very like James' own. One senses a certain compatibility of outlook between author and character in remarks such as this one about Mrs Penniman's prolonged stay in the house: 'She had given this account, at least, to every one but the Doctor, who never asked for explanations which he could entertain himself any day with inventing.' But the reader soon adopts a less sympathetic view, for the Doctor's irony is the expression of a dangerous detachment from his fellow-humans. Once the initial comedy of his disparagement of Catherine or his delight at playing the role of censorious father has worn off, these actions come to seem merely cruel. His final uncertainty as to why Morris and Catherine parted is, as James hints, a fitting punishment for a man who has shirked intimacy with other people, regarding them merely as potential sources of entertainment.

As this changing view of Doctor Sloper would suggest, *Washington Square*, for all the high spirits of its opening chapters, becomes a progressively harsh – a more obviously serious – novel. James is willing to accept the consequences of his rejection of sentimentality. The transition from blithe comedy to disillusionment is effected skillfully; one notes, for example, how carefully the reader is conditioned to accept the idea that Morris is merely a fortune-hunter. By the end, in fact, the novel has shed its tone of sparkling irony and James can sum up Catherine's dilemma in completely solemn terms that prefigure the development of some of his later heroines, like Isabel Archer in *The Portrait of a Lady*:

From her own point of view the great facts of her career were that Morris had trifled with her affection, and that her father had broken its spring. Nothing could ever alter these facts; they were always there, like her name, her age, her plain face. Nothing could ever undo the wrong or cure the pain that Morris had inflicted on her, and nothing could ever make her feel towards her father as she felt in her younger years. There was something dead in her life, and her duty was to try and fill the void.

The Portrait of a Lady

SUMMARY   While visiting New York, Mrs Touchett, an American expatriate who spends most of each year in Florence, decides to take charge of her recently orphaned niece, Isabel Archer. Isabel is delighted at the prospect of going to Europe, for she feels few ties to her own country; she has just refused her only American suitor, Caspar Goodwood, a subdued but forceful mill-owner from Boston. She is an energetic and yet serious-minded girl, with a great desire to see the world and experience it to the full. As her aunt soon discovers, she also has a great love of independence and freedom.

Isabel arrives at Gardencourt, the Touchetts' English home, when its owner, his son Ralph, and a neighbour, Lord Warburton, are enjoying tea on the lawn. Mr Touchett, a banker, is deeply attached to England, although many years' residence have not subdued his distinctively American personality. Ralph, a witty young man, suffers badly from consumption. Isabel, who has not been to England before, is charmed by the old house. She spends much of her time with old Mr Touchett, who is now badly ill, questioning him about England. She defends the country to her aunt, a resolute Anglophobe; yet in conversation with Ralph she stresses her Americanness. Though he maintains his usual ironic manner, he is fascinated by her.

Lord Warburton is also attracted to Isabel: he calls again and invites her to see his ancestral home. For her part, she is charmed by his frank and genial personality. Henrietta Stackpole, a friend of Isabel's, arrives at Gardencourt. She is a journalist, aggressively patriotic and deeply critical of Europeanized Americans like Ralph. He finds her disconcerting but likable. A few days later Isabel receives a letter from Caspar Goodwood; she cannot bring herself to reply, let alone see him. Close on the heels of this letter comes Lord Warburton with a proposal of marriage. Although she likes him, she cannot bring herself to sacrifice her freedom. Meanwhile, Henrietta, concerned that Isabel is becoming Europeanized, tries unsuccessfully to arrange for Goodwood to visit. To console herself she baits Lord Warburton when he comes to lunch, but he is irritatingly ready to agree with her criticisms of the English aristocracy.

The young people go to London where Ralph introduces Henrietta to Mr Bantling, an agreeable bachelor who takes an immediate liking to her. Caspar Goodwood calls on Isabel at her hotel. She rebukes him for pursuing her and he reluctantly agrees to return to America. When Mrs Touchett cables that her husband is gravely ill, Isabel and Ralph return to Gardencourt, leaving Henrietta with Mr Bantling. At Gardencourt Isabel meets a new guest, Madame Merle, a widowed American living in Europe. She is superbly accomplished both socially and intellectually, and soon wins Isabel's affection and admiration. Ralph proposes to Mr Touchett that he leave Isabel a generous legacy. The old man agrees and dies shortly afterwards.

Still dazed at the idea of being an heiress, Isabel goes to Paris with Mrs Touchett. She mixes with the American expatriate colony but finds them indolent and sybaritic. Predictably, Henrietta, visiting Paris with Mr Bantling, is even more censorious – and also worried that wealth will have a bad effect on Isabel. In San Remo, on her way to Florence, Isabel sees Ralph again. She lingers there happily, savouring the prospect of seeing Florence and Rome at last; she rejoices in her freedom and notices that Lord Warburton's and Caspar Goodwood's proposals of marriage seem to belong to the far distant past.

In Florence that May Gilbert Osmond welcomes his daughter Pansy back from her convent school. Osmond, a widower, is an American born and bred in Italy; he has a small income and, rather than working, dabbles in painting and collecting *objets d'art*. He is visited by Madame Merle, an intimate friend, who mentions Isabel's arrival in Florence and urges Osmond to meet her. When the two do meet Isabel is struck by his elegant manners and exquisite taste. She visits his villa to see his collection and encounters his sister, the ostentatious Countess Gemini. The Countess immediately sees that Madame Merle is trying to arrange a marriage and is alarmed, for she thinks that her brother would make Isabel a bad husband. Osmond begins to visit Mrs Touchett's house regularly to see Isabel. Ralph watches with amused interest, never doubting that she would refuse Osmond if he proposed; but Mrs Touchett is worried, for she suspects Osmond of being a fortune-hunter. Isabel and Ralph, joined by Henrietta and Mr Bantling, go to Rome. There Isabel sees Lord Warburton, who still loves her but is too good-mannered to urge his suit. Osmond comes from Florence to join them.

After touring Europe with her sister and brother-in-law and the East with Madame Merle, Isabel returns to Florence and becomes engaged to Gilbert Osmond. Most of her friends disapprove. Goodwood journeys from Boston to remonstrate with her, and Ralph is shocked into admitting that he himself loves her. Only Pansy is delighted at the marriage.

The Osmonds have now been married for two years and live in a splendid villa in Rome. Their marriage has not been completely happy, but its failings are hidden from the guests who come to the exclusive social gatherings that Osmond loves to hold. Pansy is old enough to attract suitors. The first is Edward Rosier, a dilettante-ish young American whom Isabel had met in Paris. She likes and pities him, but Osmond does not think him sufficiently prestigious. Lord Warburton arrives in Rome with Ralph, who is now badly ill. When Ralph sees Isabel he is struck by the change that intimacy with Osmond has wrought in her: her manner, once free and spontaneous, now seems studied and arranged. However, she does not see Ralph very often during his stay, since her husband disapproves.

Isabel is preoccupied by a sense of failure in her marriage: one evening she sits by the dying fire reflecting how her husband has trapped her in a cold stifling life. She notices that Lord Warburton is attracted to Pansy. Osmond is delighted at the prospect of his daughter marrying a wealthy English peer. In the event, however, Lord Warburton leaves Rome without proposing, and this leads to the first open quarrel between Isabel and her husband. He wanted her to encourage Warburton in his suit in ways that seemed to her mean and calculating; he is now sure that she deliberately sabotaged his plans.

For some time there has been a growing coolness between Isabel and Madame Merle. On one occasion, seeing Madame Merle and Osmond talking together, Isabel senses a sinister intimacy between them. This crystallizes her suspicions of the older woman: did Madame Merle, she now asks herself, deliberately arrange the marriage? Caspar Goodwood arrives urging her to leave Osmond. He and Henrietta visit Ralph; in the spring they take him to England. Soon afterwards there is a cable from Mrs Touchett, explaining that Ralph is obviously on the point of death. This causes another quarrel between Isabel and Osmond, for she insists on going to England despite his bitter opposition. As she is about to leave, Isabel meets the Countess Gemini, who explains that Pansy is Osmond's daughter not by his first wife but by Madame Merle. Stunned, Isabel visits the convent to which Osmond has temporarily sent Pansy. There she meets Madame Merle, who instantly realizes that Isabel now knows the truth. Madame Merle announces her intention of going back to America for good and, as a parting shot, tells Isabel that it is Ralph whom she should thank for Mr Touchett's legacy.

On her arrival in England Isabel is met by Henrietta, who is now engaged to Mr Bantling and plans to live in

London. She sees Ralph on his deathbed and they talk frankly for the first time in several years: he admits that the legacy was his idea and she confesses her certainty that Osmond would not have married her if she had been poor. He dies early the next morning. After the funeral she sees Lord Warburton, now engaged to an English girl, and Caspar Goodwood, who again urges her to leave Osmond and forcibly kisses her. Yet when Goodwood calls on her in London two days later he learns from Henrietta that Isabel has already returned to Rome.

CRITICAL COMMENTARY James' prefaces are always important, both as statements on the aesthetics of fiction and as inside glimpses of how he created his novels. The preface to *The Portrait of a Lady* gives a revealing account of how the idea for the novel came to him. It began not with plot, situation, setting nor even theme – but with a prevision of the character of Isabel Archer. He conceived the book 'altogether in the sense of a single character, the character and aspect of a particularly engaging young woman, to which all the usual elements of a "subject", certainly of a setting, were to need to be super-added.' In these modest terms James describes the genesis of a figure who is, by common consent, among the great heroines of fiction. For Isabel Archer has seemed to most readers the equal of Flaubert's Emma Bovary, of Hardy's Tess Durbeyfield and even, perhaps, of Tolstoy's Anna Karenina.

James speaks of Isabel as being 'particularly engaging' and the phrase (like most of his phrases) is carefully chosen. For it is central to the author's purpose that the heroine should charm the reader from the beginning, much as she charms the trio on the lawn at Gardencourt when she first meets them. James admits as much in a revealing aside near the opening of the book: 'she would be an easy victim of scientific criticism if she were not intended to awaken on the reader's part an impulse more tender and more purely expectant.' The pejorative estimate of Isabel's career is obvious: her initial confidence can seem brash and naïve, her decision to marry Gilbert Osmond hopelessly deluded, and her failure either to leave or defy him merely cowardly. But this, of course, is not the way that James makes it seem in the telling. With her warmth, her intelligence and her noble aspirations, Isabel appears a special person. In her hopes of life she is at once universal and exceptional; her delight in human contact, travel and intellectual discovery is quintessentially youthful. Her later loss of illusions – the bitter discoveries of her marriage to Osmond – seems the pattern of human development.

This account of Isabel's development does not, of course, take place in a void. James may have begun the novel simply with Isabel in mind, but he took care to locate her life in concrete settings and to introduce some of his own familiar interests into the telling. Chief of these is that 'international' theme which appears in so much of his work – his preoccupation with the relations of America and Europe, particularly with the re-discovery of Europe by an American protagonist. Isabel herself, with her freedom of manners and her endless curiosity, is ideally suited to this role, and she is placed in a context designed to demonstrate the possible responses to Europe that Americans may adopt. Henrietta Stackpole, exuberantly American, and Madame Merle, so European-ized that it is difficult to remember that she is American, represent the opposite ends of a spectrum; the various members of the Touchett family illustrate the possible inter-mediate shadings. (One notes, incidentally, the charac-teristic Jamesian irony that at the end of the book makes Madame Merle return to America and Henrietta remain in England.) Indeed, the only European in the book is Lord Warburton. As James continually stresses, the English peer is open and unaffected in his manners, whereas the Euro-peanized Americans, like Gilbert Osmond and Madame Merle, tend toward a sinister subtlety. With their assimilation into European culture and their progressive sophistication, a definite underhandedness creeps into their dealings – a striking contrast to the exuberant openness that characterizes a recent arrival from America like Isabel Archer herself.

In addition to associating his beloved 'international' theme with Isabel, James casts her career in a familiar romantic mould. The book is the history of her contact with Europe and of her love life. As James himself admits with characteristic self-irony, the plot of the novel consists of 'a succession of fine gentlemen going down on their knees to her'. Caspar Goodwood, Lord Warburton and Gilbert Osmond all make direct proposals of marriage, while Mr Touchett, Ralph and Edward Rosier are all to some degree taken with her charms. It is in her attitude to marriage that Isabel's determination to preserve her freedom is most evident; and it is one of the book's main ironies that she should accept Osmond, of all her suitors the one most likely to destroy not only her freedom but her identity. (Similarly, of course, the legacy from Mr Touchett that Ralph hopes will guarantee her independence proves its undoing.) It is not, of course, that Osmond is simply a fortune-hunter, though Isabel's money certainly attracts him. It is that he is purely a collector and aesthete; he has, as the others remark, exquisite taste, but he has only this. His taste is strengthened by no moral basis and enlivened by no human interest in his fellows. He is charmed by Isabel and adds her to his collection of beautiful objects much as he might acquire a new piece of porcelain.

Published in 1881, *The Portrait of a Lady* was the first great fruit of James' maturity as a writer. To some critics it remains his finest novel; in the opinion of all, it deserves at least to stand beside those great products of his last years, *The Wings of the Dove*, *The Ambassadors* and *The Golden Bowl*.

The Ambassadors

SUMMARY Lambert Strether, a strait-laced middle-aged American from Woollett, Massachusetts, arrives in Europe on a difficult mission. His close friend, Mrs Newsome, has become worried at the failure of her son Chad to return from Paris; it is Strether's job to free the young man from whatever entanglements have been delaying him and send him back to Woollett to take his place in the family business and marry a local girl, Mamie Pocock. Yet from the moment of his arrival in England, Strether feels a sense of freedom and a liking for Europe that threaten to conflict with this purpose. The change in him is epitomized by the way, at his hotel in Chester, he quickly and unconventionally makes friends with the charming Maria Gostrey, a Europeanized American also bound for Paris. At Chester, Strether is also joined by his friend Waymarsh, a dour New England lawyer, who quickly adds distrust of Miss Gostrey to his pre-existing distrust of everything European. In London Strether dines out with Miss Gostrey and takes her to the theatre, reflecting as he does so that the occasion has an excitement and intimacy that he never found when he took Mrs Newsome to the theatre in Boston. He explains his mission in Europe to his new friend, but she suggests that Chad might have been improved rather than corrupted by his prolonged stay in France.

In Paris he finds himself reviewing his life with irony and disappointment: middle-aged, widowed and childless, he cannot convince himself that he has achieved much. He also mentally reviews the stages of Chad's downfall: how the young American had moved from his original lodgings to the artistic Montagne Saint-Genevieve area and then to the expensive Boulevarde Malesherbes. Yet Strether likes Chad's apartment as soon as he sees it. The young man is out of Paris at the time, but another American, John Little Bilham, is looking after the apartment. Bilham, a friendly young man, invites Strether to breakfast; when he goes with Waymarsh, Strether finds the occasion and the company so pleasant that he almost suspects a trap. As he explains to Miss Gostrey when she arrives, he also feels guilty at liking so much of the way of life he had arrived to condemn.

Miss Gostrey wants to meet Bilham and arranges for him to join her party at a theatre box; but on the night Chad arrives in his place. Strether finds the young man difficult to understand. He seems shy, but this is perhaps merely good manners, for it soon emerges that he is self-confident and skillful at evading questions about his reasons for staying so long in Paris. Strether works at striking up a friendship with Chad, reporting back to Mrs Newsome all the while. Miss Gostrey is sure that there is a woman in the case, despite Chad's denials, and Strether is inclined to agree. He is struck by how polished and cultivated the young man has become, and feels a growing but guilty sympathy for him.

Chad refuses Strether's suggestion that they return to Woollett and proposes instead that Strether remain in Paris to meet two close friends, Madame de Vionnet and her daughter Jeanne. Strether immediately suspects that either the mother or the daughter is Chad's romantic attachment. He meets them at a party held in the garden of a house belonging to Gloriani, the famous sculptor. Bilham, who is also there, tells Strether that Chad is attached, though innocently, to Jeanne. Both woman prove charming -- the daughter demurely quiet and pretty, and the mother superbly cultivated. Now entirely captivated by Paris and European life, and thoroughly discontented with his own past, Strether urges Bilham to experience life while he can and not let it pass him by.

Strether learns that Maria Gostrey knows Madame de Vionnet; in fact, the two were at school together. He learns that the Frenchwoman is separated from her husband. When Strether visits her the next day she boldly tries to get him to take her side in his letters to Mrs Newsome. She also asks him to find out whether her daughter Jeanne is really in love with Chad. But when Strether speaks to the girl some days later at a party given by Chad, he gets nowhere. In conversation with Bilham at the same party he does, however, see the possibility that there is an attachment between Chad and Madame de Vionnet herself. The suspicion is confirmed a few days later when he meets her in Notre Dame; over lunch she talks of Chad with obvious affection and with great fear of losing him to the world of Woollett.

Mrs Newsome is dissatisfied with Strether's handling of affairs and sends a telegram telling him to return immediately, with or without her son. Ironically enough, Chad professes himself quite willing to go, but Strether opposes this. Miss Gostrey, like Chad, is astonished at his change of heart. Mrs Newsome now sends new ambassadors to Europe – Chad's sister Sarah, her husband Jim Pocock, and his sister Mamie, the girl whom Mrs Newsome wants Chad to marry. Awaiting the arrival of the party in Paris, Strether feels relaxed and free for the first time since he came. He is relieved to note that Sarah, the leader of the expedition, still treats him as a valued friend of the family. Jim Pocock is not angry, either; in fact, he is delighted at having an excuse to visit Paris. The new arrivals are greeted by Chad with his usual polished courtesy and by Madame de Vionnet with conciliatory gestures. Strether is shocked to discover that the two have been making arrangements, in the French manner, to marry Jeanne off. He interprets this as Chad's way of making clear that it is Madame de Vionnet, not her daughter, to whom he is attached. There is, of course, no sign of the romance between Chad and Mamie that the party from Woollett desire; indeed, Strether is only half joking when he suggests to Bilham that he should marry Mamie.

One morning Waymarsh arrives at Strether's hotel to announce that Sarah is on her way to speak to him. She explains that she is returning to America via Switzerland; her party will include Bilham and Waymarsh. For the first time she speaks frankly to Strether, revealing her contempt for Madame de Vionnet and her feeling that Mrs Newsome has been insulted. She sees nothing to welcome in the way that Chad has changed. He has told her that he would gladly return to Woollett if Strether suggests he should. But, after talking to Chad and Miss Gostrey, Strether decides not to offer any definite advice.

After the Pococks' departure, Strether decides to spend a peaceful day in the country. At a small inn he idly watches two people boating on the river. With a shock he recognizes them as Chad and Madame de Vionnet and realizes that they are pretending not to have seen him. A meeting, however, is unavoidable and proves awkward – especially since

Strether is sure that the couple are not out for the day like himself but have been spending the weekend together. After their return to Paris, he bids goodbye to the couple, warmly advising Chad to stay in Paris and continue his romance. He then takes his reluctant and wistful departure of Miss Gostrey.

CRITICAL COMMENTARY *The Ambassadors*, together with those other products of James' final phase, *The Wings of the Dove* and *The Golden Bowl*, has long been the subject of critical disagreement. In his preface to the novel the author himself pronounced it to be 'frankly, quite the best, "all round", of my productions'. Percy Lubbock in his influential *The Craft of Fiction* (1921) confirmed the common view that *The Ambassadors* is a pinnacle of James' art and one of the chief evidences of his greatness. Yet to Dr Leavis, in *The Great Tradition* (1948), it seemed to be 'not only *not* one of his great books, but to be a bad one': the subtleties and elaborations of its technique are not justified by any corresponding subtlety in the subject. Even E. M. Forster, who both admires James in general and likes *The Ambassadors* in particular, complained in *Aspects of the Novel* (1927) of the characters' narrowness: 'They can land in Europe and look at works of art and at each other, but that is all.'

Much of this disagreement has been caused by James' prose style. To some readers it has seemed subtle and refined, to others merely irritatingly difficult to read. A remorseless search for absolute accuracy of statement leads James into the habit of long sinuous sentences, dense and difficult syntax, and clusters of qualifying clauses. On occasion, of course, it has the satiric grace and concision that one associates with the author of, say, *Washington Square*. In a fine phrase, for example, James calls the dour New England lawyer Waymarsh a man of 'big bleak kindness' or gives this description of him listening to the minutiae of Strether's conscience: 'Waymarsh looked gravely ardent, over the finished soup, at this array of scruples.' The same habit of precise observation extends to the way images are used:

'He threw out the bridge of a charming hollow civility on which Strether wouldn't have trusted his own full weight a moment.'

Even some of the long and convoluted sentences which typify James' late style have an obvious flowing grace of their own:

> Why Miss Barrace, mature meagre erect and eminently gay, highly adorned, perfectly familiar, freely contradictious, and reminding him of some last-century portrait of a clever head without powder – why Miss Barrace should have been in particular the note of a 'trap' Strether couldn't on the spot have explained; he blinked in the light of a conviction that he should know later on, and know well – as it came over him, for that matter, with force, that he should need to.

This is difficult – it needs more than one reading to yield its full sense – and yet the complexity is obviously justified. The profusion of adjectives and the carefully qualified analyses attempt, with characteristic Jamesian finesse, to catch the mood of a particular fleeting moment. But what is the reader to make of a sentence like this? 'Mere discriminations about a pair of gloves could thus at any rate represent – always for such sensitive ears as were in question – possibilities of something that Strether could make a mark against only as the peril of apparent wantonness.' This, surely, is awkward, mannered and obscure. James' habit of endlessly refining his ideas can lead, on some occasions, merely to unintentional self-parody.

Whatever the disagreements about the style of *The Ambassadors*, its themes are clear. It returns to James' favourite 'international' theme – to record yet again the blundering meeting of innocent, serious Americans and graceful, wise and sly Europeans. To deliberately comic effect, James stages an almost archetypal confrontation. He creates Lambert Strether and his friend Waymarsh, two conventional small-town Americans, and launches them into Europe on a devoutly moral errand – to rescue a young friend, Chad, from the fleshpots and romantic entanglements of Paris. Yet when they arrive, although Waymarsh is massively unresponsive to his surroundings, Strether himself quickly loses his moral bearings. He is soon uneasy in the role of ambassador from Woollett, from the matriarchal Mrs Newsome, and from American business, for he is charmed by much about the way of life he has come to condemn. Despite his middle-aged respectability, he is touched by the spectacle of youth and grace. With much slipping and floundering, and with a habit of self-searching so thorough as to be almost comic, he is finally able to assert a moral position that is exactly the reverse of his initial belief: the errant Chad should stay in Paris and continue to err.

In this respect, of course, the book is a polished comedy of manners. Yet it is also a version of a favourite nineteenth-century type of fiction – the *Bildungsroman*, or novel of education. This genre usually deals with a young man's development – typically with the passage from late adolescence to adulthood. By a neat twist James writes a *Bildungsroman* about a middle-aged man, and the fact that Strether is fifty-five rather than twenty-five or fifteen makes the story at once funnier and more touching. For Strether's air of bafflement, his eager curiosity, his chopping and changing of beliefs imply at once an engaging openness and a pitifully weak sense of his own identity. As he himself is acutely aware, his own life has been a failure. His family is dead, his professional achievements are negligible, and all that awaits him on his return to Woollett is the prospect of marriage to the overbearing Mrs Newsome. Paris offers him a fuller life than he has known, but the offer comes too late. Strether cannot himself profit from his own belated development; all he can do is try to pass on his newfound wisdom to Chad or little Bilham, both young enough to benefit. This is, of course, exactly what Strether does at Gloriani's party in his speech on the traditional theme of *carpe diem*, 'gather ye rosebuds while ye may'. Such moments sound a note of anguish common in James' late fiction, and so it is no surprise to find that in the preface he singles out this part of Strether's 'irrepressible outbreak' as embodying the book's main theme: 'Live all you can; it's a mistake not to. It doesn't so much matter what you do in particular so long as you have your life. If you haven't had that what *have* you had?'

FURTHER READING Although several subsequent collections of James' work have been published, the best remains the New York Edition (twenty-six volumes; 1907–1918), which James himself supervised. There is a useful compilation of his letters edited in two volumes by Percy Lubbock (1920). The standard biography is the monumental five-volume work by that most devoted of James scholars, Leon Edel (1953–1972; revised two-volume edition 1978).

Perhaps the best critical introduction to the novels are the prefaces that James himself wrote for the New York Edition; these have been conveniently collected as *The Art of the Novel* (1934), edited by R. P. Blackmur. In addition to the essays on James mentioned in the critical discussion of *The Ambassadors*, the following specialist works are particularly useful to the student: F. O. Matthiessen, *Henry James: The Major Phase* (1944); Richard Poirier, *The Comic Sense of Henry James* (1960); Dorothea Krook, *The Ordeal of Consciousness in Henry James* (1962); and Maxwell Geismar, *Henry James and His Cult* (1964).

William Dean Howells

Although his name was later to be associated with Boston and New York, William Dean Howells was born in a small Midwestern town – Martin's Ferry, Ohio – in 1837. His family moved restlessly about the state until they settled in Columbus, where Howells began to write for the *Ohio State Journal* in 1856. In 1860 he was commissioned on Hawthorne's recommendation to write a campaign biography of Lincoln, a job which in turn gained him the American Consulship at Venice.

On his return to America in 1865 Howells lived in Boston

and worked as a journalist. He quickly gained admittance into those fashionable literary circles for which the city was famous. He became the protegé of that distinguished literatus, James Russell Lowell. Indeed, when Howells was introduced by Lowell to Oliver Wendell Holmes, Holmes is supposed to have remarked: 'Well, James, this is the apostolic succession, the laying on of hands.'

The publication of *Their Wedding Journey* in 1872 began a long and productive career as a novelist; by the time of his death in 1920 Howells had written thirty-five novels, as well as several volumes of travel, reminiscence, criticism, short stories and plays. His early work drew on his experience of Italy and is romantic in tone. But it was as a realist, and particularly as the commentator on Boston social life, that Howells found his metier. In such works as *A Modern Instance* (1882) and *The Rise of Silas Lapham* (1885) he shows a delicate understanding of both psychological and sociological nuances.

In later life Howells moved to New York where he worked for *Harper's*. With the change in locale there was a noticeable change in his outlook. He became preoccupied with social problems and was eventually converted to socialism. Where he had previously viewed American society with sunny confidence, he became progressively pessimistic. Both these tendencies are reflected in the fiction of the New York period, beginning with *A Hazard of New Fortunes* (1890).

Today Howells' name is unknown to all but specialists. Yet at the time of his death in 1920 he was regarded as a major figure in American letters. He had been a close friend and correspondent of Henry James and Mark Twain. With them he had helped to usher into American literature that new spirit of realism which replaced the earlier love of romance. His later interest in social and political ideas helped to pave the way for the work of the naturalists at the turn of the century. Indeed, he personally encouraged several of these writers – Stephen Crane, Frank Norris and Hamlin Garland – in their careers.

Yet Howells' importance is not merely historical. His best

work is a triumph of careful thought, observation and construction. It shows the realist's eye for the significance of everyday life – for the revealing gesture, nuance or detail. 'Other persons', Henry James commented, 'have considered and discoursed upon American life, but no one surely, has *felt* it so completely as he.' This praise was echoed by one of Howells' chief English admirers, Rudyard Kipling: 'The truthful and faithful fabric of his presentments . . . showed neither flaw nor adulteration, pretence nor preciosity, and the immense amount of observation and thought that has gone evenly into its texture shot and irradiated, without overloading, each strand of the design.'

A Modern Instance

SUMMARY   Bartley Hubbard, a charming young college graduate, becomes editor of the local paper in the small New England town of Equity. But he is bored by the job and dreams of making his fortune in Chicago or Boston. Bartley enjoys flirting with young women and pays particular attention to Marcia Gaylord, who readily agrees to marry him. Her father, Squire Gaylord, does not like Bartley.

The journalist is accused of trifling with the affections of Hannah Morrison, one of his typesetters. He consults Squire Gaylord about ways of preventing the affair becoming public. Marcia is a proud woman and breaks off the engagement as soon as she hears the rumours. A few days later Hubbard resigns his job and prepares to leave Equity. Marcia has already begun to regret her action – she is helplessly in love with Bartley despite his faults – and pleads with her father to effect a reconciliation. Bartley spends a few days with his friend Kinney at a nearby logging camp. The camp is visited by its owner, Mr Willett, with a party including several women. One of them, Mrs MacAllister, flirts with Bartley. He then returns to Equity and is met at the railway station by Marcia, who can no longer bear to be separated from him. They are hastily married and leave for Boston.

Bartley books them in at one of the best hotels and takes Marcia to the theatre. But when she discovers how bad their financial situation is, she insists that they find cheap rooms. Bartley writes an account of his stay at the logging camp and soon begins to make a name for himself in journalistic circles. Meanwhile, Squire Gaylord visits Marcia; she and Bartley quarrel after her father's departure.

While reporting a social gathering Bartley sees Clara Kingsbury, a fashionable young Bostonian whom he had met on a previous visit to Boston. He is offered a permanent job by Mr Witherby. This involves interviewing Mr Halleck, a successful leather dealer and the father of an old college friend. The Hallecks, who live modestly despite their wealth, invite the Hubbards to dinner, where they meet the family lawyer Mr Atherton. Ben Halleck, Bartley's friend, returns from Europe and visits the Hubbards.

Marcia has a baby, Flavia, and wants the occasion to be used for a reconciliation between Bartley and her parents. But Squire Gaylord's visit is not a success, for the old man is still ill at ease with his son-in-law. By this time Bartley has become known for being entirely commercial and unethical in his approach to his journalism. He has also begun to drink heavily and gain weight. He and Marcia quarrel violently; Ben and Atherton discuss the matter with concern. During a visit to Equity Bartley again flirts with Mrs MacAllister and upsets Marcia.

Kinney comes unexpectedly to visit Hubbard in Boston. He is charmed by Marcia and the child. After Kinney's departure Bartley writes a newspaper story about some of the logger's adventures, even though he knows that Kinney himself has been planning to do this. Marcia is worried and it takes all Bartley's persuasiveness to placate her about this unethical behaviour. Some of Hubbard's professional acquaintances are not so easily satisfied; one of them, Ricker, severs himself from him for good. The Hubbards' marriage is obviously failing and, when Marcia goes alone on a visit to Equity, Bartley realizes how much more relaxed he is in her absence. He quarrels with Witherby and loses his job.

On her return to Boston Marcia encounters Hannah Morrison in the street. Her dormant jealousy is awakened and she accuses Bartley of seeing Hannah secretly. They argue and Marcia storms out of the house in anger; Hubbard himself leaves while she is gone. He takes a train going west, with no clear plan in mind. At Cleveland he finds that his wallet (which contained money lent by Ben) has been stolen. He could not return to Boston even if he wanted to.

At about this time Halleck, who has been getting more and more depressed, decides to go abroad. Atherton, who has guessed the unspoken source of Ben's unhappiness, encourages him in this resolve. Marcia, desperate at her husband's disappearance, is beset by his many creditors. Reluctant to publicize – or even to admit to herself – that Bartley has deserted her, she consults Atherton. He takes charge, insisting that Marcia's father be informed and suggesting that Clara Kingsbury come round to comfort her. Not even Squire Gaylord can persuade her to leave the house and return to Equity: she insists on waiting for Bartley to return. The emergency draws Atherton and Clara together and they get engaged.

After two years Ben returns to Boston. He explains to Atherton that he has been fighting a losing battle against his love for Marcia. He now intends to prove that Hubbard is dead and ask her to marry him. But he soon afterwards receives a newspaper from Indiana, containing notice that Hubbard is suing for divorce on grounds of abandonment. The Hallecks and Squire Gaylord are infuriated at this latest example of Bartley's dishonesty. They persuade Marcia to come with them to Indiana and contest the suit by confronting her husband in open court. After a tiring train journey the party arrives only just in time to contradict Hubbard's story of being deserted by his wife. Squire Gaylord, acting as his daughter's lawyer, makes a fine speech that impresses the court. At its climax, however, he is taken ill with a stroke; Bartley wisely takes advantage of the confusion to escape. Subsequently he has a private interview with Ben: he has apparently guessed Halleck's feelings about Marcia, for he suggests that the two should marry. Hubbard then goes further west and is killed several months later by someone whom he had libelled in his newspaper. Squire Gaylord returns to Equity but never recovers properly from his stroke; he dies soon afterwards. Halleck, who had previously been agnostic, reverts to the religion of his family and is ordained. At the end of the novel he is still debating whether or not to ask Marcia to marry him.

CRITICAL COMMENTARY 'Commonplace? The commonplace is just that light, impalpable, aerial essence which they've never got into their confounded books yet. The novelist who could interpret the common feelings of commonplace people would have the answer to "the riddle of the painful earth" on his tongue.' This is the challenge thrown out by one of Bromfield Corey's dinner guests in *The Rise of Silas Lapham*. It is a challenge that Howells himself accepts in both that novel and its predecessor, *A Modern Instance*. Where romance – the fictional mode preferred by earlier American writers like Hawthorne and Melville – cultivates the exotic and the unusual, realism studies the commonplace. Howells' work does not deal with the past or with the lawless world of nature, and it does not use elaborate symbolic or allegorical patterns. It turns to contemporary life – specifically, to the world of polite Boston society – and to the problems of ordinary men and women. Its approach is low-keyed and ironic, studiously avoiding rhetoric and melodrama.

This attitude leads to a new and fresh handling of several traditional themes. Howells' treatment of sexual love is especially interesting. Although hardly daring by modern standards, his description of Bartley's and Marcia's courtship was sufficiently frank to shock his contemporary readers; in early editions the novel was usually heavily bowdlerized. Along with this new frankness about physical love comes a new interest in marriage. Usually romances conclude their story with a wedding: it is the conventional happy ending. But to Howells, as to a fellow realist like Henry James, marriage becomes an important theme in itself; it often begins rather than ends the novel. Here again, this leads Howells into dangerous territory. His interest in divorce – and obviously the divorce hearing in Indiana is the book's dramatic climax – identified him with advanced and controversial notions. Certainly, when the English novelist Thomas Hardy touched on the same subject some ten years later in *Jude the Obscure* he brought down on himself an avalanche of criticism which made him reluctant to return to writing fiction.

At the heart of the novel's success is the portrait of Bartley Hubbard, the cynical and ambitious young journalist who turns the trusting Marcia's love into bitter hatred. According to traditional notions of story-telling, Bartley should be the villain; at any rate he is certainly unattractive. At one point or another he hurts and betrays most of the other characters in the book by his careless selfishness: apart from Marcia herself, Kinney, Ben Halleck and Squire Gaylord all suffer at his hands.

Howells, of course, is fully aware of Bartley's failings but his treatment of him is sympathetic rather than readily censorious. He later admitted that he identified with Bartley as he wrote; while Mark Twain, without taking offence, believed Bartley to be a portrait of himself. For Hubbard is not a bad man – or at least not deliberately so. It is simply that he underrates the work and thought needed for treating other people well. He assumes too readily that good intentions are enough in life. The error is shown most clearly in the failure of his marriage; for despite his real generosity, his attitude to Marcia is increasingly self-centred and cruel. Yet it is not only his marriage that fails. After his initial success in Boston newspaper circles he is slowly ostracized: his obvious commercialism and his indifference to ethical considerations (as shown in his theft of Kinney's idea for an article) repel his colleagues. When he leaves Boston his career goes steadily downhill until his ironic death at 'Whited Sepulchre, Arizona', killed by an irate reader of his paper. In sum, the portrait is a chilling study of moral decay.

The idea for the novel originally occurred to Howells during a performance of Euripides' *Medea*; it was provisionally entitled *The New Medea*. One can see easily enough how well Bartley Hubbard corresponds to the Jason of the myth – the easygoing and charming sensualist who wins the heroine's affections only to turn them to bitterness by his careless behaviour. The matter of Marcia, the modern Medea, is more complex. Unlike the Medea of the tragedy she does not indulge in any extravagant acts of revenge. Her relationship with Bartley simply ends in separation and a sordid divorce suit; and, at the end of the book, her future is left deliberately indefinite. Much of the development of her character is finely etched – from unformed young girl, only too ready to trust the men in her life, to embittered and independent woman. Yet the portrait never comes into focus completely and it lacks the conviction of Howells' presentation of Bartley. As in the case of Hardy's portrait of Sue Bridehead in *Jude the Obscure*, one feels that the writer is working, however bravely, out of his range. Howells is obviously fascinated by Marcia, but ultimately puzzled and rather awed by her.

The ending of the novel is no less typical of Howells' realism than his interest in divorce and in the subtleties of human psychology. He refuses to give the story a conventional conclusion: rather than tying up the loose ends neatly, he leaves things deliberately doubtful and indeterminate. Hubbard and Squire Gaylord are both dead, and Marcia is at last disillusioned about her husband. But it is not clear whether Ben Halleck, Marcia's timid and upright admirer for most of the book, will summon up the courage to ask her to marry him, or whether she would accept if he did. In this respect Howells is attempting to be faithful to life, as he and his contemporary realists saw it. Life, they liked to argue, did not arrange itself into convenient plots: it was a continuous process without obvious beginning or ending. The true artist should try to imitate this effect of process and not impose a sense of stylized and artificial form.

The Rise of Silas Lapham

SUMMARY Bartley Hubbard (see *A Modern Instance*), a cynical young Boston journalist, interviews Silas Lapham, the wealthy paint manufacturer. Lapham is an impressive figure: homely and unsophisticated but with an instinctive business sense. He was born in Vermont and brought up on his father's farm. Encouraged by his wife Persis, he exploited a mineral paint mine on his land and soon made himself a fortune.

Lapham has recently become conscious of the need to move in good society – it will benefit his daughters Irene and Penelope – and has begun to build an expensive house in the exclusive Back Bay area. The Laphams visit its site after his interview with Hubbard. On the way they meet Rogers, Silas' ex-partner. Silas is bitter towards Rogers and cuts him; Mrs Lapham does not approve of her husband's conduct, for she believes that he treated Rogers badly when they were colleagues. Normally the happiest and most sensible of couples, the Laphams quarrel.

Now reconciled, they again visit the new house with their daughters the next day. They meet Tom Corey, a young man from an exclusive Boston family, and Silas shows him around the partly completed building. As he explains to his father that evening, Tom wants to join Lapham's business. Bromfield Corey, an elegant and cultivated gentleman, is privately horrified at the idea of this connection with trade but knows better than to oppose his son's wishes.

The paint manufacturer is delighted and flattered at the idea of someone from so genteel a background joining his business, and he takes Tom home to dinner to show him off to the family. The Laphams notice that Tom pays attentions to both their daughters and seems especially attracted to Irene, the younger, shyer and prettier of the two. After dinner it is decided that the young man should join the firm, using his fluency with foreign languages to help in the export trade. Mrs Corey is shocked when she hears of this step but her husband stops her from intervening.

Tom is puzzled by Miss Dewey, Lapham's secretary: she is a mysterious figure who seems to have a special relationship with her employer. The young man enjoys his work and pleases Lapham. However, Bromfield Corey's failure to make any gesture of social acknowledgement offends the paint manufacturer. Tom himself visits the Laphams regularly and shows an interest in Irene. Finally the older Corey calls to see Lapham at his office and their meeting is cordial, if hardly relaxed. At this time Lapham is loaning money to his ex-partner Rogers, which pleases Mrs Lapham greatly.

Mrs Corey and her daughters, back in Boston after their summer holiday, worry about Tom's attentions to Irene. She resolves to visit the Laphams to see her possible future daughter-in-law. However, Irene is out and Mrs Corey is received by Mrs Lapham and Penelope. The mother is flustered and ill at ease but the daughter is her usual cool and ironic self; indeed, Penelope's self-possession irritates the visitor. When the Laphams dine at the Coreys they commit a solecism by allowing Penelope to absent herself unexpectedly from the party at the last minute. After dinner Silas, usually a teetotaller, drinks too much and becomes talkative; he boasts of his new house, his wealth and his paint.

When Tom calls at the Laphams one evening he is received by Penelope and, to her surprise, confesses his love for her. She and her parents are disturbed to learn that Penelope, not Irene, is the object of Tom's affection. In despair they seek the advice of Mr Sewell, a clergyman whom they had met at the Coreys' dinner party. He comforts them and stresses that Penelope should not be prevented from marrying Tom by pity for Irene. When Irene hears the news she is devastated and goes to the family farm in Vermont to recover. The Coreys are far from pleased at the prospect of having Penelope as a daughter-in-law.

A new firm has developed a method of manufacturing paint that underprices Lapham's product. His business begins to slacken and he becomes worried and secretive. To make matters worse, he has been making further loans to Rogers; now he suspects that his ex-partner has been trying to swindle him. He is soon in deep financial trouble and with great reluctance decides to sell the house at Back Bay. He visits the place one evening and, lighting a fire in the unused grate, sits down to think the matter out. Later that night the house burns down. It is a crippling blow for Lapham – financial as well as emotional, since the building was uninsured. Yet the disaster rouses his fighting spirit and he goes to New York to visit the rival paint firm. His competitors offer to let him buy his way into their business, but ask a high price. Lapham is tempted to join Rogers in a dishonest deal to raise the money, but he resists this.

The progressive failure of the business has placed a great strain on Mrs Lapham. This is intensified when she receives an anonymous letter dropping innuendoes about her husband's relationship with his secretary. When Silas refuses to answer these charges Mrs Lapham goes to the office to confront Miss Dewey. She realizes that the secretary is the daughter of Jim Millon, a Civil War colleague who had saved Lapham's life; in gratitude Lapham has supported Millon's feckless family ever since. Mrs Lapham falls ill with shock in her husband's office and is escorted home by Tom Corey.

At last Lapham goes bankrupt. After the months of protracted anxiety the final crash comes almost as a relief. The Laphams are forced to sell their Boston house and return to the Vermont farm from which Silas had started out many years ago. He continues in the paint business, though in a modest way. Soon he is taken over by his new and successful rival. The firm keeps him on as a local manager and, at Lapham's recommendation, hires Tom Corey. By this time Tom has married Penelope. Originally she tried to refuse his proposal out of guilt about her sister, but Irene intervened and insisted that Penelope marry. Lapham himself is aged and depressed but not destroyed by his business failure. He lives a quiet life, nostalgic for his former success but not entirely discontented with his present lot.

CRITICAL COMMENTARY   In *A Modern Instance* Howells' instinct for realism had led him to tackle the controversial and timely subject of divorce. In *The Rise of Silas Lapham,* written a few years later, he dealt with an equally topical though rather less controversial subject: the self-made businessman. His hero is an archetype of the breed: the son of a humble Vermont farmer, Lapham is anxious to break into the exclusive circles of Boston society. Such men, indeed, were typical of the times in which Howells was writing. The American Civil War, like most wars, had made the society more fluid, even in traditional areas like Boston. Fortunes were made (and lost) quickly, and men could rise on the social scale with a speed and ease which would have been unthinkable only decades before.

Yet Howells' interest in the subject was also personal, for he was himself the equivalent in the literary world of self-made businessmen like Lapham. He had been born in Ohio and it was only later in life that he won admission into Boston society. He always regarded such circles with that mixture of attraction and repulsion which commonly attaches to the outsider. *Silas Lapham,* although not an auto-biography in any literal sense, is written out of deep personal experience. Henry James noted the way that Lapham himself is 'understood down to the ground, inside and out'.

Howells was thus in a unique position to portray both Boston society and the feelings of a social upstart who wishes to break into it. It is this ability to sympathize with both sides – with Lapham and with the 'proper Bostonians' – that gives the novel its characteristic strength. It is not simply a satire on the snobbery of traditional Boston in the name of the values of the new business world, nor a satire on the crass, uncultivated businessman in the name of old school gentility. The portrait of Bromfield Corey, for example, is a finely rendered study of a certain type of Boston gentleman. Although the family fortune is based on trade, Corey has chosen to be a man of leisure – travelling around Europe in his youth, dabbling (but only dabbling) in painting and cultivating a reputation as a dinner-table wit. He has real elegance and a real intelligence that the reader is asked to admire. At the same time, however, Howells is sufficiently detached from Corey's world to render Lapham's reactions at the dinner party with real vividness. From Lapham's initial confusion about his gloves (which he feels make his hands look like 'canvased hams'), to his nervous attention to the table manners of his fellow guests, to his final bragging drunkenness, the reactions of an outsider to genteel society are caught with sympathetic accuracy.

Howells, of course, is by no means blind to the faults of Lapham and the business world in which he is at home. The manufacturer's pride in his paint is touching but has a dangerous naïvety, like his failure to see that his advertisements painted on rocks deface the landscape. He has a fatal belief in the power of his purse – this is especially evident when he talks about the cost of his projected house at Back Bay – and he can be tempted to dishonest dealing. Yet for all this, *Silas Lapham* does not belong to that tradition of American fiction which reaches its climax with Sinclair Lewis' *Babbitt*: the novel of businessman-baiting. Despite his vulgarity, his bragging and his social pretensions Lapham represents at root the soundest values in the book. He has a calm good sense and a laconic honesty, bred in him not by high society or big business but by his humble background in Vermont. Silas and Persis have a way of talking together – Howells catches their idiom superbly – that epitomizes these qualities: their conversations are blunt, good-humoured and sensible. Once the importance of these values is understood the book's title becomes comprehensible. For, of course, the novel does not describe a 'rise' in the usual sense of the term: during most of the action Silas is losing money and falling socially. Yet he is rising morally. Adversity toughens him as well as wounding him. During his Indian summer back at his old farmstead, he achieves a stability and peace that had deserted him during his years of material success.

FURTHER READING There is no complete collection of Howells' works, but most of the better-known novels are readily available in modern editions. The long-felt need for a proper biography has recently been filled by Kenneth Lynn's excellent *William Dean Howells: An American Life* (1971), which also contains some of the best criticism of Howells' work. The writer's correspondence with Mark Twain has been edited by H. N. Smith and W. M. Gibson (two volumes; 1960).

Howells has not yet found the criticism or the recognition he deserves; only Mr Lynn's study goes some way towards remedying this injustice. Nevertheless, the works by D. G. Cooke (1922), O. W. Firkins (1924), Van Wyck Brooks (1959) are useful introductions. By far the best short discussion is Lionel Trilling's essay, 'William Dean Howells and the Roots of Modern Taste', in *The Opposing Self* (1955).

Edith Wharton

Born in New York in 1862, Edith Wharton (née Jones) was brought up in an affluent, snobbish and fashionable world very like the setting of most of her novels. Her familiarity with the world of the American aristocracy was increased by her marriage in 1885 to Edward Wharton, a Boston banker. Like most Americans of her background she visited Europe several times in her youth, and in 1907 she settled permanently in France. She died in 1937.

Edith Wharton's life, beginning in exclusive American society and ending in European exile, resembled that of her friend and near-contemporary Henry James. Critics have also been struck by the similarities between their work: indeed, Edith Wharton has often been called 'Henry James' heiress'. Beginning in 1899, she published novels that view upper middle-class New York society in a wry and detached, though not absolutely hostile, manner. Her subject, she said, was 'a field as yet unexploited by any novelist who had grown up in that little hot-house of traditions and conventions'. The best of her books about fashionable life are *The House of Mirth* (1905) and *The Age of Innocence*, awarded the

Pulitzer Prize on its publication in 1920. But *Ethan Frome* (1901), her most popular novel and also her own favourite, deals with a very different sort of subject: it turns from upper middle-class life to record a stark and simple tragedy taking place in a poor New England village.

Ethan Frome

SUMMARY The narrator stays in the small isolated Massachusetts village of Starkfield for the winter whilst working at the power-house at nearby Corbury Junction. He becomes curious about Ethan Frome, an aged and partly crippled ruin of a man who calls each day at the post office. From Harmon Gow he learns that Frome owns an unprofitable farm and saw-mill in the area, that he was badly hurt in an accident, and that he has been in some way trapped in Starkfield. The narrator's landlady, Mrs Ned Hale, is usually talkative and friendly, but she is reticent when Frome's name is mentioned.

For all his curiosity, the narrator still has not had any personal contact with Frome. But when the livery stables disappoints him one week, he decides to hire Frome to drive him to and from work each day. On these journeys he covertly observes the farmer. Frome is a quiet, melancholy and impressive-looking figure. His reserve breaks down only occasionally: once he mentions that he has been to Florida and once he shows an interest in science. One evening the snow is so bad that Frome cannot drive the narrator back into Starkfield: he has to offer him accommodation at his own farm. That night, the narrator explains, he learns the story of Frome's life.

Although still a young man, Ethan Frome already feels trapped and burdened by cares. He has to abandon his training as an engineer to nurse his sick parents, and at their death he inherits a farm and saw-mill that he cannot sell. His marriage to Zenobia (or Zeena) has little joy about it, for his wife is a prematurely aged hypochondriac. Ethan's only pleasure comes from the company of the pretty Mattie

Silver, his wife's cousin, who lives with the family. As he goes to collect Mattie from a local dance one evening, Ethan broods on his wife's insinuation that the young girl will soon marry Denis Eady, the son of a local merchant. But his jealousy is quickly assuaged, for Mattie chooses to walk home with him rather than accept a ride from Denis. On the way Ethan hopes that Mattie returns his secret love. But his affectionate thoughts are driven out of his head when they reach the farm and are greeted churlishly by Zeena.

The next day Zeena announces that she is going into the next town to consult a new doctor and will need to be away for the night. Ethan is secretly overjoyed at being able to spend time alone with Mattie but annoyed at the prospect of more medical bills. He asks for cash payment on some wood he delivers to Andrew Hale but is genially refused; he is too proud and too shy to press the matter. He returns home to dine alone with Mattie. They are both embarrassed in each other's presence and, in her nervousness, she breaks a favourite pickle dish of Zeena's. Yet for Ethan the evening is still a delicious glimpse of what life could be like without his wife. But Zeena returns unexpectedly early the next day and, after brooding alone in her room for a while, abruptly breaks shocking news to Ethan. The doctor has told her to avoid housework and so she has hired a maid; this will mean turning Mattie out of the house. Ethan is horrified and when he tells the news to Mattie their constraint breaks down: they kiss and embrace for the first time.

Alone in his study that evening Ethan debates leaving his wife and running away with Mattie. He even begins to write Zeena a latter of farewell. But he is restrained in these dreams by the thought of his own poverty: he can leave Zeena nothing and can offer Mattie nothing. The next day, despite his anguish, Ethan cannot bring himself either to oppose or to leave his wife; he watches helplessly as preparations are made for Mattie's departure. He insists on driving her to the station and on the way he learns that Mattie has found the discarded letter to Zeena. The couple talk openly of their love for the first time. To delay her departure, he suggests that they borrow a sledge and coast down the hill. When they come to the bottom, they only just miss an elm tree dangerously near the track. This puts a desperate idea in Frome's head and he talks Mattie into taking another ride with him, planning to run into the tree and kill them both. The sledge hits the tree but Ethan and Mattie are injured, not killed.

When he arrives at the farmhouse many years later in Ethan's company, the narrator is introduced to the aged and paralysed Mattie Silver. On his return to the lodgings, he talks to Mrs Hale, who tells him about the aftermath of the accident. Mattie was brought to stay with the Fromes and nursed by Zeena, who set aside her hypochrondria to take care of her husband and cousin. However, Mattie has become a soured and embittered woman over the years.

CRITICAL COMMENTARY *Ethan Frome* is a short, simple novel. It is an American *Wuthering Heights*: a stark tragedy of defeated love that takes place against a background of isolated rural life and harsh turbulent nature. Edith Wharton is best known for her poised and ironic novels of fashionable life, but here she shows herself equally accomplished at evoking the passions of poor, inarticulate people and at describing the daily rhythms of country life. Her achievement was based on personal experience rather than scholarly research: '*Ethan Frome* was written after I had spent ten years in the hill-region where the scene is laid, during which years I had come to know well the aspect, dialect and mental and moral attitude of the hill-people.'

Appropriately enough, the story is told by an outsider to the community of Starkfield – just as *Wuthering Heights* is told by a visiting dandy from the city. The narrator of *Ethan Frome* is never named and only the barest facts about him are indicated (he is an educated man, interested in science); but his presence has an important effect on the book. Most obviously, he distances the reader from Ethan Frome and his story: we never see the events themselves, but only the narrator's interpretation of them. He never explains how he actually learns the story of Frome's life during his visit to the farm, for he merely says cryptically that he 'found the clue to Ethan Frome and began to put together this vision of his story'. At the same time, the fact that the storyteller is himself a stranger to the community provides an excuse for the careful detail with which the picture of rural life is constructed. The gaunt, unfriendly landscape, perpetually shrouded in snow; the silent and laconic manners of the natives; the pervasive atmosphere of grim suffering and endurance: all these are tellingly rendered. Indeed, the village's very name – 'Starkfield' – is emblematic.

This backdrop is appropriate to the human drama that the narrator reconstructs. The story is about defeat and disappointment, about how people are forced to submit to an alien fate. The narrator's first glimpse of Ethan Frome provides, in symbolic form, the key to his life: he has a lameness 'checking each step like the jerk of a chain'. Frome is a trapped man: trapped first by the illness of his parents that thwarts his education, then by the legacy of the unsaleable farm and saw-mill, and then by his marriage to the begging and hypochondriac Zeena. When the narrator first sees him, Frome is dragging out his days in a depressed town from which, as Harmon Gow says, 'most of the smart ones get away'.

The central event in this sequence – the one on which the story concentrates – is the failure of Frome's love for Mattie. Her name, 'Silver', is no doubt intended to be symbolic, for she is the one source of light and beauty in the book. Ethan's love for her is unsentimentally and movingly rendered; Edith Wharton does not simplify matters by indulging in shallow moralizing, or by making Frome's wife into a villainous caricature. The reader is invited to sympathize with all three – Frome, Zeena and Mattie – as helpless victims. Frome is as powerless to escape his marriage as he is to escape the rest of his fate. Even his attempt to kill Mattie and himself misfires: they are left mutilated and embittered to drag out their lives. This is the last, disquieting irony in a bleak and sombre tragedy.

FURTHER READING   Although there is no collected edition of Edith Wharton's works, there are many editions of her best-known novels and two useful selections: *The Edith Wharton Treasury* (1950), edited by Arthur Hobson Quinn, and *The Best Short Stories of Edith Wharton* (1958), edited by Wayne Andrews. There is an excellent biography by R. W. B. Lewis (1975). Her work has attracted a good deal of distinguished criticism: Percy Lubbock's *Portrait of Edith Wharton* (1947), Blake Nevius' *Edith Wharton: A Study of Her Fiction* (1954) and the volume of essays edited by Irving Howe (1962). Q. D. Leavis' *Scrutiny* essay, 'The Importance of Edith Wharton' (1938), is an excellent introduction.

4 Naturalism

The term 'naturalist' is commonly applied to the generation of writers, men like Frank Norris and Theodore Dreiser, whose work began to appear in the late 1890s and early 1900s. There is, however, no clear-cut chronological division between the American naturalists and the American realists: Norris' *McTeague* appeared before Edith Wharton's *Ethan Frome*, and Dreiser's *Sister Carrie* before James' *The Ambassadors*. Nor is there any rigid critical distinction between the two schools. Although the naturalists often liked to present themselves as rebels and pioneers, they were in many ways the logical and inevitable successors to the earlier generation of realists.

This point is illustrated by the later life of William Dean Howells. By the mid-1880s Howells was firmly established in his position of 'Dean of American Letters', the writer who had done most to make realism the dominant mode of American fiction. Yet, as his detractors were quick to point out, there was an air of smugness and narrowness about even Howells' best work. For all his determination to portray American life, he still dealt mainly with exclusive Boston society. Moreover he had, in a rash phrase, committed himself to the opinion that American novels should deal with 'the more smiling aspects of life'.

Howells himself was uneasily aware of his limitations. In 1887 he broke away from the cloistered world of Boston and went to live in New York. He became increasingly involved in the political turbulence of the age. The 1886 Haymarket Riots in Chicago led to an extensive witchhunt against communists and anarchists. Howells wrote to a friend: 'It's all been an atrocious piece of frenzy and cruelty, for which we must stand ashamed before history. But it's no use. I can't write about it. Some day I hope to do justice to these irreparably wronged men.' His later fiction makes a brave attempt to deal with these new subjects that the age had forced on his attention; but it fails. Howells' contemporary Underwood Johnson complained:

> One might have expected that the man who pleaded for the lives of the Chicago anarchists would have done more in fiction to present the claims of working men and the proletariat. The fact of it is, perhaps, that his sympathy came from the kindness of his heart and from his conclusions in his study, rather than from close contact with the laboring classes in their everyday life. He was not a slumming novelist.

The naturalists *were* slumming novelists. Their knowledge of the lives of millions of urban Americans was based on personal experience, not scholarly investigation. Theodore Dreiser came from a poor German immigrant family in Indiana, while Jack London was the illegitimate son of a California fortune-teller. Unlike Howells and many of the other realists, these writers were not assimilated into the genteel life of the East Coast. With the emergence of naturalism, the American literary scene lost forever its air of an exclusive fashionable club. Fiction began to deal with cities like Chicago and San Francisco as well as Boston, with working-class characters as well as middle-class intellectuals.

The central inspiration of the naturalist movement, then, was the desire to describe the lives of ordinary people in American cities. Its mood was documentary. Warner Berthoff notes in *The Ferment of Realism* (1965): 'All at once it seemed, as if by common consent, that a new effort of honesty and plain speaking had to be made.' Using deliberately blunt and unliterary language, the naturalists piled factual detail on factual detail in an attempt to recreate the very look, texture and smell of contemporary America.

Beneath this documentary air, there lay a deep pessimism. The picture of life that emerges from naturalist fiction is sordid and depressing. Characters drift about aimlessly, fail, or simply remain trapped in oppressive environments. Much of this view derived from nineteenth-century scientific thought: like the Darwinists and Spencerians, the naturalists saw man as a pawn in a game over which he had no control. Yet there was also a special disillusion with America. Behind the relentless examination of contemporary society lay the fear that America did not in fact provide the liberty, equality and chance of happiness that it had promised.

Stephen Crane

Unlike most American novelists of his generation, Stephen Crane (1871–1900) was born not in the Midwest but in an East Coast state, New Jersey. He spent most of his childhood in New York State, where his father was a Methodist clergyman. After brief periods at Lafayette College and Syracuse University, he moved to New York City and, like many writers of the time, worked as a journalist.

The response to his first book, *Maggie: A Girl of the Streets* (1893), was discouraging; it sold few copies and excited little interest among the critics. But *The Red Badge of Courage* (serialized in 1894 and published as a book in 1895) won him immediate acclaim. Crane was hailed as a literary 'golden boy', the promising young writer of his time. Joseph Conrad, one of his English admirers, remarked shrewdly: 'He has outline, he has colour, he has movement, with that he ought to go very far. But – will he?'

In the next five years Crane brought out three more novels, several volumes of short stories (the story, 'The Open Boat', based on his own ordeal at sea, is considered one of his best works), an historical study and two collections of poems. He also continued to work as a journalist, specializing in war reporting. Although he had no personal experience of war when he wrote *The Red Badge of Courage*, he subsequently covered the Spanish–American war in Cuba and the Greco–Turkish war; he also worked in the Southwest and in Mexico. Crane has been compared to Keats in the precosity of his development; he also resembles the poet in that he died of tuberculosis at an early age.

The strength and variety of Crane's talents is suggested by the fact that figures as diverse as Ernest Hemingway and John Berryman, the poet, have been amongst his modern admirers. His forceful presentation of the realities of war helps to explain his attraction for Hemingway and many other readers. He has also been highly praised for his realistic treatment of the sordidness of city life in *Maggie*. In both his poetry and his novels there is a considerable talent for creating striking images. The poems, which were influenced by the New England poetess Emily Dickinson, in turn influenced Imagist poets like Ezra Pound, and Crane is often seen as an important precursor of that school of modern poetry.

The Red Badge of Courage

SUMMARY Henry Fleming is a young private in the Northern (Union) army during the American Civil War. Despite opposition from his mother, his dreams of glory have led him to enlist in the war. Along with the rest of his regiment, he listens to a tall soldier, Jim Conklin, who is authoritatively predicting that they will fight at last. Despite all of his fantasies of heroic deeds, Fleming realizes that he is afraid of battle and doubtful of his own ability to fight bravely. He discusses the forthcoming engagement with several other soldiers, particularly Jim Conklin; one recurrent topic in their conversation is whether any of the soldiers will become frightened and run away. Fleming's friend Wilson (often merely called 'the loud soldier') has a premonition that he will be killed and asks Henry to deliver a packet to his family.

Jim Conklin's initial predictions about the imminence of fighting prove wrong, but the battle at last occurs and Henry is proud of himself for participating in the bloody ordeal. Just as he is congratulating himself, however, the enemy charges again. He is frightened and runs away.

As he slinks through fields and woods, he hears a Northern general announcing that his side has won the battle; this victory makes Henry consider his retreat even more inglorious. He wanders along, overcome with shame. At the entrance to a peaceful part of the forest he comes across a putrefying corpse and runs away from it in horror.

Henry joins a group of wounded soldiers and is befriended by a man described simply as the Tattered Soldier. But when his new friend asks him what wounds he has received, his sense of humiliation increases. He longs for a wound, which he sees as a 'red badge of courage'. He then encounters Jim Conklin, who has been severely hurt in the battle. Though Fleming agrees to help support Conklin so that he will not be run over by passing wagons, the dying man lurches away from his companions, and Henry watches helplessly as Conklin dies in agony. He sees a group of frightened and wounded men and tries to question them; one of their number gets angry and hits him on the head with a rifle. The wound is serious but Fleming is helped by a friendly soldier, who guides him back to his regiment.

Fleming has been afraid that the other members of his regiment will mock him for his cowardice. Instead, they assume that he has been fighting with another group, and that the wound on his head was honourably acquired. Encouraged by their reaction, Fleming begins to boast of imaginary feats of valour, but becomes ashamed of these lies when another soldier accuses him of bragging.

A second battle starts soon afterwards. Fleming at last fulfills his desire to fight bravely; in fact, he becomes so involved that he continues to fire when the other soldiers have stopped. While Fleming and Wilson are getting water, they overhear an officer describing their regiment as 'mule drivers'. Fleming is enraged by this slur and sets out to disprove it in the ensuing conflict: he dashes into battle ahead of his comrades, and he and Wilson take over the flag from the dead colour sergeant. Someone overhears a lieutenant and a colonel commending Fleming and Wilson and repeats the conversation to the proud young soldiers. Other battles follow; in one of them, Wilson grabs another flag.

At last the fighting ceases, giving Fleming time to contemplate his experiences. Vivid mental images pass through his mind: when he thinks of the tattered soldier he recalls his cowardice, but then he remembers his deeds of heroism. As he reflects on these conflicting memories, he feels convinced that he has become a man. At the point when he reaches this decision, a ray of sun breaks through the clouds.

CRITICAL COMMENTARY Crane's first novel, *Maggie: A Girl of the Streets*, was a pioneer work of naturalism, antedating both Frank Norris' *McTeague* and Theodore Dreiser's *Sister Carrie* by several years. *The Red Badge of Courage* also has many of the characteristics of this type of fiction. It is animated by a desire to get to grips with the actualities of life; and it uses animal imagery, stereotyped characters and colloquial English. Naturalists are usually detached and scientific, and no less an authority than Joseph Conrad described the author of *The Red Badge of Courage* as 'the most detached of men'.

Yet Crane's talent was in many ways idiosyncratic and the label 'naturalist' does not fit *The Red Badge of Courage* entirely. Novelists of that school tend to emphasize the influence of environment on their characters more than Crane does. Moreover, the naturalists usually deny the possibility of free will and moral choice, and many readers have seen the novel as a study of how Fleming fulfills his determination to become a hero.

One of Crane's main interests is the psychological life of

Henry Fleming. Like so many nineteenth-century English and American novels, the book is a *Bildungsroman*: it traces the development of a young man from immaturity to maturity. Crane portrays Fleming subtly and dramatically; one of his most effective techniques is the description of the images of glory that crowd through the young man's head when he thinks about war.

An incident in the forest represents a particularly significant moment in Fleming's development. Just as he thinks he has found an idyllic grove, he stumbles across the rotting corpse of a soldier. The forest here clearly epitomizes a hope of getting away from the tensions and complexities of everyday life. Yet, like so many American writers, Crane is rejecting pastoral escapism as well as presenting its attractions. Fleming cannot ultimately solve his problems in the forest, just as Huck Finn cannot rely forever on the raft.

Crane's prose style is one of the achievements of the book. He once declared – 'my chiefest delight was to write plainly'; and certainly the narrative style of *The Red Badge of Courage* is simple and straightforward. Of course, behind his directness lies considerable artistry: he chooses every word carefully. As one reads the imagery of the novel, as well as when one reads Crane's poetry, one can understand why the Imagist poets were so impressed by him: his figures, like theirs, are vivid isolated pictures. One purpose of many of the images is to suggest the dehumanizing effect of war; for example, the soldiers are often compared to animals or inanimate objects.

Though the power of *The Red Badge of Courage* is unmistakable, readers disagree about the interpretation of some central episodes. One of these controversial questions is whether Jim Conklin is intended to be a Christ figure. The initials of his name suggest he is, and the description of his death is filled with references to Christianity. Further, he plays a suggestive role in Fleming's moral development: he is the saviour and guide who teaches the young man about war. Yet the description of Conklin's death seems to stress the brutality and meaninglessness of war, rather than hinting at the redemption a saviour might bring. It seems possible that instead of presenting a Christ figure seriously, Crane is parodying the death of Christ to indicate the total absence of spiritual values in the brutal world of the Civil War.

The central critical problem of the book, however, is its ending. Are we to accept Henry Fleming's assertion that he has become a man on face value? Some readers feel that Fleming's analysis of his experiences is quite correct: through his struggles he has truly attained the 'soft and eternal peace' that he feels. Others argue that Crane must intend the conclusion ironically: Fleming's belief that he has attained maturity is another delusion, not unlike his dreams of glory. Yet another possibility is that Crane did not intend to criticize Fleming but wrote an ending that suffers from dramatic falsity because the reader has not been convinced by Fleming's view of himself. Even if the ending is a failure, though, the book as a whole is a remarkable achievement – and we are even more impressed when we recall that Crane was in his early twenties when he wrote it.

FURTHER READING   The standard collection of Crane's work is edited by Wilson Follett (twelve volumes; 1925–1926). The same scholar also edited Crane's poems (1930). *The Red Badge of Courage* is published in a number of useful editions, notably R. W. Stallman's *Stephen Crane: An Omnibus* (1952). In collaboration with L. Gilkes, Stallman edited Crane's letters (1960); another important collection is *Stephen Crane's Love Letters to Nellie Crouse*, edited by Edwin H. Cady and Lester G. Wells (1954). Biographical analyses may be found in the studies of Crane by Thomas Beer (1923) and by the poet John Berryman (1950). Beer's book includes an introduction by Joseph Conrad. Daniel G. Hoffman's book on Crane's poetry (1957) is one of the most significant critical studies.

Frank Norris

Frank Norris was born in Chicago in 1870 and brought up in San Francisco. After studying art in Paris he entered the University of California (1890), where he began to write *McTeague*. He continued the novel while at Harvard in 1895, encouraged by his instructor, Lewis E. Gates, to whom the book is dedicated. At Harvard he also began another novel, *Vandover and the Brute*, left unfinished at his death and published under his brother's supervision in 1914. Subsequently, he reported the Boer War in South Africa and the Spanish–American War in Cuba, and had a romantic novel, *Moran of the Lady Letty* (1898), serialized in a San Francisco magazine, *The Wave*. Although a visit to the Big Dipper mine in 1897 inspired him to finish *McTeague*, the novel did not easily find a publisher. It was finally issued in 1899 by Doubleday, Page, for whom Norris was working as a manuscript reader. The same firm also published *Blix*, a semi-autobiographical novel, later that year. After writing a romantic novel, *A Man's Woman* (1900), Norris planned a trilogy, 'The Epic of Wheat'. However, only two parts – *The Octopus* (1901) and *The Pit* (1903) – were completed before his unexpected death in 1902.

Although publishers were originally reluctant to issue *McTeague*, Norris' work enjoyed great popularity and respect in the years immediately before and after his death – far more than it does today. His reputation now stands below that of a contemporary like Stephen Crane – whose *The Red Badge of Courage* has passed smoothly into the list of American classics – or of a successor like Theodore Dreiser, whom he advised and influenced. Yet Norris deserves to be remembered as a pioneer of American naturalism.

> The muse of American fiction, [he wrote] will lead you far from the studios and the aesthetes, the velvet jackets and the uncut hair, far from the sexless creatures who cultivate their little art of writing as the fancier cultivates his orchids ... straight into a world of Working Men, crude of speech, swift of

action, strong of passion, straight into the heart of a new life, on
the borders of a new time, and there only will you learn to
know the stuff of which must come the American fiction of the
future.

His own work amply fulfills this robust claim. It deals with
the lower, rather than the upper reaches of society; with
coarse and usually inarticulate people; and with primitive
or even brutal emotion. The narrative style is as simple
and direct as the subject. The result can sometimes be a
deliberate oversimplification of life's subtleties, or even
lurid melodrama. Yet at its best, as in *McTeague* or *The
Octopus*, Norris' work illuminates areas of society and of
human psychology that the American novel has previously
shunned.

McTeague

SUMMARY Each Sunday afternoon McTeague relaxes in his
dental parlour in San Francisco. After a heavy lunch at a
cheap restaurant he sits in his dentist's chair, smoking,
drinking and sleeping. Sometimes he plays his concertina,
which reminds him of his youth at the Big Dipper Mine
where his father was a shift-boss and his mother a cook. His
present one-room surgery is the realization of his life's
ambition. McTeague is a slow man, stupid but not vicious,
animal-like in his immense physical strength.

On Monday he returns to work. His first patient is
Miss Baker, an elderly spinster who lives in the same
building and is secretly in love with her next-door neighbour,
Old Grannis. During the morning McTeague's friend
Marcus Schouler brings in his cousin, Trina Sieppe, to have
two damaged teeth repaired. The dentist's initial hostility
yields and he becomes friendly; after she has visited him
several times he proposes to her. However, Trina refuses and
the two become cold and distant.

Maria, the maid, goes from flat to flat collecting junk.
She bullies the tenants, especially Miss Baker and Old
Grannis, into giving her things which she can sell to Zerkow,

the local scrap dealer. She tells the avaricious Zerkow about a gold dinner service that supposedly belonged to her family in her youth.

McTeague confides to Marcus that he still loves Trina. Marcus is surprised, for he had been courting the girl himself, but he grandiloquently relinquishes his claim. The next day the two men join Trina and her family for a picnic and McTeague replaces Marcus as the girl's acknowledged suitor. Trina finally agrees to marry the dentist. As a celebration McTeague takes her, Mrs Sieppe and her little brother August to the music hall. The evening is unnerving for McTeague – he is unused to such grand occasions – and it is made worse when August wets his trousers during the performance. When the party get back to the dentist's flat they learn that Trina has won five thousand dollars in the lottery. There is an impromptu party during which McTeague announces his engagement and makes an embarrassed speech. He dreams of spending the money all at once, but Trina insists that they invest it. The interest, together with McTeague's earnings and her pay for carving wooden toys, will make a good income.

However, Marcus now becomes jealous of McTeague for acquiring so much money and tries to provoke a fight with him at Freena's bar. McTeague's anger is mollified when, on his return home, he finds that Trina has sent him a huge imitation gold tooth as an advertising sign. A few weeks later the two friends are reconciled, but their friendship never completely recovers and Marcus refuses to be McTeague's best man.

The couple are married in their new flat and the ceremony is followed by an immense wedding breakfast. Afterwards the Sieppe family leave for the southern part of the state, where they plan to start a new life. The McTeagues are happy. She is occasionally surprised at herself for marrying so gross and animal a man but her affection grows. McTeague himself becomes more refined. Trina, however, is growing miserly and the couple begin to argue about money.

Trina hears from Miss Baker that Maria and Zerkow are to be married. McTeague makes friends with Heise, a harness-maker, and a picnic is arranged. Trina's cousin Selina is invited and she brings Marcus, who has been courting her. During the picnic Marcus and the dentist quarrel; McTeague goes berserk and breaks Marcus' arm. The marriage between Maria and Zerkow goes badly, for he becomes obsessed with her stories of the gold dinner service and comes to believe that she is hiding it somewhere in the house. Meanwhile the Sieppe family has been getting into financial trouble, but Trina is too mean to help them. Marcus finally leaves San Francisco to become a rancher.

The State authorities stop McTeague practising dentistry since he has no diploma. They auction their belongings, except the concertina and the advertising tooth, and move into cheap rooms. He takes to drinking and maltreating Trina to extort money from her. She becomes friendly with Maria and the two women commiserate about the brutality of their husbands. One day Trina finds Maria dead with her throat cut; that night Zerkow's body is found floating in the river. Shortly afterwards Miss Baker and Old Grannis marry.

Trina insists that they move into Zerkow's house to save money. In these squalid surroundings she becomes slovenly herself; her only interest is hoarding money. At last McTeague leaves her, taking her precious savings with him. She collapses with hysteria and Miss Baker takes care of her. The doctor notices that several of Trina's fingers have blood-poisoning and need to be amputated. After the operation she becomes the caretaker of a kindergarten, leading a more miserly life than ever. She even has her prize money withdrawn from the bank, so that she can actually see the coins. When McTeague returns starving she refuses to let him in or even help him. One day he sees his concertina in a shop-window and realizes that his wife must have sold it. Enraged, he goes to her house, kills her and takes all the money.

McTeague goes to the Big Dipper Mine, but a sixth sense soon warns him to move on. The Sheriff and his deputies arrive just after his departure. McTeague heads for Mexico, stopping on the way to go prospecting for gold. He tries to cross Death Valley but the heat proves insufferable. He is stopped by Marcus, who has heard about the murder and set out to hunt down his former friend. The two men fight. McTeague wins but before his death Marcus manages to handcuff him. McTeague is left in the midday sun of the desert manacled to a corpse.

CRITICAL COMMENTARY Those who like exquisite and polished works of art will not like *McTeague*. Deeply flawed, it is obviously a young man's novel: its style wavers and changes, the story moves by fits and starts and the author's grasp of his central figure is far from sure. Yet at the same time it has the virtues of a young man's novel: it is energetic, deeply committed to its task and deliberately adventurous. *McTeague* has something genuinely new to say.

Norris' naturalistic approach is immediately apparent in his writing style. He once wrote: 'I detest "fine writing", "rhetoric", "elegant English" – tommyrot. Who cares for fine style! Tell your yarn and let your style go to the devil. We don't want literature, we want life.' In *McTeague* the style, despite its occasional lapses into grandiloquence, aims at simplicity and directness. The vocabulary is unlatinate, the sentences short and the grammatical structures simple – habits which Norris' experience as a reporter would have encouraged. At its best the result is a fine vehicle for conveying a sense of life's physical surface. Norris is an expert in the tactile and the tangible:

> Once in his office, or, as he called it on his signboard, 'Dental Parlors', he took off his coat and shoes, unbuttoned his vest, and, having crammed his little stove full of coke, lay back in his operating chair at the bay window, reading the paper, drinking his beer, and smoking his huge porcelain pipe while his food digested; crop-full, stupid, and warm.

This has the detailed neutral accuracy of a photograph. It is not surprising that *McTeague* was made into an excellent film, *Greed*, by Erich von Stroheim.

Indeed, neutrality is one of Norris' main aims. Where earlier writers moralize or nudge the reader into a particular emotional response, he tries to remain unimpassioned and objective. The account of Trina's death, as Larzer Ziff points out in *The American 1890s* (1967), is an especially effective example of this: 'Trina lay unconscious, just as she had fallen under the last of McTeague's blows, her body twitching with an occasional hiccough that stirred the pool of blood in which she lay face downward. Towards morning she died with a rapid series of hiccoughs that sounded like a piece of clockwork running down.'

Naturalism implies a subject as well as a manner. There is no reason, of course, why the life of the poor should be more 'real' than the life of the rich, and yet most literary movements of 'naturalism' have assumed this to be so. Norris is no exception. In *McTeague* he sets out to recreate life on lower middle-class Polk Street in San Francisco. His feeling for this milieu is one of the best things in the book, and leads to some of its unqualified successes: the description of the wedding breakfast, for example. What personal experience or observation could not supply, scholarship could: whilst at Harvard Norris read dental manuals in order to get the details and the terminology of his hero's trade right.

Yet when he ventures into the psychology of his main characters, Norris is on considerably less firm ground. His naturalism here creates a preference for elemental or primitive emotion: violence, lust and greed. The handling of sexual emotion is the least satisfactory. Although outspoken enough to have shocked many contemporaries, it seems prim to the modern reader: 'But for all that, the brute was there. Long dormant, it was now at last alive, awake. From now on he would feel its presence continually; would feel it tugging at its chain, watching its opportunity. Ah, the pity of it!' The descriptions of Trina's greed are far more effective. Her progressive degradation from lower middle-class girl concerned to pile up a family nest egg to a crone who derives quasi-sexual pleasure from lying naked amidst her gold is finely rendered. In fact, gold is referred to continually: it is largely responsible for the characters' degeneration. In the city McTeague yearns for the gold tooth to hang outside his surgery, while his wife hoards gold dollar pieces. On the run at the end of the book McTeague goes back to the Big Dipper Mine, and then goes prospecting for gold himself. By a typical irony, it is money – the fortune that McTeague carries in his saddlebag – that precipitates the fight with Marcus and the final disaster.

FURTHER READING   The standard edition of Norris' *Works* was issued in ten volumes in 1928. However, the best-known novels – *McTeague*, *The Octopus* and *The Pit* – are available in a variety of editions. A collection of Norris' critical essays was published as *The Responsibilities of the Novelist* (1903). There is only one biography, by Franklin Walker (1932).

Ernest Marchand's *Frank Norris: A Study* (1942) is a useful general introduction. Naturalism is discussed by Malcolm Cowley, 'Not Men. A Natural History of American Naturalism' in the *Kenyon Review* (1947), and Philip Rahv, 'Notes on the Decline of Naturalism' in *Image and Idea* (1949). William Dean Howells wrote two friendly and influential reviews of Norris' work when it first appeared: 'A Case in Point' in *Literature* (1899), and 'Frank Norris' in the *North American Review* (1902).

Theodore Dreiser

Dreiser was born in Terra Haute, Indiana, in 1871, of a family of intensely religious German immigrants. His childhood seems to have been unhappy for many reasons, not the least of which was his parents' poverty. Supported by one of his former school teachers, he spent a year at the University of Indiana. He then held a series of newspaper jobs in the Midwest. On his arrival in New York in 1894, however, he had trouble finding work. Dreiser records that the portrait of Hurstwood in *Sister Carrie* was inspired by his own economic fears at this time; indeed, he tends to include many autobiographical characters in his novels.

In December 1899 he married Sallie White. Like many other realists, he had difficulty getting his fiction published. At first Doubleday accepted *Sister Carrie* on Frank Norris' recommendation, but one of its senior editors tried to reverse the decision. Dreiser held the firm to its original agreement and the novel appeared in 1900. Under the circumstances, it is not surprising that the publishers made little effort to promote the book. Its failure almost drove Dreiser to suicide, but he recovered from his despair and lived to see the novel widely acclaimed.

After *Sister Carrie* was published, he continued to work as a journalist and wrote several more novels: *Jennie Gerhardt* (1911), *The Financier* (1912), *The Titan* (1914), *The 'Genius'* (1915) and *An American Tragedy* (1925). The last novel is usually considered the best. In middle age Dreiser was attracted to socialist ideas, and eventually became a Communist. He wrote several books about politics, the best of which is *Dreiser Looks at Russia* (1928). His other writings include poetry, sketches of New York and philosophical essays. He died in 1945.

Like many of the realists and naturalists, Dreiser was deeply impressed by scientific thought, especially the work of Huxley and Spencer. He aimed, in fact, to give his fiction the precision of a scientific statement. Its view of society or of people would be true and completely objective. To this end, rather like the English writer Thomas Hardy, Dreiser developed several quasi-scientific theories of his own. The most important was the theory of 'chemisms', essentially ruling passions or forces that govern human conduct, like sexual desire or greed. These are frequently invoked in his novels to explain the characters' conduct and to shape the progress of the story.

The controversy surrounding Dreiser's reputation demonstrates the problems that naturalism poses for the reader.

In fact, when generalizing about those literary movements in America, critics often choose Dreiser as their prime example. Many praise him for his harsh, unsentimental portrait of American life and for his rejection of the genteel tradition in American letters. Other critics, however, argue that the importance of Dreiser's subject does not excuse the many failings of his style. Similarly, while some laud him because of the 'Americanness' of his subject matter and attitudes, others maintain that this is hardly a valid criterion for judging literature.

Sister Carrie

SUMMARY   Caroline Meeber ('Sister Carrie'), an innocent eighteen-year-old from a small town, is travelling by train to Chicago. She is planning to find work in the city and live with her sister and brother-in-law, Minnie and Sven Hanson. On the train she meets Charles Drouet, a travelling salesman, whose sophistication and affluence charm her. She gives him her address and he promises to look her up in Chicago.

Carrie approaches the city dreaming of the glamorous life she will lead there, but is soon disillusioned. Her hard-working sister shows little affection; she and her husband live in a dowdy apartment and lead a dull life, beset by continual financial anxieties. Quickly realizing that they would disapprove of her relationship with Drouet, Carrie writes to him telling him not to see her. After much difficulty, she finally gets a job in a shoe factory. The conditions are very unpleasant, and Carrie finds that her salary is too small to allow her the pleasures she had associated with urban life.

Carrie becomes ill and so loses her job. As she wanders around in search of a new one, she meets Drouet. She is impressed by his geniality and, after having a meal with him, accepts money from him to buy clothes. The salesman helps her to find a room to live in; soon afterwards she begins to live with him. He vaguely promises to marry her.

Drouet encounters George Hurstwood, an affluent businessman, and invites him home to meet Carrie. Hurstwood is not happy with his own home life; he is unfaithful to his wife during a trip to Philadelphia, and finds his children, Jessica and George Jr, irksome. He visits Carrie and Drouet several times, and becomes attracted to Carrie. He takes to visiting her during Drouet's absence, and finally declares his love for her. Another of Carrie's acquaintances during this period is Mrs Hale, whose preoccupation with wealth and status influence the impressionable young woman.

Drouet suggests that Carrie act in a play that his fraternal lodge is producing; wishing to conceal his relationship with her, he introduces her as 'Carrie Madenda'. Despite her initial hesitation, she takes part in the production and does very well. Hurstwood becomes even more infatuated with her as he watches her performance.

Hurstwood's wife accuses him of infidelity and leaves him. Drouet is also becoming suspicious of Carrie's relationship with Hurstwood, and confronts her with accusations. They quarrel and Drouet leaves in a temper. Assuming that he has abandoned her, Carrie begins to look for theatrical work. In fact, Drouet returns to the apartment hoping for a reconciliation; but Carrie is not there, and he leaves without seeing her. Carrie feels bitter toward Hurstwood, both because he has caused the estrangement from Drouet and because she has discovered that he is married, a fact that he has tried to conceal from her. She writes to Hurstwood, telling him that she does not want to see him again.

Hurstwood is depressed at losing both his wife and Carrie. In a rash moment he removes ten thousand dollars from the company safe. While he is debating whether or not to steal the money, the safe door accidentally swings shut and the decision is made for him. By pretending that he is taking her to a hospital where Drouet lies ill, he manages to trick Carrie into going away with him. It is only when she is on the train that she realizes she has been deceived. Hurstwood does not tell her about the stolen money.

Shortly after they arrive in Montreal, a detective finds

and confronts the embezzler. Hurstwood agrees to return most of the money to his firm, and so they do not prosecute. Taking the name of Wheeler, he marries Carrie, though the ceremony is not valid. The couple move to New York, and Hurstwood goes into partnership in a bar with Shaughnessy. Meanwhile, Carrie becomes friendly with her neighbours, the Vances. Like Mrs Hale, Mrs Vance encourages Carrie in her dreams of an affluent and glamorous life. Carrie meets Bob Ames, Mrs Vance's cousin. She likes the idealistic young man, but is confused by his contempt for the riches that she values so highly. His praise of the theatre increases her desire to be an actress.

Hurstwood's bar does not succeed. Moreover, he learns that the land on which it stands has been sold to someone who plans to demolish the building. He has comparatively little capital left and cannot find a new job. He and Carrie begin to quarrel about money. In the course of one of these arguments, Carrie discovers that her marriage is not legally valid.

Carrie decides to go on the stage to earn money. Her work there further estranges her from Hurstwood. She begins to spend time with a friend in the chorus, Lola Osborne, through whom she meets some flirtatious young men. She feels increasingly resentful about devoting her salary to supporting Hurstwood. Desperate for work, he decides to take a job as driver on the trolley lines, replacing striking workers. Despite the police protection that he has been promised, a fight with the strikers starts, and Hurstwood is wounded and badly shaken.

As his fortunes fall, Carrie's continue to rise: she becomes a popular actress and earns more money. Unaware that her friend is living with Hurstwood, Miss Osborne suggests that they share a room together. Carrie is at first reluctant to abandon Hurstwood, but he angers her by recommending yet another drop in their standard of living, and so she decides to leave him.

Carrie's career becomes even more successful. Her photo appears in the paper, she upstages one of the leading actors, and the critics praise her. Now living in great poverty, Hurstwood bitterly reads about her triumphs. Mr Withers persuades Carrie to take a room in his showy new hotel, at the same time as Hurstwood is hired by a different hotel to do menial jobs. Despondently, he goes to the entrance to Carrie's theatre to beg for money, but he cannot find her. Instead he joins a group of down-and-outs on whose behalf a charity worker is begging.

Carrie is surprised in her dressing room one day by an unexpected visit from Drouet. He takes her to dinner, and through him she learns for the first time about the money that Hurstwood embezzled. The salesman is eager to see Carrie again but she discourages him. On the same night she sees Hurstwood, a broken and pitiful man, and gives him money. Shortly afterwards she leaves for a tour of London. On her return she again meets Bob Ames; he suggests that she abandon comedy for serious theatre, but the main effect of his advice is to stir up vague discontents.

Hurstwood tries once again to see Carrie in order to beg from her, but he is rudely refused admission by the stage doorkeeper. Bankrupt and friendless, he kills himself. Despite the success of her career, Carrie never loses an intangible sense of dreams yet to be fulfilled.

CRITICAL COMMENTARY In a sense 'An American Tragedy', the title of one of Dreiser's later novels, would also be appropriate for *Sister Carrie*. Dreiser's ability to portray the unpleasant realities of American life in the 1890s accounts for no small part of the book's success. He skillfully conveys the atmosphere of various parts of America by piling up a series of small details; in fact, his use of these lists has reminded many readers of the poet Walt Whitman.

Yet Whitman wrote about 'man in the open air', in his own phrase, while Dreiser, like most naturalists, concentrates on life in the city. The book focuses on Chicago and New York, where he finds examples of many contemporary social problems. He strikingly contrasts the sordidness of the factory in which Carrie works with the artificial glamour of the restaurants and bars nearby. His descriptions of the discomforts and humiliations suffered by down-and-outs in New York are also impressive.

Dreiser's deep understanding of the deprivations of poverty and the drive for wealth – themes that Balzac, one of his favourite writers, also examined closely – lends power to the book. But his frequent discussions of another human drive, the sexual urge, dismayed many contemporary readers; indeed, it was this element that almost prevented the book's publication in the first place. Sister Carrie shows little regret about losing her virginity; in fact, throughout the novel she seems merely to be drifting aimlessly, and she drifts casually into her affair with Drouet. Moreover, Carrie is not punished for her sins as 'fallen women' usually are in the fiction of the period. Instead the book traces her rise to stardom.

Modern readers are usually concerned about a different type of problem: Dreiser's reliance on philosophical speculation. Here, as in *An American Tragedy*, he tends to analyse the characters both through the thought of determinists like Spencer and Huxley and through his own theories about human nature. While his family background led to a deep hatred of religion, he was always intrigued by science, and several times in *Sister Carrie* uses images drawn from chemical physiology to describe Hurstwood's mental state. But the passages in which Dreiser presents his own philosophical ideas are usually vague and incoherent, and these abstract analyses prove much less successful than the passages of concrete description. In particular, the chapter titles exemplify the imposition of philosophical speculations on the immediate events that he paints so vividly.

The main problem posed by the book, however, is its extremely awkward style. Dreiser's prose has been both criticized and defended as the epitome of the simple straightforward narrative favoured by the naturalists. One contemporary reviewer declared: 'The author writes with a startling directness. At times this directness seems to be the frankness of a vast unsophistication.' Yet Dreiser's style is more often stiff and formal. The novelist tends to rely on over-long sentences and on vague pompous phrases. A typical passage reads:

> Carrie had the air of one who was weary and in need of protection, and, under the fascinating make-believe of the moment, he rose in feeling until he was ready in spirit to go to her and ease her out of her misery by adding to his own delight.

Several explanations for Dreiser's stylistic problems have been put forward. Supported by some of the writer's own comments, some people have argued that Dreiser did not care much about the technique of writing. He believed that an author's main responsibility is to present the facts about how people live, and that the particular manner of expression is not especially significant. Another possible explanation is that Dreiser, whose parents were German, never felt completely in command of the English language. Perhaps the most likely theory is that Dreiser, insecure about his lack of formal education, set out to impress his readers with what he imagined to be polished English. One critic suggests that in choosing between two words, as in choosing between two pieces of furniture, Dreiser would always select the more expensive-looking.

Despite its stylistic flaws, the novel remains a powerful document. Probably one reason for its success is that Dreiser, who spent so much of his own life struggling to attain money and status, could identify with all three of the major characters.

An American Tragedy

SUMMARY Asa and Elvira Griffiths run a shabby religious mission in Kansas City. Their son Clyde dreams of becoming wealthy and hopes that his rich uncle will help him. When his sister Esta runs away with a travelling actor, Clyde is strengthened in his desire to escape. His job as bellboy in a local hotel is well-paid and gives him a glimpse of a glamorous and affluent world. He spends his salary extravagantly and leads a progressively dissolute life. Clyde becomes infatuated with Hortense Briggs, a conceited and coquettish girl. Because he is spending money on Hortense, Clyde is annoyed when his mother asks for a loan. He soon discovers that this is to help Esta, now pregnant and living secretly in a cheap room in the neighbourhood.

Clyde takes Hortense on an outing with the other bell-boys. They go in a luxurious car which a friend, Sparser, has secretly borrowed from his employer. Hurrying home, Sparser accidentally knocks down and kills a young girl. He drives on in panic until, several miles further on, he crashes the car. Clyde runs away before the police arrive.

Several years later Samuel Griffiths, Asa's affluent brother, returns from Chicago to his home in Lycurgus, New York, with the news that he has met his nephew Clyde. The young man seemed intelligent but shy and Griffiths has invited him to work in the family shirt-collar factory. Griffiths' son, Gilbert, is jealous, and gives his cousin a menial job in the shrinking room. Clyde is lonely: he hesitates to mix freely with his workmates or the fellow-lodgers at his dull boarding-house.

He is given a supervisory job in the stamping room, and takes this to be a sign that the Griffiths family plan to promote him to executive level. Gilbert stresses that he should have no social contact with the young girls under his command. Clyde does, however, become interested in Roberta Alden, a shy newcomer to the department. She is also secretly attracted to him, though neither dare show any sign of interest in the other.

After meeting accidentally out of working hours, they begin to see each other regularly; they are soon infatuated. Clyde insists that their relationship be kept secret. When one of Roberta's friends, Grace Marr, becomes suspicious, Roberta moves out of her boarding-house and takes a single room on her own. Clyde takes advantage of this to try to seduce her and, after a quarrel, she yields.

Clyde becomes acquainted with Sondra Finchley, a beautiful young socialite. He is overjoyed at mixing in exclusive circles and tries to combine this with his clandestine romance with Roberta. But his interest in the working-class girl wanes and he begins to neglect her in favour of Sondra. Just as he is about to make a complete break with Roberta, she discovers that she is pregnant. When Clyde's attempts to arrange an abortion fail, Roberta demands that he marry her. But he is too deeply in love with Sondra to consent readily.

A newspaper account of a boating accident gives Clyde the idea of murdering Roberta; he yields to temptation and sets about plotting her death. He pretends to agree to marriage and, when she returns from a visit to her parents, takes her to the nearby lakes for a holiday. After registering at a hotel under an assumed name he takes Roberta on the lake, planning to drown her and leave his own hat on the water in the hope that people will think he has also drowned. When the moment for the murder actually arrives, Clyde revolts from the idea; but he does strike her accidentally, toppling her into the water and capsizing the boat. Roberta cannot swim and Clyde leaves her to drown.

The next day Roberta's body is discovered by the local coroner, Fred Heit, and his assistant, Earl Newcomb. Their suspicion of foul play grows when they fail to discover a second body. Orville W. Mason, the district attorney, takes over the case and contacts Roberta's parents. Mrs Alden gives Clyde's name to Mason, for the girl had talked about her love affair with her mother. Mason goes to Lycurgus and discovers that the young man is at a local holiday resort with Sondra and her friends. Clyde is tortured by guilt and anxiety, and Mason's arrival to arrest him for murder comes almost as a relief. He admits to having taken the girl out on the lake but insists that her death was accidental.

The case is headline news. The Griffiths and the Finchleys work to minimize the scandal: Sondra is sent away and Smillie, the family lawyer, is instructed to talk to Clyde in prison. He reports that the young man is obviously guilty. Mr Griffiths, however, decides to retain two lawyers, Belknap and Jephson, as Clyde's counsel. Belknap is a warm and friendly man, whose temperament leads him to sympathize with Clyde; his partner Jephson, though a colder person, quickly gains Clyde's trust and respect. Together the two lawyers evolve a plausible story. According to this, Clyde took Roberta on holiday intending to persuade her to leave him alone, but had a change of heart and agreed to marry her; the boating accident occurred and, despite Clyde's attempt to save her, Roberta was drowned. Jephson drills his client in this version of the facts word by word.

The trial is a great ordeal for Clyde. Mason is fanatically dedicated to securing a conviction and he has pieced together a thorough case. In reply, Belknap and Jephson have to rely more or less completely on putting their client in the witness box. At first Clyde's story appears credible enough, but it is badly shaken by Mason's savage cross-examination. Inevitably, Clyde is found guilty.

There is great public dislike of Clyde and only his mother, whom the press eagerly interview, really believes in his innocence. Samuel Griffiths, planning to leave Lycurgus to avoid scandal, refuses to pay for an appeal. Clyde's mother persuades a newspaper to pay for her travel expenses and is in court to hear her son sentenced to death. Belknap and Jephson, struck by her evangelical manner, suggest that she give public lectures to raise money for the appeal. These are unsuccessful but the lawyers still decide to go ahead with their attempts to save Clyde. He is getting used to the tedious routine of life on 'Murderers' Row' in the State Prison. The Rev Duncan Macmillan visits him and Clyde turns to religion for consolation. He finally brings himself to confess the truth of Roberta's death. Macmillan comforts him when both the formal appeal and the personal plea to the Governor fail. Clyde is executed. His parents, now in San Francisco, continue their drab religious life, taking Esta's illegitimate son Russell out hymn-singing on the streets just as they had taken Clyde when he was young.

CRITICAL COMMENTARY During the first quarter of this century Dreiser's reputation mounted steadily. The young

Scott Fitzgerald thought that he and H. L. Mencken, the caustic critic and essayist, were 'the greatest men living in the country today'. Dreiser's popularity reached a peak with the publication in 1925 of *An American Tragedy*, which was widely acclaimed as the masterwork not just of the author but of modern American fiction. Dreiser's deep longing for recognition was at last realized; the novel's commercial success even brought him a measure of affluence. For all this, however, *An American Tragedy* does not represent any break with Dreiser's previous work. It has, in fact, much the same faults and the same virtues as his first novel, *Sister Carrie*, published some twenty-five years before.

The main fault that has not changed is the clumsy and inexpressive prose style. Just as much as its predecessors, *An American Tragedy* shows a love of pompous words – like 'vouchsafe', 'asseverate' and 'eventuate' – and awkward phraseology:

> Neither could tolerate the socialistic theory of capitalistic exploitation. As both saw it, there had to be higher and higher social orders to which the lower classes could aspire. One had to have castes. One was foolishly interfering with and disrupting necessary and unavoidable social standards when one tried to unduly favor any one – even a relative.

> One of the things that Roberta soon found was that her intuitive notions in regard to all this were not without speedy substantiation.

Some of this, of course, is caused by the speed at which Dreiser worked: he wrote about 3000 words a day and revised little. But it also shows a deep insensitivity to the nuances and subtleties of language. Almost alone amongst major novelists, Dreiser apparently gets very little pleasure out of handling words.

An American Tragedy also shows the author's fondness for scientific theory. He will, for example, introduce Asa Griffiths as 'one of those poorly integrated and correlated organisms, the product of an environment and a religious theory'. Or he will comment about Orville Mason's broken nose – 'this had eventually resulted in what the Freudians are accustomed to describe as a psychic sex scar.' This is awkwardly done, and the jargon contributes very little to the reader's understanding of the character. Much the same is true of Dreiser's insistence on his theory of 'chemisms', the passions that govern human conduct. It seems more like an unnecessary editorial intrusion than a vital part of the narrative.

Yet it is too easy just to enumerate Dreiser's faults. As Alfred Kazin remarked, Dreiser lacks everything a novelist needs except genius. For all the obvious lack of technical skill, *An American Tragedy* still succeeds. Despite its great length, the story grips the reader and becomes, in its later stages, a deeply moving and sobering document. Even faults like the awkward prose style manage to contribute to the novel's total effect of gritty, unattractive integrity. The writer is determined, one feels, to tell the truth as he sees it without prettifying or omitting anything.

Much of this air of unglamorous truth comes from Dreiser's habit of using real-life incidents. The story of Clyde Griffiths' murder of Roberta Alden is based on the Chester Gillette case of 1906. Similarly, much of the description of Clyde's youth is drawn from Dreiser's own experience. His own parents were intensely religious (though they were Catholics rather than evangelists) and very poor. But if his appreciation of Clyde's desperate desire to escape from his background is based on first-hand knowledge, Dreiser still handles it in a cold, dispassionate way. With his respect for the scientific viewpoint, he aims at an objective study of the drive towards wealth and power. Even in the final stages of the action, when Clyde is in the condemned cell awaiting execution, Dreiser does not indulge in either sentimental sympathy or moralizing about his hero. Like a good scientist, he merely gives the facts.

It is in this scientific view of people as the helpless victims of their own 'chemisms' that the novel's revolutionary quality lies. At the time of its publication *An American*

Tragedy was considered daring for its free handling of sexual matters. Yet the public outcry was surely mistaken, for few things could be less erotic than Dreiser's clinical attitude to sex. As H. L. Mencken stressed, the real affront to conventional morality was of a different sort:

> It will probably astound posterity to hear that ... *An American Tragedy* was forbidden as obscene in Boston. It is, in fact, no more obscene than a table of stock prices. But it is undoubtedly profoundly immoral, for if it teaches anything at all, it is that committing a murder is a sort of biological accident, like breaking a leg or becoming a father.

FURTHER READING Despite Dreiser's stature there is no standard edition of his works. R. H. Elias edited the novelist's letters (three volumes; 1959), while Louise Campbell issued a volume of the letters addressed to her (1959). W. A. Swanberg published a full-scale biography in 1965. Other studies are by Ford Madox Ford (1937), R. H. Elias (1949), F. O. Matthiessen (1951) and Charles Shapiro (1962). Mr Shapiro and Alfred Kazin jointly edited an important collection of critical essays about Dreiser's work (1955). One of the most significant (and most controversial) critiques is Lionel Trilling's 'Reality in America' in *The Liberal Imagination* (1953).

Jack London

The early life of Jack London (1876–1916) was extraordinary, even for a country which specializes in writers with chequered and adventurous youths. The illegitimate son of a quack fortune-teller, he was brought up on the tough Oakland waterfront in California and left school at the age of fourteen. After earning a living by stealing oysters from the beds in San Francisco bay, London became in turn a sailor, a tramp, a student at the University of California, and a prospector in the Klondike gold rush of 1897.

He returned from the Klondike without a fortune but with a determination to be a writer and threw himself into his new career with all the frenetic energy of the writer-hero in his novel, *Martin Eden*. His short stories based on his own adventures quickly found a market in San Francisco magazines. During the rest of his short life he poured out a ceaseless stream of novels and political treatises. His best works are the adventure stories, *The Call of the Wild* (1903), *The Sea-Wolf* (1904) and *White Fang* (1906), the semi-autobiographical novel, *Martin Eden* (1909), and the autobiography, *John Barleycorn* (1913). He committed suicide at the age of forty.

Today London is usually remembered as the man who wrote boys' adventure stories about dogs. This is unfortunate, for he wrote much more than *The Call of the Wild* and *White Fang*. His work, though ragged and uneven, is always vivid and energetic; his best novel, *Martin Eden*, would by itself establish him as an important and serious writer. Seen in its historical context, London's work combines the perennial American love of romance and adventure with the naturalism made fashionable at the turn of the century by writers like Frank Norris and Theodore Dreiser. Like the naturalists, London writes out of political commitment (he was an ardent socialist) and is interested in working-class life. Like them, too, he is consciously frank and unsentimental, and his prose style is deliberately direct and unadorned. But where the naturalists usually write about urban life and show their characters being crushed by external forces, London deals with a primitive world of nature and celebrates the assertion of individual will. For all his socialism, London was deeply influenced by the work of the German philosopher Nietzsche, and this coloured his view of society and the natural world. Human, as well as animal, relations are seen in deliberately primitive terms: life is a deadly struggle in which only the fittest survive. This often gives an air of brutality and sadism to his writing, just as London's lack of a formal education can make him seem arrogant and doctrinaire. But for all these faults, his power as a writer is undeniable: his descriptions are always vivid and precise, while (as *Martin Eden* shows) his grasp of human psychology can be surprisingly sensitive.

Martin Eden

SUMMARY The young sailor Martin Eden is uncouth and uneducated, but has an instinctive love of culture and a burning desire for knowledge. When his genteel friend Arthur Morse invites him to dinner at home Martin feels awkward and embarrassed, for the Morses' refined way of life is completely alien to him. At the same time he is deeply impressed. Arthur's sister Ruth becomes a symbol of the culture to which he aspires. For her part Ruth finds Eden's brute strength attractive, though she is sheltered enough to be appalled at his coarse manners. When he returns home to his lodgings with his sister Gertrude and her husband, Bernard Higginbotham, Martin is struck by the narrowness and cheapness of their existence.

Martin resolves to undertake a programme of self-education. At the local library, he is depressed at the sight of all the books he has not read and probably could not understand, but he still perseveres, reading the poetry of Kipling and Swinburne. He also becomes cleaner in his personal habits and neater in his dress. In all these efforts at self-improvement he is inspired by the thought of Ruth. He sees her once in the distance at a theatre, but instead of talking to her he picks up two working-class girls.

At last he plucks up courage to go and see Ruth again to return some books she had lent him. She is pleased to see him and encourages him in his desire to be educated. Her attitude to Martin is contradictory: at the same time she both finds his animality attractive and wants to refine him. With her encouragement, he studies grammar and mathematics, literature and music. When his money runs out, he signs up on a new voyage. After thinking things over at sea, he determines to be a writer. Back in San Francisco he sets eagerly to work, writing an account of the voyage and an adventure story based on his experience of whaling, and sending them off to the newspapers. When Ruth sees him again she is enchanted at his improvement in speech, manners and dress.

Martin fails his high school exam, but neither this nor the newspaper editors' rejection of his stories deters him. He throws himself into his writing with gusto, taking off only one afternoon a week to see Ruth. By chance he comes across the writings of Herbert Spencer and quickly becomes a disciple of the Victorian philosopher. He is impressed by Spencer's use of the evolutionary theory to account for human society as well as animal life, and by his skill at synthesizing disparate ideas. The one disappointment during this period of his life occurs when he reads some of his writing to Ruth. She is too sheltered not to be disgusted by the brutal realism of his fiction.

None of his work has yet been published and his money has run out, so Martin is forced to take a job in a hotel laundry. It is back-breaking work, leaving him none of the free time for reading and study that he had hoped. Only the friendliness of his co-worker, Joe Dowson, makes it endurable. Martin realizes that his recent education has created a gulf between him and the working-class life with which he used to be so familiar. As he continues in the laundry, however, he finds himself slipping into a bestial routine of work, sleep and alcohol. He leaves the job in disgust. Ruth, meanwhile, has been trying to convince herself that she is not in love with Martin, but on his return they can deny their affection for each other no longer.

Mr and Mrs Morse inevitably oppose the engagement – they think Martin too coarse for their daughter – but decide not to interfere. Martin, anxious to raise the money to get married, turns to hack writing but this fares no better with the editors than his serious work. When various small things he has written are at last accepted, Martin is depressed at the meagreness and unreliability of the pay. Ruth visits him at his new lodgings and is appalled at their squalor. For a long time she has been disturbed by the unconventionality of her fiancé's way of life, and now she begins to urge him to abandon writing and take a respectable job. He angrily refuses. In the meantime the Morses have been organizing gatherings of young people, designed to show Martin up in Ruth's eyes. Martin is disappointed and bored by the guests: the Morses no longer seem the epitome of culture to him.

Martin is desperately lonely in his new intellectual life. Ruth does not believe in his writing and is shocked by some of his ideas, while his relatives ostracize him; his brother-in-law Bernard even writes abusive anonymous letters to magazine editors. At last, he does find a companion, Russ Brissenden, a cynical young writer dying of tuberculosis. Russ praises Martin's work and introduces him to an intellectual community whose members sit up late into the night discussing philosophy, politics and literature. After one of these occasions, Martin goes to dinner with the Morses and the contrast between his intellectual friends and the pompous Judge Blount, who ignorantly criticizes Spencer, is too much for him: he shuts the Judge up rudely, shocking Ruth and her parents. Brissenden's efforts to convert Martin to Socialism fail. When they go together to a Socialist meeting, Martin makes a speech championing Spencer's idea that 'the survival of the fittest' should apply in society as well as in the jungle. A journalist misreports the speech, however, and makes Martin seem a revolutionary Socialist. Mr and Mrs Morse seize this opportunity to persuade Ruth to break off the engagement, and even the neighbours ostracize Martin.

Brissenden's master-poem, sent privately to a magazine by Martin, is accepted. But when Martin rushes round to Brissenden's hotel with the good news, he finds that his friend has just killed himself. When the poem is published, the magazine presents it so vulgarly that Martin is glad his friend is not alive to see it. Just as he is too disillusioned with magazines to care, his own work begins to succeed. Several stories and articles are accepted and a leading publisher agrees to bring out one of his philosophical essays as a book.

For all this, Martin is lonely. He begins to dream of returning to the South Sea Islands he had visited during his days as a sailor. He goes to the local park and tries to renew his friendship with some of his old working-class companions. He meets Lizzie Connolly, a girl he used to know, and fights with her boyfriend. Other people join in and a streetfight breaks out. Martin leaves, feeling alienated from this way of life.

His book is wildly successful. At least his money worries are over: he can live comfortably and even spare money to help his relatives and his landlady. Martin notes that people who had earlier criticized him or avoided him, now court his company: Judge Blount, Bernard and even Mr Morse all eagerly invite him to dinner. He is at first puzzled and then tormented by this hypocrisy. The realization that he is admired not for himself or his work, but for his fame, depresses him further and makes him feel even lonelier. Ruth visits him and suggests they resume their engagement; still angry at her earlier desertion of him, he rebuffs her. He takes a ship for Tahiti, planning to live in peaceful exile. On the way his depression finally overwhelms him and he deliberately drowns himself.

CRITICAL COMMENTARY *Martin Eden* is Jack London's best (though probably not his best-known) novel. It shows him deserting the sort of rugged outdoors adventure story that had made him famous for a more complicated and introspective form. *Martin Eden* is a version of the familiar *Bildungsroman*: it describes the development of a young writer, and is based on London's own life. Martin's working-class background and his frenetic programme of self-education are London's own, while the affair with Ruth resembles a youthful romance with the genteel Mabel Applegarth. The ending of the novel was no doubt suggested by London's earlier attempt at suicide; it was also unintentionally prophetic, for London did finally die by his own hand.

The autobiographical novel about a young artist is a

familiar form in modern literature. It has produced notable achievements like James Joyce's *Portrait of the Artist as a Young Man* and D. H. Lawrence's *Sons and Lovers*. As Arthur Calder-Marshall has pointed out, the resemblance between *Martin Eden* and *Sons and Lovers* is especially striking. In both books the hero's development as an artist is accompanied by a rise in the social scale: he leaves his working-class background behind him as he becomes more educated. And in both books the intellectual development and the social rise are accompanied by a love affair with a genteel and sophisticated girl: Ruth Morse in London's novel and Miriam in *Sons and Lovers*. Both Martin and Lawrence's hero, Paul Morel, begin by adulating these women and end by rejecting them scornfully.

Yet perhaps *Martin Eden* is not that far away from the world of his adventure novels. For all its self-absorption and its serious themes, the book is never cerebral or reflective. Like everything Jack London wrote, it is sudden, rash and unforgettably vivid. Martin's growth is told as a breathless and headlong adventure. London is superb at conveying his hero's sense of discovery and enthusiasm: his eager accumulation of knowledge, his acquisition of better social manners and his passion for Ruth. His style always goes straight to the point and lets the reader into the hero's mental world. Here, for example, is Martin dining out in genteel company for the first time:

> The process of getting into the dining-room was a nightmare to him. Between halts and stumbles, jerks and lurches, locomotion had at times seemed impossible. But at last he had made it, and was seated alongside of her. The array of knives and forks frightened him.

Like many *Bildungsroman*, *Martin Eden* is at root a novel of disappointment and lost illusions. Martin begins eager and confident; he ends by killing himself. He succeeds as a writer, but only when he has become disgusted by the hypocrisy of the literary world. He wins Ruth's love but comes to feel that the girl, once the pinnacle of his dreams, is merely prissy and narrowly educated. Martin becomes affluent and socially accomplished, but he feels contemptuous of middle-class society and nostalgic for the working-class life from which he is irrevocably separated. If the novel begins with freshness and enthusiasm, it ends in moody disenchantment.

Martin Eden has large and obvious faults. It makes one-sided and arrogant judgements, it is full of blustering rhetoric and it has an unpleasant streak of cruelty. In these respects, indeed, it is a more accurate reflection of himself than Jack London ever supposed. Moreover, like most of London's work it bears obvious signs of hasty writing and a lack of planning. Yet for all this, it is an impressive and haunting work. *Martin Eden* has a raw and vivid honesty that is more important than technical polish.

FURTHER READING There is no complete edition of Jack London's works, but Arthur Calder-Marshall had edited a useful selection, *The Bodley Head Jack London* (four volumes; 1963–1966); this includes *The Call of the Wild*, *John Barleycorn* and *Martin Eden*. Charmian London, the writer's second wife, wrote a biography, *The Book of Jack London* (two volumes; 1921); but Irving Stone's *Sailor on Horseback: The Biography of Jack London* (1938) is less biased. H. L. Mencken, the caustic essayist and friend of Theodore Dreiser and Sinclair Lewis, contributed a valuable essay in *Prejudices* (1919).

Sinclair Lewis

Sinclair Lewis (1885–1951) was born and brought up in Sauk Center, Minnesota, the sort of small American town he satirized in his best-known novel, *Main Street*. His early career followed a pattern familiar in novelists of his generation. He left Minnesota for the East Coast, studied at Yale, became a hack writer and journalist, and published a string of minor novels before the success of *Main Street*, his fifth book, in 1920. *Main Street* sold a million copies and was translated into twelve languages. Its success was partly a matter of notoriety, for the novel attacked many American shibboleths and earned Lewis a reputation as an iconoclast. This was confirmed by *Babbitt* (1922), which dealt in similar vein with the world of American business. Three more novels, *Arrowsmith* (1925), *Elmer Gantry* (1927) and *Dodsworth* (1929), secured his reputation.

By the end of the decade Lewis was one of America's most respected writers, hailed in his own country by Theodore Dreiser and Scott Fitzgerald, and in England by H. G. Wells and Hugh Walpole. In 1930 he became the first American writer to receive the Nobel Prize for Literature. The Secretary of the Nobel committee used the occasion to welcome America into the forum of important world literature. 'Yes – Sinclair Lewis is an American,' he grandly proclaimed – 'He writes the new language – American – as one of the representatives of a hundred and twenty million souls. He asks us to consider that this nation is not yet finished or melted down; that it is still in the turbulent years of adolescence. The new great American literature has started with national self-criticism. It is a sign of health.' Lewis replied in an equally confident manner: 'The American writer ought to perceive that he has . . . the most exciting country in the world.'

After these grand proclamations Lewis' subsequent career was a disappointment. His later novels are sound and uninspired expressions of an interest in contemporary problems and a belief in liberal values; as art they are insignificant. This decline was accompanied by difficulties in Lewis' personal life: he was married twice and became an increasingly heavy drinker. The latter problem was partly responsible for his death in Rome in 1951.

Lewis' name has often been linked with the writers of the 'Lost Generation', men like Scott Fitzgerald and Ernest Hemingway. Certainly his career followed the same pattern as theirs, with youthful success yielding to progressive literary sterility and personal problems. His early work exudes the same air of savage cynicism found in novels like *Fiesta* and *This Side of Paradise*. Yet Lewis belonged to a slightly older generation – he was born ten years before Hemingway and Fitzgerald – and he is best viewed as a transitional figure between the naturalists and the Lost Generation. He derived much of the characteristic strength of his early fiction from the work of Norris and Dreiser. *Main Street* takes that favourite naturalist theme, the individual's entrapment in an oppressive environment. Both *Main Street* and *Babbitt*, moreover, use the naturalists' love of documentary detail for satiric purposes: American styles of dress, speech and architecture have rarely been captured with a more merciless accuracy.

Main Street

SUMMARY   Carol Milford, artistic and enthusiastic, marries Dr Will Kennicott and goes with him to live in his hometown of Gopher Prairie, Minnesota. Although she knows little about American small-town life, Carol arrives full of vague dreams about changing Gopher Prairie: she will transform it with fashion, beauty and culture. But she is quickly disappointed. The town itself is a small cluster of houses around an ugly Main Street of unimaginative shops. Kennicott's house is barren and gloomy. The people, though ebulliently friendly, turn out to be conservative and dull. Only Vida Sherwin, a schoolteacher, and Guy Pollock, a lawyer, seem at all interesting to Carol. Kennicott is unaware of her disappointment; though a kindly man, he is unimaginative and completely immersed in the rituals of small-town life.

Carol bravely redecorates her living room in a modern style and holds a party, where she cajoles the guests to slip out of their usual respectability and play lively games. But social life in Gopher Prairie quickly returns to its usual round of small talk about farm prices, motor cars, and hunting. In the winter she tries to organize sports parties but the townspeople prefer bridge. She feels ill at ease and excluded at the meetings of the Jolly Seventeen, a local women's club. From Miss Sherwin Carol learns that her alien ways and her attempts to change the town have simply caused suspicion. When she turns to her husband for consolation, she finds that he agrees with the local criticism. Her original arrogant self-confidence collapses and she goes about the town fearing the judgements of her neighbours. She no longer wants to change Gopher Prairie, merely to be tolerated by it.

The one kindred spirit she discovers is Miles Bjornstam, a local handyman popularly known as 'the Red Swede' because of his radicalism. The example of Bjornstam's rebellion gives her renewed courage. She tries to get her husband to appreciate poetry, but he is good-naturedly uncomprehending. She dutifully attends meetings of the Jolly Seventeen, playing bridge badly. Her hopes are revived when she hears that a local society, the Thanatopsis, holds literary meetings; but these turn out to be banal and uninspired. The only aspect of life she enjoys in Gopher Prairie is the open-air days of the summer.

Still looking for something in Gopher Prairie to respect, Carol becomes enthusiastic about the pioneer days and goes to visit Mr and Mrs Champ Perry, who remember the town in its infancy. She is appalled by the narrowness of their outlook, which is based on a love of the Baptist Church and the Republican Party, and a dislike of Socialism and Bohemianism. She cultivates her friendship with Guy Pollock, the shy and cultivated lawyer who accepts philosophically the fact that he is trapped in small-town life. She fights down the temptation to flirt with Pollock, but quarrels with Will, who is still angry at her supercilious attitude to his local friends. Penitently, she dedicates herself to being the country doctor's wife and idolizes Will's work. She redecorates his waiting room, goes on rounds with him and even assists at a messy emergency operation. She develops a real respect for his patience, skill and kindness – but is still discontented.

Carol has a new idea for bringing culture to the town:

she will organize a Dramatic Society and put on local plays. In her enthusiasm she persuades Will to take her to an avant-garde theatre in Minneapolis; he is bored and puzzled. Back in Gopher Prairie she organizes a committee, but is astonished when it vetoes her own choice of play (Bernard Shaw's *Androcles and the Lion*) in favour of a popular low-brow comedy. She dedicates herself to the production but is disappointed at the result. Similar hopes about her role on the committee of the library board and about the Chautauqua, a travelling lecture group, are dashed.

Her criticism of small-town life is now fully formulated: Gopher Prairie is mediocre, spiritually and mentally dead. The birth of her baby, Hugh, and the arrival in the town of Will's Uncle Whittier and Aunt Bessie, two elderly gossips, make her feel completely trapped. Percy Bresnahan, a local boy who became an executive in Boston, returns to the town for a week's holiday. The local people idolize him, and he in return elaborately plays the part of the small-town boy who has only reluctantly become a city-dweller and still remains a nature-lover at heart. He senses Carol's discontent with Gopher Prairie, flirts with her and then attacks her radicalism with his conservative businessman's philosophy. She lapses into a discontent that is only partly relieved by her decision that she and Will should occupy separate bedrooms. Meanwhile Will is in his quiet way equally discontented, and has begun an affair with a patient, Maud Dyer.

Carol's only real friend is Miles Bjornstam, who is now married to Bea, Carol's ex-maid, and leads a lonely, ostracized life. But Bea and their child, Olaf, catch typhoid; after their death Miles leaves Gopher Prairie, still execrated for his radicalism. Carol then becomes interested in a young newcomer to the town, Erik Valborg. Despite his lowly job as a tailor's assistant, Erik is elegant and cultivated. Together with Fern Mullins, a young schoolteacher, Carol and Erik form a small artistic set in the town. Despite herself, Carol becomes increasingly attracted to Erik. Gopher Prairie begins to buzz with gossip. The sanctimonious Mrs Bogart stirs up rumours against Fern and forces the local school-board to get rid of the teacher. Appalled at this witchhunt, Carol resolves not to court further scandal with Erik. Despite her attempts to avoid him, they are quickly drawn together again. Kennicott, who has heard the local gossip, intervenes. He insists that Erik leave town and takes Carol away on a holiday to California.

When she gets back to Gopher Prairie, her discontents return immediately: nothing has been solved. To celebrate the end of the First World War, the town begins an expansion drive under the guidance of James Blausser, a coarse land speculator. Carol is revolted by the town's new mood of aggressive arrogance and by the resurgence of conservatism. These objections precipitate a quarrel with Kennicott and their hidden resentments flood to the surface. They agree to separate, and Carol goes to Washington with her child. In some ways her new-found freedom is empty and dissatisfying; but it also allows her to put Gopher Prairie and its faults in perspective. The town now seems petty rather than intimidating. With this sense of distance a new acceptance emerges and, after a year, she decides to return to a much subdued Will. Gopher Prairie is predictably unchanged, and she settles down and has a new baby.

CRITICAL COMMENTARY   *Main Street* is Sinclair Lewis' revenge for his boyhood. Born and brought up in a small Midwestern town – Sauk Center, Minnesota – he came to view this milieu as absurdly narrow and provincial. So it was natural that in his first successful novel he should have shown the dreary life of a small town stifling his central character, Carol Kennicott. It is not fanciful to detect in the book an undercurrent of 'There but for the grace of God goes Sinclair Lewis.' Yet the book is not merely Lewis' attempt to come to terms with his own past. The subject also attracted him because places like Gopher Prairie and Sauk Center seemed representative of the American way of life. 'Main Street is the climax of civilization,' he warned in a prefatory note. 'That this Ford car might stand in front of the Bon Ton

Store, Hannibal invaded Rome and Erasmus wrote in Oxford cloisters.' The mediocre, he feared, had inherited the earth.

The novel owed much of its notoriety to the fact that small towns, however much intellectuals like Sinclair Lewis might disdain them, were still revered and idolized in the popular imagination. It was natural that Americans, always ready to believe that God made the country and the devil made New York City, should feel a special affection for places like Sauk Center and Gopher Prairie. They were the ideal compromise between those two otherwise conflicting American values, nature and civilization. The small town stood on the edge of the prairie or the forest, in close and healthy contact with virgin nature. Yet at the same time it was evidence of the steady march of progress and civilization; it owed its existence to that source of all American good, the sturdy pioneer spirit. In the popular mind it was the bastion of all that was best in American culture: religion, patriotism, honesty in business, and happiness at home.

It is this tradition that Lewis sets out to debunk, much as the English writer Stella Gibbons attacked the idealization of English village life in her excellent novel, *Cold Comfort Farm*. His heroine, Carol Kennicott, arrives in Gopher Prairie with the naïve optimism of an ill-informed missionary. She believes that, however much small towns might be in need of improvement, they will be responsive and can soon be made into little paradises on earth. What she finds is a town of narrow and hypocritical religion, illiberal politics and third-rate culture. Its past is represented by Mr and Mrs Champ Perry, crabbed and narrow-minded pioneers, and its future by James ('Honest Jim') Blausser, the coarse land speculator who leads the campaign to 'Make Gopher Prairie Grow'.

Even the celebrated small-town friendliness is seriously qualified by gossip and intolerance. Mrs Bogart, the Kennicott's sanctimonious neighbour, begins as a comic figure but by the end of the book, after the episode of Fern

Mullins' expulsion from the school, she has become a grotesque monster. All the valuable or sensitive spirits in Gopher Prairie – Carol, Fern, Erik Valborg, Miles Bjornstam – are victims of some sort of witchhunt. Nor is Gopher Prairie redeemed by being picturesque. It is as much a part of the culture of cheap mass-produced goods as New York, with its 'cheap motor cars, telephones, ready-made clothes, silos, alfalfa, kodaks, phonographs, leather-upholstered Morris chairs, bridge-prizes, oil-stocks, motion-pictures, land-deals, unread sets of Mark Twain, and a chaste version of national politics'.

Carol's relations with Gopher Prairie move from idealistic hope to disillusion, to entrapment, to a final sense of acceptance. This is a familiar situation in modern fiction. Realism and naturalism have always been concerned about the relationship between character and environment, and hence have often shown an individual being stifled or trapped in an unsuitable social milieu. Usually this individual is a woman, if only because the social position of women has rendered them much less in control of their lives than men – much more likely to be crushed by an externally imposed fate. Lewis, then, is touching on a broad and familiar theme, and Carol Kennicott takes a humble place beside the heroines of Flaubert's *Madame Bovary*, George Eliot's *Middlemarch* and Chekhov's *The Three Sisters*.

Yet the invocation of these grand names serves as a reminder of Lewis' limitations. His portrait of Gopher Prairie is superbly exact, but his handling of Carol's emotional life is relatively unsure. It is essential to Lewis' intentions that the reader should see Carol, despite her naïvety and condescension, as obviously superior to the rest of the townspeople. She is supposed to be not just fashionable and urbane but, in a deeper sense, 'cultured'. This is everywhere asserted, but never adequately dramatized. Although Lewis persistently belabours the people of Gopher Prairie for their lack of culture, he never gives any very clear or convincing picture of what culture is. The most he does is to include an occasional scene showing Carol being inspired to solemn fantasies by reading a Yeats poem. The vagueness is damaging: it robs much of his attack on Gopher Prairie of precise grounding and makes the satire appear too easy and too slick.

Babbitt

SUMMARY   George F. Babbitt is a successful estate agent in Zenith, a typical American city. One morning he wakes feeling irritable and gets more depressed as he contemplates his ageing wife, Myra, and dresses amidst the affluent modern gadgets in which his house abounds. At breakfast he indulges in the usual ritual squabbling with his elder children – Verona, a Bryn Mawr graduate whose political views seem dangerously close to Socialism in her father's eyes, and Ted, still at school, who is always wanting to borrow the family car. After the meal, when his youngest child Tinka has been taken upstairs, Babbitt reads the paper and makes his usual right-wing comments on the news.

On the way to work he greets his neighbours Sam Doppelbrau and Howard Littlefield, a tame intellectual who works for a local company. At the office Babbitt writes the firm's regular newsletter and holds a business conference. He lunches at the Zenith Athletic Club with his oldest friend, Paul Riesling. Although successful in business, Paul feels discontented. He is unhappily married (his wife Zilla is continually criticizing him) and is acutely aware of the limitations of life in Zenith. On his way back to the office Babbitt meets his father-in-law, Henry T. Thompson, an old rugged Yankee, and reflects complacently that his own generation of businessmen is much more polished and cultured. His bad temper still remains, however, and that afternoon he is rude to one of his salesmen, Stanley Graff. At home that evening he and Ted discuss university education, agreeing that much of it is too impractical to help in modern business.

Later that spring the Babbitts hold a large dinner party,

whose guests include Howard Littlefield and T. Cholmondley ('Chum') Frink, a poet whose sentimental doggerel is syndicated in several newspapers. Although such grand occasions make the Babbitts nervous everything goes well. After dinner the guests hold a seance and try to summon the spirit of Dante. The Babbitts spend an evening with the Rieslings, who squabble with each other; Babbitt upbraids Zilla and takes Paul's part. The incident confirms him in the belief that Paul, like himself, needs a holiday away from his wife. They go to Maine together for a week and Babbitt aggressively plays the role of experienced backwoodsman. The idyll is shattered when they are joined by their families.

Babbitt throws himself into the public life of Zenith with renewed gusto. He attends a state conference of estate agents and makes a speech championing the dignity of their calling. At election time he campaigns hard against Seneca Doane, a liberal lawyer. He delivers the annual address to the local association of estate agents, lectures to the YMCA and builds up a considerable reputation as an orator. Yet he still feels excluded from the highest social circles and longs for the friendship of Charles McKelvey, a local millionaire. He sees McKelvey at an alumni gathering and seizes the chance to invite him to dinner. The occasion is strained and unnatural and no return invitation is forthcoming. The Babbitts jealously read accounts in the local paper of the McKelveys entertaining Sir Gerald Doak, a visiting English magnate.

Babbitt is flattered when the local Presbyterian pastor, Rev John Drew, invites him and Chum Frink to join William W. Eathorne on the Sunday school committee. The work is uninteresting but Babbitt is thrilled at associating with somebody as prestigious as Eathorne, the living representative of Zenith's oldest banking family. The Church's press agent, an intellectual young man named Kenneth Escott, begins to court Verona. Another romance is going on between Babbitt's son Ted and Eunice, the daughter of Howard Littlefield. When Ted holds a party for his friends Babbitt is appalled to see them smoking and drinking.

Babbitt sacks his salesman, Stanley Graff, for dishonesty.

Now Ted is almost of age to go to university a new intimacy has sprung up between father and son, and Babbitt takes him on a business trip to Chicago. After Ted has gone back to Zenith Babbitt meets Sir Gerald Doak, the former guest of the McKelveys. The Englishman turns out to be friendly and the two enjoy Chicago nightlife together, a fact which Babbitt boasts about on his return. He is alarmed to see Paul Riesling in a Chicago restaurant with another woman; he visits Paul at his hotel and persuades him to return to Zenith. Yet soon afterwards Babbit is horrified to hear that his friend has shot Zilla, almost killing her. Zilla recovers but Paul is jailed.

With his best friend in prison and his wife away visiting relatives, Babbitt's discontent returns and he resolves to rebel. He takes time off from work and indulges in adulterous fantasies about his secretary Miss McGoun and Eddie Swanson's wife, Louetta. He visits Paul and finds him already deadened by prison life. Soon after his wife's return to Zenith Babbitt goes on holiday to Maine again. On the way he dreams of getting back to nature and never returning to his family and business, but when he arrives he feels sad and unwelcome; he goes home early. On the train he meets Seneca Doane, the liberal lawyer. Like most of the Zenith businessmen he has always despised Doane as a trouble-maker, but the two enjoy a friendly conversation. This starts in Babbitt a temporary conversion to liberalism, which is encouraged by a local strike. While most of his friends condemn the strikers, Babbitt comes out in tentative support of them.

Babbitt begins a discreet love-affair with Mrs Tanis Judique, a widow whom he has met through his work. He joins her group of boisterous and fun-loving friends and gets in the habit of drinking heavily. His infidelity does not go completely unsuspected: on her return from visiting relatives Myra is worried, and Virgil Gunch finds occasion to speak to him about his disorderly life. Soon Tanis begins to seem as enslaving and demanding as Myra and Babbitt breaks off the affair. When he is approached by a group of business colleagues he refuses to join the Good Citizens' League, a conservative vigilante group. His friends begin to avoid him and his business declines.

One night Myra is taken ill with acute appendicitis. In the crisis Babbitt is suddenly reminded of his affection for her, and his friends flock round him. Anxious to be re-accepted, he quickly forgets his new-found liberalism and joins the Good Citizens' League. Soon afterwards Ted Babbitt secretly marries Eunice Littlefield. Most of the relatives are appalled but Babbitt, with a last flash of defiance, supports his son's rebellion.

CRITICAL COMMENTARY Where *Main Street* dealt with the small town, *Babbitt* turned its attention to American cities and businessmen. The subject had already been explored in Edith Wharton's good but little-known *The Custom of the Country* (1913) and Lewis acknowledged his debt by dedicating *Babbitt* to Mrs Wharton. Yet *Babbitt* never seems derivative. On the contrary, his portrait of the average American businessman shows at their best all those qualities that earned Lewis respect as a writer: his exact, almost photographic eye for the physical appearance of American life, his ear for clichés of dialogue, and his passionate dislike of philistinism, cant and injustice.

When *Babbitt* was first published in England the novelist Hugh Walpole expressed in a preface the fear that the novel might prove incomprehensible to non-American readers: 'Let us admit at once that the English reader will find the first fifty pages difficult, the dialogue strange, the American business atmosphere obscure and complicated.' Indeed, the English edition even contained a glossary of 125 American-isms. That was in 1922, and today, with the growth of international communications and the Americanization of so many aspects of European life, *Babbitt* is an easier book for the Englishman to read. It has not lost its relevance to American life, however. In his portrait of George F. Babbitt Lewis set out to satirize the American businessman and through this, to attack a whole sector of American middle-class life – the milieu which is now commonly called 'middle America' or 'the silent majority'.

Babbitt is the upholder of everything that is conservative, conventional and respectable. He is a member of the Presbyterian Church, the Republican Party, and innumerable local organizations associated with a belief in God and Country: the Elks, the Boosters' Club and the YMCA. He talks about business in solemn – almost religious – terms, but this piety is only skin-deep, for his business ethics are cut-throat. He detests everything that is Bohemian, liberal and intellectual. He identifies liberals and trade unionists with communism, for which he has a patriotic abhorrence. Although proud of being a university graduate, he is suspicious of the intellectual life. Lessons in literature and poetry are impractical, he tells his son. Chum Frink, the local writer of doggerel and advertising copy, is a great artist while Dante is merely old-fashioned and funny. Babbitt's social manner is equally coarse: he is gruff, loud and aggressively jolly, a back-slapping, rib-digging good fellow. In short, he is the epitome of smug American philistinism.

Lewis' eye for this milieu is superbly exact. This, for example, is his comment about Babbitt's alarm-clock:

> It was the best of nationally advertised and quantitatively produced alarm-clocks, with all modern attachments, including cathedral chimes, intermittent alarm, and a phosphorescent dial. Babbitt was proud of being awakened by such a rich device. Socially it was almost as creditable as buying expensive cord tyres.

His mastery of Babbitt's ideals and beliefs is equally sure:

> If you had asked Babbitt what his religion was, he would have answered in sonorous Boosters'-Club rhetoric, 'My religion is to serve my fellow men, to honour my brother as myself, and to do my bit to make life happier for one and all.' If you had pressed him for more detail, he would have announced, 'I'm a member

of the Presbyterian Church, and naturally, I accept its
doctrines.' If you had been so brutal as to go on, he would have
protested, 'There's no use discussing and arguing about
religion; it just stirs up bad feeling.'

Yet for all this, Babbitt is far from being a contemptible
figure. Rather like Shakespeare's Falstaff, he begins as a
satiric butt and ends by endearing himself to the reader.
His charm, perhaps, lies in his naïvety and utter lack of
self-knowledge. He is forever swearing that he will give up
smoking and heavy eating, forever approving Prohibition
and drinking illicit cocktails, forever turning new leaves
with complete unawareness that he will certainly fail. The
reader can easily find some reflection of his own foibles and
vanities in all this; Babbitt is not a monster but a comic
version of ourselves. Moreover, he is made even more
sympathetic by his residual discontent with himself and his
way of life. He tries to break away from the business world
and get back to nature: he breaks away from domestic life
in his affair with Tanis Judique and from conventional
Zenith politics in his brief burst of liberalism. In all these
attempts at rebellion he is destined to both failure and complete surprise at his failure.

Babbitt, of course, is not without its faults. Its structure
is episodic. Indeed, the book lacks any central plot and its
incidents almost break down into a series of short stories
or vignettes: 'Babbitt at Home', 'Babbitt in Politics',
'Babbitt Becomes A Liberal' and so forth. Several critics
have argued that Sinclair Lewis' grasp of character is
superficial rather than profound. His characters have very
little real emotional life, for they are ingenious caricatures
rather than in-depth studies. This is certainly true, and the
final impression left by *Babbitt*, as by most of Lewis' work, is of
an immense talent restricted within very narrow limits. In
The Last of the Provincials (1947) Maxwell Geismar has commented: 'Not often before, in the history of our letters, has
an artist been able to see so much and see so little, or been so
rigidly constrained to do the only thing he can do.'

FURTHER READING It is too early for Lewis' works to have been published in a collected edition, but his best-known novels have been more or less continually in print since their first appearance. Some of his letters have been published as *From Main Street to Stockholm* (1952), edited by Harrison Smith. Mark Schorer has written an excellent biography, *Sinclair Lewis: An American Life* (1961), which also contains useful discussions of the novels. Further criticism is found in *The Last of the Provincials* (1947) by Maxwell Geismar.

5 The Lost Generation

Gertrude Stein, the American authoress who spent most of her adult life in Paris, told the young Ernest Hemingway: 'You are all a lost generation.' Hemingway was struck by the comment and used it as one of the epigraphs to his early novel, *Fiesta* (called *The Sun Also Rises* in America). With the success of that book the phrase passed into popular currency as the label for the group of writers who had been born near the turn of the century and reached maturity during World War I. It was applied to poets like Ezra Pound and e e cummings, and even extended by courtesy to English writers like Aldous Huxley and Wyndham Lewis. Above all, however, it was used for the novelists of the age: Hemingway himself, Scott Fitzgerald, Thomas Wolfe and John Dos Passos.

Today the 'Lost Generation' has come to seem an over-worked catchphrase. Used indiscriminately in its own era, the title has been claimed by successive generations of writers and applied retrospectively to earlier schools, such as the American naturalists. Yet the term remains useful in discussing the novelists of the 1920s, if only because it epitomizes the way they liked to see themselves. In this respect, as Malcolm Cowley has pointed out in *Exile's Return* (1961), the noun is as important as the adjective. Artists of Hemingway's and Fitzgerald's generation felt profoundly cut off not only from older figures like Dreiser but also from near-contemporaries like Sinclair Lewis.

Their unique and common experience was a disillusion bred by the First World War. They returned from that conflict to a society whose values seemed hollow and artificial by comparison with the harsh realities of the battle-field. Their alienation from America often took the form of exile and expatriation: Hemingway and Dos Passos spent most of their early adult lives in Europe, while Scott Fitzgerald and Thomas Wolfe were frequent visitors. It would hardly be an exaggeration to say that Paris became the extra-parliamentary centre of American culture in the 1920s. It was the shrine to which most ambitious young writers of the era made their pilgrimage.

Disillusioned with society in general and America in particular, the novelists of the Lost Generation cultivated a romantic self-absorption – a deliberate retreat into private emotion. They became precocious experts in tragedy, suffering and anguish. The early novels of Hemingway and Scott Fitzgerald are peopled by sad, bitter young men who have lost all illusions at an early age; Amory Blaine of *This Side of Paradise* and Jake Barnes of *Fiesta* are the prime examples. They are haunted by war memories and by images of violence, cynical about idealism in any form, and given to only the most cryptic and laconic expressions of feeling.

But the nihilism and the suffering are only half the picture. The years following the Great War were also a time of financial boom and extravagance, from which writers as well as businessmen benefited. Novelists no longer had to undergo the penury and lack of recognition that had initially greeted an earlier figure like Dreiser: at the age of twenty-four Scott Fitzgerald was earning $18,000 a year. Their new-found affluence encouraged writers to don a mask of hedonism. The novelists of the Lost Generation were also the pioneers of the Jazz Age; they were bent, as Scott Fitzgerald proclaimed, on 'the greatest, gaudiest spree in history'. The mood of the times was neatly expressed in one of its popular songs:

How are you goin' to keep 'em down on the farm
After they've seen Paree
How are you goin' to keep 'em away from Broadway
    Jazzin' around
        Paintin' the town.

The characters of Lost Generation novels live in restless pursuit of excitement and pleasure. Their Europe is not the gallery of cultural objects found in Hawthorne's and James' fiction: it is a Europe of elegant restaurants, picturesque bars and intriguing local customs. They delight in kicking over the conventional traces (and in the resultant cries of middle-class horror), indulging in heavy drinking and casual sex. In *The Great Gatsby* Scott Fitzgerald found a metaphor for an entire era when he portrayed Gatsby's world as an endless extravagant party. Yet for the Lost Generation writers, as for Gatsby, the pursuit of pleasure has a frenetic quality. 'It's a great life if you don't weaken,' says one of the characters in Dos Passos' *USA*, summing up the note of desperation underlying the age's gaiety.

The Lost Generation is only a brief chapter in American literary history. Its characteristic blend of public suffering and private pleasure begins to disappear with the onset of the 1930s. By the end of that decade Scott Fitzgerald was dead, the golden legend of his youth overshadowed by the 'crack-up' of his later life. Moreover, the Depression, the Spanish Civil War and the outbreak of the Second World War altered the mood of American culture. This can be seen clearly in Hemingway's later work, with its shift to involvement in public issues and social causes, and in the career of John Dos Passos, who adds a sense of political commitment to the characteristic qualities of Lost Generation writing. The movement that would lead to 'social conscience' novels like John Steinbeck's *The Grapes of Wrath* was already underway.

F. Scott Fitzgerald

Although his life and writings are associated with the fashionable East Coast, Francis Scott Fitzgerald (1896–1940) came from the staid American Middlewest. He was born and brought up in St Paul, Minnesota. His first real taste of a different life came when he went to Princeton, at that time one of the most socially exclusive and traditional of American universities. During his college years he was active in theatrical circles and formed important friendships with the poet John Peale Bishop and the critic Edmund Wilson. His first novel, *This Side of Paradise* (1920), written at Army training camp during the First World War, established him as the leader and poet laureate of the Jazz Age. He and his wife Zelda, whom he married in 1920, threw themselves enthusiastically into a round of parties, dances, drinking and trips to Europe. It was a hard, bright, fashionable way of life. His literary reputation was further established by another novel, *The Beautiful and the Damned* (1922), and two collections of short stories, *Flappers and Philosophers* (1920) and *Tales of the Jazz Age* (1922).

Scott Fitzgerald's next novel, *The Great Gatsby* (1925), shows a great advance in seriousness. Today it is recognized as his finest work. Precise and compact in its form, it gives a finely objective portrait of the hedonistic world in which the Fitzgeralds themselves lived, capturing both the frantic gaiety and the underlying sadness. The years after the publication of *The Great Gatsby* saw a gradual deterioration in Fitzgerald's life: from being the darling of the Jazz Age, he became its chief victim. He himself was an alcoholic, while his wife Zelda was permanently hospitalized in 1934 after a series of schizophrenic breakdowns. The troubles of these years are reflected in his next novel, *Tender Is the Night* (1934), and in the autobiographical essay, *The Crack-Up*, posthumously published in 1945. In the final years of his life Scott Fitzgerald struggled to recover his lost literary reputation and to establish a career as a Hollywood scriptwriter. *The Last Tycoon* (1941), a novel left incomplete at the time of his premature death in 1940, is a powerful reminder that even in decay his talents were considerable.

Fitzgerald's parents christened him 'Francis Scott Key' after the composer of 'The Star-Spangled Banner', a remote ancestor. This proved to be a particularly appropriate choice, for Fitzgerald spent most of his life wrestling with the American Dream. In his progress from Princeton to Hollywood via Long Island and the French Riviera, he sampled most aspects of the Jazz Age. In his youth he was its main celebrant. 'The rich are not as we are,' he grandly told his friend Ernest Hemingway. (Hemingway retorted: 'No. They have more money.') This is not a worship of money for its own sake, but for the style, elegance and charm it can buy. By the time of his best novel, *The Great Gatsby*, this attitude had changed; his descriptions of Gatsby's extravagant parties are closer to satire than eulogy. In *Tender Is the Night* Fitzgerald turned on the fashionable world that had failed him so badly with all the fury of a disillusioned romantic.

Inevitably, the main impression left by his career is one of waste. Like so many American writers, he never completely fulfilled the promise of his youthful work. But in his best fiction he shows himself to be one of the best American writers of this century. For all the romantic extravagance of his themes, he shows a surprisingly painstaking craftsmanship. His writing style is simple but graceful and he excels in creating striking literary metaphors. (Is not Gatsby's mansion itself the best metaphor yet coined for a whole era of American history?) These powers never entirely deserted Scott Fitzgerald and his later work shows flashes of tragedy as powerful in its way as the earlier social comedy had been.

This Side of Paradise

SUMMARY Beatrice Blaine brings up her son Amory unconventionally, interrupting his formal education to take him on tours of Europe and encouraging him in snobbish and amoral attitudes. As a result Amory is a precocious and egotistical child. When Beatrice has an alcoholic breakdown and Amory is sent to stay with relatives in Minneapolis, he has difficulty adjusting to this provincial environment. His sense of superiority makes him disliked and he is unhappy until he learns to hide his feelings beneath a conventional exterior. He experiences the same difficulty at his exclusive preparatory school in New England. During this period, however, he derives much comfort from his friendship with the worldly and cynical Monsignor Darcy, an old friend of Beatrice who is now an influential Catholic priest.

He loves Princeton from the start: the university's ancient traditions, high academic standards, social exclusiveness and reputation for gay elegance are precisely to his taste. He makes friends quickly – his closest companions are Burne and Kerry Holiday and Alec Commage – and is consumed with the desire to succeed. He is deeply affected by his contact with Thomas Parke d'Invilliers, a serious young undergraduate who publishes poetry in various university magazines. For all his cleverness, Amory had not previously taken literature seriously; now Tom introduces him to poetry, especially the work of the Romantics and the Decadents. Amory's ambition is satisfied when he joins the Triangle Club, a fashionable club which stages musical comedy, and tours in one of their shows. He has a youthful taste of romance when he meets Isabelle Borge at the end of a university vacation. They flirt with self-conscious sophistication before being parted when Tom returns to Princeton.

Here Tom is elected to a prestigious social club at the beginning of his sophomore (i.e. second) year and embarks on a gay and elegant social life. This is temporarily over-shadowed by tragedy: motoring back to the University one night he and his friends come upon the scene of a motor accident in which a friend, Dick Humbird, has been killed. The next day Isabelle and her mother arrive for the end-of-term dances. Afterwards, the young couple go to Isabelle's summerhouse on Long Island where, after a few days of delicious intoxication, their romance ends. The next term

Tom, never an industrious student, fails his exams. As a result of this disgrace he abandons his candidacy for the chairmanship of the college newspaper and sinks into social obscurity. His father's death further increases his discontent and he almost resolves to leave university, but is dissuaded by Monsignor Darcy. He becomes more interested in literature and he and Tom encourage Tanaduke Wylie, before the younger poet's work gets too Bohemian for their taste.

Princeton has now become considerably less conventional and Tom is delighted to find that many of the new freshmen share his own secret feelings of rebellion. The freshmen stage a boycott of the exclusive social clubs, led by Burne Holiday. In his quiet and unassertive way Burne has been maturing intellectually – reading Tolstoy, Whitman and other radical thinkers – and Amory now finds himself envious of somebody he had always previously patronized. Burne's stand against the social clubs loses him prestige and he becomes reclusive and eccentric, shunned by the rest of his class. At this time Amory is having his first completely serious experience of love. At Darcy's request he goes to see Clara Page, a young widowed relative living in nearby Philadelphia, and finds her charming. He goes again and again, joining the small court of male admirers who habitually gather around Clara. He falls in love and even begins to dream of marriage but when he speaks to Clara she gently rebuffs him.

The war begins to affect Princeton. Burne Holiday completes his social ostracism by taking a pacifist stand. Amory and Tom, now the closest of friends, say goodbye as they leave university for different training camps. During the war Beatrice dies, Kerry is killed and the group loses sight of Burne. However, Tom, Amory and Alec meet again in New York at the end of the conflict and share a flat together. Amory visits Alec's home and meets his sister Rosalind, a young debutante. She is imperious, enthusiastic and beautiful; Amory quickly succumbs to her spell. For a while she appears to return his love but then she decides to marry Amory's richer rival, Dawson Ryder. Amory is shattered by the blow; he spends several days touring the bars of New York getting more and more drunk and then resigns his job with an advertising agency.

Amory is now thoroughly bored, cynical and restless. He and Tom, who works for a fashionable literary magazine, spend hours together discussing the current state of litera-ture: they join in grand denunciations of its shallowness and lack of talent. Amory goes to see an uncle in Maryland. During his visit he meets Eleanor, a vivacious and literary-minded girl with whom he quickly falls in love. But even at the height of their romance he is aware that it is less intense than his affair with Rosalind. Moreover, he is scared by a wild and crazy streak in Eleanor's personality. When he leaves Maryland Amory does not see her again. He goes to Atlantic City, a popular seaside resort, where he meets Alec with a group of girls. That night the house detective raids Alec's hotel room – he has one of the girls with him – but Amory manages to take the blame for the incident. The detective does not inform the police but merely throws him out of the hotel.

Amory arrives in New York to be greeted by two pieces of bad news. His investments in public transport companies, the main source of his income, have failed and left him penniless. Monsignor Darcy, his mentor for so many years, has died. After attending Darcy's funeral, Amory finds his discontent with life reaching a climax. He heads back towards Princeton, forced by lack of money to hitchhike. On the way he is given a lift by two affluent businessmen. He launches into a tirade against their way of life, but they merely find him eccentric. At last Amory sees the familiar scene of the Princeton campus before him and he realizes that, whatever else he may lack, he has at least achieved a measure of self-knowledge.

CRITICAL COMMENTARY   When it was first published in 1920 *This Side of Paradise*, Scott Fitzgerald's first novel, was an immediate success with both the public and the critics. It is not difficult to see why: with his elegantly disillusioned hero and his hints of romantic sadness beneath the polished charm, Fitzgerald had captured the mood of his times perfectly. As Alfred Kazin noted in *On Native Grounds* (1942), he was 'not so much a novelist as a generation speaking'.

The life of Amory Blaine (obviously a romanticized version of the life of Scott Fitzgerald) is typical of the Lost Generation. Amory is born into a privileged world – the world of the American aristocracy – with the natural advantages of good looks and intelligence. His mother, the fashionable Beatrice Blaine, encourages him in a pose of aristocratic disdain towards life. His years at Princeton University intensify this secret rebellion against stodgy middle-class propriety. At that time the university was dominated by the concept of the 'Christian Hero' – a devout, clean-living undergraduate who throws himself impartially into work and sport – but Amory and his friends take a different course. He abandons his interest in football during his first term and fails his exams at the beginning of his second year, for his energies are devoted to the pursuit of style and social prominence. His friends drive fast cars, drink too much, flirt with girls in a way that would have been unthinkable only a few years earlier, and dabble in literary interests.

The effect of the war is to harden this pose of casual cynicism into a rock-bottom despair. The early parts of the novel convey an atmosphere of gay enchantment, but this vanishes with the hero's departure from Princeton. The New York sections of the book recount a series of reverses in Amory's life: his abortive romance with Rosalind, his loss of his private income and his job, and the death of Monsignor Darcy, his adviser for so many years. Amory talks at one point in the story about books that describe quests. If the reader sees *This Side of Paradise* in these terms, it is a quest that destroys rather than establishes certainties about life. Amory's surreal journey back to Princeton at the end of the novel is a final expression of his extreme emotional turbulence.

For all its novelty, *This Side of Paradise* has precedents in

earlier literature. Scott Fitzgerald is particularly influenced
by the work of Oscar Wilde, the English Decadent. Indeed,
Wilde is several times mentioned with obvious respect in
the literary conversations of Tom and Amory. With his love
of bright and cynical epigrams, his fascination with gilded
youth, and his occasional surreal touches (like the scene
where a drunken Amory meets the Devil), Scott Fitzgerald
sometimes seems to be a latter-day member of the Decadent
movement. But he was also subject to more modern influences, especially that of James Joyce. Joyce's *Portrait of the
Artist As a Young Man* also described a young man's development or 'quest' and its experimental style obviously impressed Fitzgerald. In the middle section of *This Side of
Paradise* he temporarily breaks with conventional techniques
of narration to present part of the story through letters and
stage dialogue.

It is unlikely, however, that readers will today be as
impressed by *This Side of Paradise* as Scott Fitzgerald's contemporaries were. Edmund Wilson, a lifelong friend of the
author, voiced an important criticism when he described
the novel as 'a phantasmagoria of incident which had no
dominating intention to endow it with unity and force'. At
times it seems more like a scrapbook of undergraduate
memories than a planned work of art: a contemporary
reviewer facetiously hailed it as 'the collected works of Scott
Fitzgerald'. Moreover, the novel's outlook on life is often
immature. Fitzgerald's cynicism seems like a shallow pose,
while his ceaseless straining after brilliant epigrams quickly
becomes irritating. In spite of these very real faults, *This Side
of Paradise* remains an important and memorable book. It
expressed the mood of a generation and it introduced, in
however crude and immature a form, a novelist who was to
become one of the major writers of the age.

The Great Gatsby

SUMMARY   The story is told by Nick Carraway, a quiet young
man whose habit of reserving judgement on others often

encourages them to confide in him. The son of an affluent Midwestern family, Nick comes east to work on the New York stock exchange and commutes to the city each day from the nearby island of West Egg. His own house is modest enough, but it is next to an extravagant and vulgar mansion built in imitation of a French château, owned by the fabulously wealthy Jay Gatsby.

Although he does not know the millionaire, Nick chances to mention Gatsby's name when he is dining one evening with Tom and Daisy Buchanan who live on the adjacent East Egg, a more fashionable island. Like Nick, Tom is a wealthy young Midwesterner who has recently come east; he is a hard arrogant man. His wife, Daisy, is charming and polished in her social manners. Despite this there is a tense moment during dinner when Tom goes out to answer the telephone. Daisy hurries nervously out of the room after him and Jordan Baker, Nick's fellow guest, explains that the phone call must be from Tom Buchanan's mistress. On his return home that night Nick Carraway sees his neighbour for the first time. Gatsby is standing on his lawn looking out across the harbour, but his manner is so preoccupied that Nick decides not to interrupt him.

Nick is also destined to meet Tom's mistress soon. One day the two men are travelling together by train to New York when Tom insists that they get off at an intermediary stop. He takes Nick to a shabby garage in a poor neighbourhood, where he talks to Wilson the proprietor. But it soon becomes evident that Wilson's wife Myrtle is the real reason for his visit. In her husband's absence Tom makes an arrangement to see Myrtle in New York that day. Nick is present at this meeting, which is held in Myrtle's New York flat; Myrtle's sister Catherine and some neighbours, the McKees, are also there. It develops into a drunken party that ends abruptly when Tom, angered at the mention of Daisy's name, hits Myrtle.

That summer Gatsby holds a succession of extravagant parties at his house. He provides unlimited food and drink, hires large bands and invites a wide circle of New York celebrities and socialites. When Nick goes to one of these parties he meets Miss Baker again and begins a mild romance with her. He finds that Gatsby is a mysterious figure to all of the guests. The air is thick with extraordinary rumours: Gatsby is a German spy, Gatsby recently killed a man and so forth. But when Nick actually meets him he finds the millionaire to be a pleasant, self-effacing young man with an elaborately formal manner.

Soon afterwards Gatsby takes Nick to New York in his expensive car and talks about his past. He claims to have graduated from Oxford and to have spent many years touring the European capitals trying to forget a tragic disappointment he has suffered in life. Nick is suspicious of the story for it sounds too much like a cheap romance. In New York he learns that Gatsby wants a favour of him. Miss Baker, a long-time friend of Daisy Buchanan, explains that Gatsby was Daisy's first love. Gatsby has never stopped loving Daisy and has taken the house in West Egg to be near her. Now Gatsby wants Nick to invite both him and Daisy to tea.

Gatsby arrives at the tea-party desperately nervous and embarrassed, but after Nick has left him alone with Daisy for a while he becomes radiantly cheerful and insists on showing them around his elaborate house. Clearly, Gatsby is overjoyed to feel that he has Daisy back again. But soon Tom Buchanan becomes suspicious and insists on accompanying Daisy to one of Gatsby's parties. Daisy finds the party too raucous for her taste. Afterwards Gatsby talks to Nick about Daisy's reluctance to leave her husband. He shows, as usual, a childlike faith in his ability to bring back the past and live it again. He also suddenly changes his style of life, discontinuing his season of parties and employing a smaller staff of servants.

On one of the hottest and most uncomfortable days of the summer Nick and Gatsby go to the Buchanans for lunch. After a tense meal during which Tom obviously begins to realize that Daisy is in love with Gatsby, the group goes for a drive. On the way into New York, Tom stops at Wilson's garage; the proprietor, who looks ill, mentions that he is planning to return to the west with his wife very soon. The party decide on impulse to hire a suite at the fashionable Plaza Hotel, so that they can sit and drink out of the heat. The atmosphere becomes increasingly edgy, with Tom persistently taunting Gatsby. At last Gatsby blurts out that Daisy never loved Tom. But Daisy corrects him: she has loved both of them, she claims.

On the way back to West Egg Gatsby's car hits Myrtle Wilson and does not stop. Wilson had at last become suspicious of her fidelity and had begun to bully her: in panic she ran into the road and under the wheels of the car. Tom Buchanan, driving up shortly after, sees the corpse and is badly shaken. When he is dropped outside the Buchanans' house that evening, Nick finds Gatsby waiting in the shadows. They talk about the accident and Gatsby reluctantly admits that Daisy, not he, was driving; now he has stayed behind to check that she is all right.

When Gatsby returns to his house in the early hours of the morning he and Nick again talk. This time Gatsby at last reveals the truth about his past life: his real name is James Gatz and he is a poor boy from the west who began to succeed through the help of a corrupt elderly millionaire, Dan Cody. He also talks about his first meetings with Daisy and his shock on hearing that she had married Buchanan. That day Nick forces himself to go to work, studiously avoiding Wilson's garage.

After an anguished night Wilson has now set off to avenge the death of his wife; he arrives at Gatsby's house late that afternoon when the owner is in his swimming pool. On his return home from work Nick finds Gatsby dead in the pool and Wilson's body in the grass nearby. Nick now takes on his shoulders the melancholy task of winding up Gatsby's affairs. It is a lonely business, for all of Gatsby's acquaintances desert him: the Buchanans leave town, business colleagues claim to be too busy and the party guests vanish. The only other person to go to the funeral is Gatsby's father, Henry Gatz, who arrives from Minnesota. Months later Nick meets

Buchanan and realizes that it was he who told Wilson where to find Gatsby.

CRITICAL COMMENTARY   *This Side of Paradise* and its successor, *The Beautiful and the Damned*, established Fitzgerald as the literary spokesman of the Jazz Age. He was the Golden Boy of those determinedly gay and resolutely cynical days that followed the Great War. Yet these novels, like the age that produced and adulated them, are essentially light: they deal in striking poses rather than substantial emotions. This makes Fitzgerald's third novel, *The Great Gatsby*, all the more of a surprise. It is subtle yet precise in its artistry, rich in feeling: a carefully polished jewel of a book. To T. S. Eliot, never a hasty or extravagant critic, it seemed 'the first step that American fiction has taken since Henry James'. Today it is obviously the work by which Fitzgerald's name is destined to be remembered, and one of the classics of modern American literature.

T. S. Eliot's invocation of Henry James is entirely appropriate. For Scott Fitzgerald, previously a sprawling and disorganized writer, showed in *The Great Gatsby* that he had developed into a controlled and careful craftsman. One notes, for example, how skillful is the handling of the narrative. The story is told not by an impersonal and omniscient narrator or from Gatsby's viewpoint, but by Nick Carraway, Gatsby's friend. As befits a novel that expresses both fascination and disillusion with Gatsby's world, Nick Carraway is neither insider nor outsider. He attends Gatsby's parties and feels at ease amidst the elite social world of the Buchanans. Yet he himself is neither rich nor leisured in the way many of his friends are. Similarly, he shows an interesting blend of ignorance and knowledge about Gatsby. Gatsby makes Carraway his confidant, but Carraway does not find out the complete truth about the millionaire's past until near the end.

Fitzgerald's literary style is precise and polished. He likes, for example, to make Nick Carraway sum up a chapter or section with a graceful epigram: 'Everyone suspects himself of at least one of the cardinal virtues, and this is mine: I am one of the few honest people that I have ever known.' The crucial episodes in the story remain sharply etched in the reader's mind – the scene where Gatsby hurls his expensive shirts about the room to impress Daisy Buchanan, for example, or the scene where Daisy and Tom sit together in sinister intimacy after the accident in which Tom's mistress has been killed. The story, moreover, is dominated by several compelling visual images: Gatsby standing in his darkened garden staring at the green light of Daisy's house across the harbour, or the eyes in the poster advertising Doctor T. J. Eckleburg's spectacles.

This technical advance is accompanied by an emotional maturity that is also new in Fitzgerald's work. *The Great Gatsby* is his summative comment on the Jazz Age of which his own career was so prominent a part. The book expresses neither shallow criticism nor thoughtless praise but a delicate blend of enchantment and disenchantment. Like Nick Carraway himself, Scott Fitzgerald is both an outsider and an insider in Gatsby's world. He is passionately attracted to its glamour while being deeply aware of the pettiness and suffering that underlie its tinsel.

At the centre of this glamorous but insecure world, its very epitome, is Jay Gatsby. He is ridiculously rich, so rich that he possesses an almost magical power to conjure up whole worlds of enchantment. He can hire or fire a whole retinue of servants at the snap of his fingers. He can convert his life at the extravagant mansion in West Egg into an endless party, continually fuelled with exotic food and drink and peopled by the cream of New York society. He has a house like a French château, a man to send him clothes from Europe by the score, a hydroplane, and a car like an armoured tank. Gatsby is the apotheosis of the American dream of wealth.

Fittingly enough, there is more than a smack of vulgarity about all of this. If Gatsby's life is the fulfillment of a romantic dream, it is a dream based on coarse and popular appetites. His very nickname, 'The Great Gatsby', suggests the circus showman rather than the aristocrat. His house is a bad imitation of a French château, while his car, with its excess of ostentatious gadgetry, is ridiculous. Moreover, Gatsby himself turns out on close inspection to be distinctly ill at ease in his own fairytale kingdom. Significantly, Nick Carraway talks to him at the party for a while without realizing who he is; for Gatsby can never quite live up to the magnificent role he has created for himself. His suit is cheap-looking (Fitzgerald memorably describes it as 'a pink rag') and his manners are nervous and overly formal.

In a sense, however, the subtle wrongness of Gatsby's personality only adds to the mystery that surrounds him. The end of the book gives the hard, disillusioning facts: Gatsby's real name is James Gatz and he is a bootlegger. But this is concealed for most of the action. Gatsby appears to have sprung up out of nowhere and his parties hum with bizarre and unlikely speculations about him. Is he a graduate of Oxford? Is he a murderer? Obviously a man so hard to place is an impressive figure, whatever the real truth about him may be.

Although Gatsby's life seems both mysterious and glamorous to spectators, its mainspring is almost touchingly simple. Gatsby is the last of the great romantics, devoting his life to thoughts of Daisy Buchanan, his youthful love. He attempts to woo her in a characteristically extravagant manner. His parties are designed to attract her attention and win her love, and when he finds that they have failed in this he abandons them at a stroke. There is an alarming naïvety in such adolescent romanticism beneath so impressive a façade. This is especially apparent in the scene where Gatsby sees Daisy again at Nick Carraway's tea-party. First of all, there is the elaborate way that Gatsby arranges the occasion; then the typically grandiose gesture of sending round a servant to mow Nick's lawn. Finally, Gatsby himself arrives in a pitiable state of nerves, more like a schoolboy at his first dance than an experienced man of the world.

It is this innocence that seals Gatsby's fate, for it makes him vulnerable. In this respect, despite all his wealth, he resembles the Wilsons. Just as Gatsby's car can sweep

Myrtle Wilson down without noticing, so the hardness of Daisy and Tom Buchanan can destroy Gatsby. The simultaneous death of Wilson and Gatsby – fellow victims of the same tragedy – is thus a fitting irony as well as a superb dramatic touch. Nick Carraway understands the reasons for Gatsby's destruction. He sees the essential callousness of the gay brittle life of the Jazz Age:

> They were careless people, Tom and Daisy – they smashed up things and creatures and then retreated back into their money or their vast carelessness, or whatever it was that kept them together, and let other people clean up the mess they had made...

Tender is the Night

SUMMARY The film actress Rosemary Hoyt arrives at a Cannes hotel with her mother, Mrs Elsie Speers. On the beach Rosemary meets Dick and Nicole Diver and their friends Abe North and Tommy Barban. Dick himself is polite and superbly sensitive to other people's feelings; Rosemary is immediately attracted to him. She is invited to a party at the Divers' new house, the Villa Diana. Under their hosts' expansive influence the guests shed their anxieties and give their best to the occasion. The only exception is McKisco, an egocentric literary critic and novelist. Rosemary feels more and more intimate with the Divers as the evening progresses, and at its end Dick asks her to accompany them to Paris to say goodbye to Abe North, who is returning to America. She tells him that she is in love with him, but he passes the matter off jokingly.

Later that night Rosemary learns that there has been an argument between McKisco and Tommy Barban. Apparently Violet McKisco had begun dropping innuendoes about the Divers; Barban, coming ferociously to his friends' defence, challenged McKisco to a duel. Abe North has been appointed McKisco's second. He and Rosemary visit the writer in his room and find him frightened and half-drunk.

However, McKisco manages to pull himself together in time for the duel and in the event nobody is wounded.

In Paris Rosemary is disturbed to notice that North is a heavy drinker. Apparently he was once a promising composer and has now resorted to alcohol to assuage his sense of failure. She again confesses her love for Dick, but he gently rebuffs her, explaining his sense of loyalty to Nicole. The next day Rosemary takes her friends to a film studio to see a private screening of *Daddy's Girl*, the film that made her famous. They are joined by Collis Clay, a raw young man who had been Rosemary's boyfriend in America. He now seems gauche and uninteresting in comparison with Dick.

After a succession of parties Abe North is seen off at the Gare du Nord. There is a shooting incident on the platform and Dick insists on helping, partly to impress Rosemary. The next day Abe North reappears in Paris and goes on an extended tour of the bars. Finally he arrives at the Divers' hotel, still drunk and now desperately asking for help. He has become involved with a group of Negroes who are trying to get money from him; one of them, Peterson, accompanies North to the hotel and waits outside the room. Shortly afterwards Rosemary finds Peterson dead in her room; apparently he has been killed in a quarrel with one of the other Negroes. Dick again takes charge and skillfully manages to prevent any scandal attaching to Rosemary. When she goes to thank him she finds Nicole in a frighteningly hysterical state.

The narrative now shifts abruptly to the past, when Dick Diver arrived in Zurich at the end of the First World War. He was a young psychiatrist of great promise. During the war he had been receiving letters from a young girl in the Zurich clinic, Nicole Warren, whom he had only briefly met. The director Dr Dohmler explains that Nicole had been brought in several years before by her father, a wealthy and influential American. The girl had been exhibiting symptoms of schizophrenia, which Dohmler was able to trace back to a sexual assault on her by her father. Diver begins to see Nicole regularly; they fall in love and marry.

Back in the present, Dick meets Mrs Speers in Cannes and explains that he has begun to fall in love with her daughter. He is now back at the villa working hard on a psychiatric textbook, trying not to think about Rosemary and to be as gentle as possible to Nicole, whose mental condition remains precarious. When the Divers go for a holiday in the Alps they meet Franz, a friend from medical school, who proposes that Dick join him in establishing a private clinic. Dick agrees and invests some of his wife's considerable fortune in the venture.

He is soon immersed in his new work. One day, however, Nicole receives a poison-pen letter accusing her husband of committing adultery with one of his patients. Nicole had already been jealous of Rosemary and this accusation adds to her increasing instability. She deliberately crashes the car when she is out driving with Dick and the children, but fortunately nobody is hurt. The incident leaves Dick so shaken that he decides to leave Nicole in Franz's care and take a holiday by himself. In Munich he learns from Tommy Barban that Abe North has been killed in a bar-room fight in New York. Dick's father dies and he goes to America for the funeral. On his return he encounters Rosemary in Rome and takes her out to dinner. He suddenly realizes that their tentative romance is over. Depressed, he goes out drinking and gets involved in a fight; he spends an unpleasant night in an Italian jail.

Back at the clinic he tries desperately to throw himself into his work but his depression persists and he begins to drink heavily. Franz readily agrees when Dick suggests that he should resign from the partnership. At the Villa Diana Dick finds it harder and harder to work on his book and relies increasingly on alcohol. Nicole is slowly falling out of love with him and when Tommy Barban arrives to stay with them this process is completed. Tommy has long been secretly in love with Nicole and she now readily begins an affair with him. Eventually she explains that she wants a divorce and Dick sadly returns to America. Nicole never sees him again, but she hears through mutual friends that he is practising psychiatry with less and less success in obscure provincial towns.

CRITICAL COMMENTARY Scott Fitzgerald's own description of *Tender is the Night* as a 'novel of deterioration' is apt in more ways than one. He wrote the book at a time when his own life, once the epitome of the gaiety and glamour of the Jazz Age, was becoming messy and unhappy. His wife Zelda had already suffered several schizophrenic breakdowns, while he himself was fighting a losing battle against alcoholism. *Tender is the Night* stands on the edge of the abyss. After its publication Fitzgerald wrote several good short stories and an interesting unfinished novel, *The Last Tycoon*, but on the whole his talent sadly declined. These are the years so movingly described in the autobiographical essay, *The Crack-Up*. After Zelda's permanent confinement in a sanatorium, he lived a life of lonely heavy drinking and financial anxieties. A desperate attempt to establish himself as a Hollywood scriptwriter brought further suffering and no relief to his money worries.

Tender is the Night was relentlessly attacked by contemporary reviewers: it was the first major work by Scott Fitzgerald that was not an immediate success. The chief burden of complaint was that the book was messy and formless. This is largely justified, for the structure of *Tender is the Night* (especially after the precision and compactness of *The Great Gatsby*) is a great disappointment. Probably the most striking fault is the long opening section describing the initiation of Rosemary Hoyt into the Divers' social circle. One can see why Fitzgerald wanted to begin with a glimpse of Dick and Nicole before their troubles set in, but unfortunately the effect is to muddle the reader. It is quite a while before it becomes clear that the novel is about Dick rather than Rosemary herself. Scott Fitzgerald was fully aware of this weakness and in his extensive revisions of the novel after publication he transposed the Rosemary Hoyt section to the middle of the book. Even this major surgery did not satisfy him and it seems likely that if he had lived longer he would have returned to revise *Tender is the Night* again.

Surrounded by waste and suffering in Fitzgerald's own life, and itself showing signs of a decline in skill, *Tender is the Night* actually takes deterioration as its main theme. It describes the gradual transformation of Dick Diver from a promising and hard-working doctor to a genteel playboy on the French Riviera, and then to a medical hack practising in obscure American provincial towns. Much of the story, of course, draws on his own experience – his alcoholism and his wife's illness – and on his fears about himself. Yet it also expresses a larger disillusion with the gay world of parties, dancing and drinking in which Scott Fitzgerald had spent much of his life. In *This Side of Paradise* he had adulated the Jazz Age; in *The Great Gatsby* he had expressed a wistful disenchantment with it; in *Tender is the Night* he is its most visceral critic.

The opening sections on the beach near Cannes show this world on the point of decay. Through Rosemary's reactions the reader is made to understand the charm of so elegant and fashionable a way of life. The long, lazy afternoons on the beach, the parties at the Villa Diana and the meals in fashionable restaurants are a seductive pastoral idyll. Dick Diver is the epitome of this world: not merely rich and stylish, but with an innate sense of courtesy towards other people. In a sense he is the last gentleman alive, a naïve and gentle figure too frail to survive the frantic merrymaking of the Jazz Age. Dick's surname – 'Diver' – contains an implicit warning of the disasters to come, and the cracks in the happy picture soon begin to show. There are hints of Nicole's mental illness and of marital disagreements between the couple.

The smash-up of the Divers' world is expressed in images of literal violence. In the opening section at Cannes, the writer McKisco and Tommy Barban fight a duel on the golf links one morning. It is more like a children's game than a real issue of life and death. But violent realities quickly intrude into the Divers' sheltered world. There is a shooting on the railway platform in Paris; a few days later the sinister

Peterson is found dead in Rosemary's hotel room. Later Dick learns with horror that Abe North has been beaten to death in a New York bar. Dick himself becomes the victim of violence: first Nicole deliberately crashes their car and then he is involved in a fight with the Italian police. Towards the end of the book he can sadly survey the wreckage of his own and his friends' lives and warn: 'I guess I'm the Black Death ... I don't seem to bring happiness any more.'

For all its obvious faults – the incoherence of its structure and the self-pitying tone – *Tender is the Night* is a moving and memorable work. In some respects, indeed, it surpasses Fitzgerald's most widely praised book, *The Great Gatsby*. Written out of deep disappointment and betrayal, *Tender is the Night* goes far towards achieving what Fitzgerald himself called a 'wise and tragic sense of life'.

FURTHER READING Scott Fitzgerald's writings are easily available in Penguin Books and in the six-volume *Bodley Head Scott Fitzgerald* (1958–1963), edited by J. B. Priestley and Malcolm Cowley. Penguin Books use the revised text of *Tender is the Night*, while the Bodley Head prints the original version. Inevitably, Fitzgerald's life has attracted a great deal of attention. There are two excellent biographies, by Andrew Turnbull (1962) and Arthur Mizener (1965). These are supplemented by two specialist studies, Nancy Milford's biography of Zelda Fitzgerald (1970) and Aaron Latham's account of Fitzgerald in Hollywood, *Crazy Sundays* (1971), and a host of interesting 'association items': Hemingway's remarks about Scott Fitzgerald in *A Moveable Feast* (1964), Zelda's autobiographical novel about her marriage, *Save Me the Last Waltz* (1932), and Budd Schulberg's fictionalized account of one of Fitzgerald's drunken sprees in *The Disenchanted* (1951). Andrew Turnbull has edited Scott Fitzgerald's letters (1964); those addressed to his daughter Scottie, a particularly revealing collection, are also included in the second volume of the Bodley Head edition.

Fitzgerald has been less well served by literary criticism. Arthur Mizener has edited a collection of essays (1963) and there are useful full-length studies by Sergio Perona (1968) and James Miller (1965).

Ernest Hemingway

Although he died only in 1961, Hemingway's life has become a modern myth which continues to interest and move even those who have never read his books. Born in Oak Park, Illinois in 1899, he trained as a reporter in Kansas City; thereafter he began to lead the sort of active and adventurous life that is so often the subject of his fiction. During the First World War he served in France and Italy, suffering serious injuries. In 1922 he returned to Europe as a journalist and mixed in the literary circles for which Paris was famous in the 1920s. He became a close friend of Ezra Pound, Gertrude Stein and Scott Fitzgerald. This society formed the background of his first major novel, *Fiesta* (called *The Sun Also Rises* in America), published in 1926. For his next important work, *A Farewell to Arms* (1929), he turned to his war experiences in Italy. During this period he also wrote a number of short stories, a genre in which he excelled, and went on to write two important works of non-fiction which reflect his life-long interest in violent sports: *Green Hills of Africa* (1935), about big game hunting, and *Death in the Afternoon* (1936), about bullfighting.

The novel *To Have and Have Not* (1937) showed the beginning of an interest in social and political issues which was confirmed by his experience as an observer in the Spanish Civil War. This provided material for the play *The Fifth Column* (1940) and *For Whom the Bell Tolls* (1940), commonly regarded as his masterpiece. But the decade following this novel was one of silence. It seemed to bear out Hemingway's own gloomy maxim about America: 'We do not have great writers. Something happens to our good writers at a certain age.' The impression that Hemingway's inspiration had deserted him was confirmed by his next novel, *Across the River and Into the Trees* (1950). A measure of critical esteem was regained when his last work of fiction, *The Old Man and the Sea*, appeared two years later. In 1953 Hemingway was awarded the Nobel Prize. In the last years of his life he wrote little except for a reminiscence of his early days in Paris, *A Moveable Feast*, posthumously published in 1964. Hemingway committed suicide in 1961.

Hemingway's early work – the short stories and the three novels, *Fiesta*, *A Farewell to Arms* and *For Whom the Bell Tolls* – won wide critical acclaim. By the time of the Second World War he was accepted as the grand old man of modern American fiction. In later life he paid dearly for this position, for there was no lack of detractors to call his preoccupation with violence and courage a bombastic pose, his emphasis on romantic love reminiscent of Hollywood, and his terse literary style philistine. The charges were encouraged by Hemingway's own transformation from a serious writer into a public figure bent on asserting his prowess as sportsman, drinker and playboy.

Much of this criticism is justified, but it obscures the very real contribution that Hemingway made to American literature in the 1920s and 1930s. In the words of the poet Archibald MacLeish, he 'whittled a style for his time'. This may be taken literally, for his style of writing was one of his most influential characteristics. With his simple diction, his terse sentences, and his vivid colloquialisms he cleansed and invigorated the American language. His subjects and his themes spoke for his generation. Profoundly affected by the First World War, his early work is cynical and disillusioned; it deals in irony and understated suffering. Thereafter Hemingway embarked on a literary and spiritual pilgrimage that finally led him to a resigned stoicism. His vivid experience of war and his love of violent sport made death seem omnipresent: it was the ultimate and perhaps the only reality. He most admired those qualities which help man meet his end: courage, dignity and the power to endure.

Fiesta (The Sun Also Rises)

SUMMARY The story is told by Jake Barnes, an expatriate American working as a journalist in the Paris of the 1920s. In the First World War he received a wound that made him impotent and now, despite his frenetic social round of drinking, parties and dancing, his life is frustrated and embittered. One of his casual friends in Paris is Robert Cohn, a shy young New York Jew whose first novel has recently made a hit; he lives with a grasping and possessive woman, Frances.

One evening Jake picks up a prostitute, Georgette, at a café and takes her to dinner, hoping to find her conversation amusing, but he is disappointed. After the meal they go to a local dancing-club with Robert, Frances and the Braddocks, a naïve and respectable American couple. Shortly after his arrival Jake sees Brett (Lady Ashley), an English friend. They immediately leave together and drive around in a taxi; as they talk it becomes clear that they are in love but Jake's impotence has destroyed any chance of a relationship. Now they try to forget their love and avoid each other. Jake leaves Brett in a bar and goes sadly back to his flat. Lying awake in bed that night, unable to sleep, he thinks bitterly of the war and of his meeting with Brett when she was a hospital nurse in England. In the early hours of the morning he is awakened by Brett. Now completely drunk, she bursts into his flat to tell him about an Italian count whom she has met at the bar where he said goodbye to her.

The next day Jake lunches with Robert Cohn. The novelist, a quiet sedentary man, has recently become scared of growing old; he now has a desperate urge to travel and see the world before it is too late. He has also fallen in love with Brett, whom he saw briefly the previous evening. He eagerly questions Jake about her but receives only bitter replies; apparently Brett has already been married once, is in the process of getting a divorce and plans to marry Mike Campbell. Later Jake sees Frances, who tells him that

Robert is planning to leave her. She launches into a tirade against Robert, who endures it patiently. Jake flees their company as soon as possible. That evening he again sees Brett. She calls at his flat with her Italian count; he insists on taking them out to dinner. The three spend a convivial evening together, but again on returning home Jake is depressed and insomniac.

Shortly afterwards both Brett and Robert leave Paris and Jake throws himself into his newspaper work. An American friend, Bill Gordon, visits and one evening they meet Brett, unexpectedly back in Paris to see Mike, the man she plans to marry. Mike, a bankrupt and a heavy drinker, greets them effusively but Jake and Bill decide to spend the evening at a boxing-match together. Robert Cohn returns to Paris with the suggestion that he and Jake go to the Pamplona fiesta in Spain. Jake also invites Bill, Mike and Brett. At first she is reluctant to come and confesses to Jake that she and Robert left Paris together and had a brief affair; but Robert does not seem worried at the idea of Brett joining the party.

Jake drives down to the Bayonne with Bill and Robert; the trio wait for Mike and Brett to join them. Bill quarrels with Cohn, whom he finds annoyingly serious and humourless. Jake, still hurt by Brett's confession about her affair with Robert, gets pleasure out of Robert's discomfiture. Bill and Jake go to Burguete together for a holiday. They stay at a small inn in the hills, fish in the daytime, and drink and play cards each evening with a fellow guest at the hotel, an Englishman named Harris. In Robert's absence they can relax together and indulge in their familiar ironic badinage. They arrive back in Pamplona in time for the festival, to find that Mike and Brett have at last arrived.

Jake is an *aficionado* – a lover of bullfighting – and he takes his friends to see the bulls being unloaded. The maddened animals are driven from their travelling cages into a corral, where they attack and gore the waiting steers. Jake explains the finer points of bullfighting to the others as they watch. Mike begins to goad Robert. He is jealous of the other man's affair with Brett and even more annoyed at the way Robert continues to hang around her in the hope that their romance might continue. In his shy, vulnerable way Cohn receives the insults in silence and offers no answer. The pair are reconciled with difficulty and the party dine together that evening.

When the fiesta starts the town explodes with noise and movement. The foreigners find themselves sucked into a singing, drinking, dancing crowd of friendly Spaniards. Brett loves the bullfights and Jake expertly explains their lore to her. Mike, who is often bad-tempered when drunk, begins to abuse Cohn; even Brett, who loves male admiration, is annoyed at the way Cohn follows her around.

Brett has been attracted by Pedro Romero, a handsome young matador who has distinguished himself in bull-fighting. Jake introduces them and leaves Brett to seduce the shy young Spaniard. When Cohn gathers what has happened he attacks Jake; later that evening Jake sees Cohn lying on his hotel bed crying uncontrollably. The next morning he learns that Cohn had sought out Brett and Romero, found them in bed together, and given the young matador a bad beating. It is the last day of the bullfighting. The bulls are driven through the streets, goring and killing a man on the way. Romero insists on going into the ring despite his bruises and again distinguishes himself. He gives the ear of his third bull to Brett. That evening Jake learns that Robert has left Pamplona quietly and that Romero and Brett have run off together. Now only Bill, Mike and Jake himself are left of the original party; they spend the evening drinking sadly together.

The trio drive back towards France. Jake stays in a quiet hotel in San Sebastian, recovering from the nervous strain and the heavy drinking of the Pamplona fiesta. But he is soon summoned to Madrid by an urgent telegram from Brett. He finds her in a hotel, deserted by Romero. As so often before he takes care of her – paying the bill, taking her out to dinner and trying to comfort her. Each is embittered by the thought of the happy life together that has been denied them.

CRITICAL COMMENTARY   Published in 1926, *Fiesta* (*The Sun Also Rises*) was Hemingway's first novel of any importance; previously he had confined himself to a few poems, some short stories and a slight, satirical novel called *The Torrents of Spring* (1926). Today *Fiesta* is usually neglected in favour of later works like *A Farewell to Arms* and *For Whom the Bell Tolls*. Yet on its first appearance the book was received with extravagant enthusiasm. It became, as Malcolm Cowley testifies in *Exile's Return* (1961), a 'craze': 'young men tried to get as imperturbably drunk as the hero, young women of good families took a succession of lovers in the same heartbroken fashion as the heroine, [and] they all talked like Hemingway characters.' It remains a central text for students of the Lost Generation; in *The Last of the Provincials* (1947) Maxwell Geismar notes that if Scott Fitzgerald's *This Side of Paradise* was 'the generation's masculine primer', *Fiesta* was 'the second reader for both sexes'.

The newcomer to Hemingway's work will first be struck by the style in which *Fiesta* is written. Its language is spare, terse and idiomatic. Like so many modern novelists Hemingway reacted against earlier notions of literary style, finding them ornate and pretentious. His aim was to tell his story as simply and cleanly as possible. This led him not to add to the language but to diminish it, to cut out redundant or 'literary' words and get back to a simple but expressive vocabulary. The result can be astonishingly vivid and Hemingway remains virtually unequalled amongst modern writers for his ability to make scenes of action and adventure come alive for the reader. In *Fiesta* itself the descriptions of the bullfight in which Romero kills the bull for Brett, the boxing-match that Bill Gorton goes to in Vienna and Robert Cohn's fight with Romero are outstanding.

The fact that the last two of these incidents are presented as inset anecdotes told to the other characters by Bill Gorton highlights another important characteristic of Hemingway's style: he abandons literary usage and formal manners in order to try and recreate the sound of the language as it is actually spoken. To this end he uses a variety of techniques: the repetition of a word several times within a single sentence; the stringing together of successive clauses by the conjunction 'and'; and above all, a vivid command of colloquial idiom. These characteristics can be seen not just in the inset anecdotes but in the main narrative by the hero, Jake Barnes. Here for example is the casual and informal way that Jake opens the story:

> Robert Cohn was once middleweight boxing champion of Princeton. Do not think that I am very much impressed by that as a boxing title, but it meant a lot to Cohn. He cared nothing for boxing, in fact, he disliked it, but he learned it painfully and thoroughly to counteract the feeling of inferiority and shyness he felt on being treated as a Jew at Princeton. There was a certain inner comfort in knowing he could knock down anybody who was snooty to him, although, being very shy and a thoroughly nice boy, he never fought except in the gym.

This may sound easy and flowing but it is an art that conceals art.

Even in the brief quoted passage Jake Barnes establishes the viewpoint that he expresses throughout the novel. He is wry and sardonic: a man who finds Princeton boxing titles and 'thoroughly nice guys' merely amusing. In its pervasive mood of cynicism and disillusion with established values *Fiesta* caught the mood of its times. Its characters are rootless and homeless expatriates, Americans and English who move from hotel room to hotel room around Europe. Superficially their lives seem to be a gay social whirl – a continuous round of parties, dinners and pleasure trips. Yet it does not take long to sense the desperation that underlies their pleasure-seeking. In their heavy drinking, their reckless spending and their promiscuity they are trying to forget their own pain, or to find a happiness that persistently eludes them. The central example of this despair is Jake's frustrated love affair with Brett. He has been rendered impotent by a war wound – a situation made all the worse, as he wryly points out, by the fact that it is usually regarded as a subject for ribald comedy rather than tragedy. Jake's wound is a concrete symbol of the legacy of suffering that blights his present life.

The book is notable for its preoccupation with violent sport. Bill Gorton gives a vivid and racy account of a boxing match in Vienna, while he and Jake choose to go to one in Paris rather than spend the evening with Brett's drunken fiancé, Mike. Bill and Jake later escape from the stresses of urban life – and from the irritating company of Robert Cohn – on a peaceful fishing trip in Spain. The book's climax centres on the bullfighting at the fiesta. In these respects the novel prefigures much of Hemingway's later work; he later wrote non-fictional accounts of both bull-fighting (*Death in the Afternoon*) and big game hunting (*The Green Hills of Africa*). In the mood of cynicism engendered by the war Hemingway and his generation often turned eagerly to violent and dangerous sport. By hunting or watching bullfights they could escape from artificial society and phoney values into an elemental world where death, danger, courage and technical skill were the only realities.

This preoccupation with the primitive life was to play a crucial role in Hemingway's fiction. In *Fiesta* itself he is content to concentrate on the artificiality and desperation of the life bred by the First World War; the idyllic fishing trip and the magnificent bullfights merely hint at different ways of living. In later works he was to show man returning to nature and to primitive forms of reality: in *For Whom the Bell Tolls* Robert Jordan is a guerilla fighter in the Spanish Civil War, while in *The Old Man and the Sea* Santiago is a deep-sea fisherman. From their elemental struggles the heroes of these later novels emerge with a positive code of ideals which, simple and stoical though it is, shows a great advance on the despair of Jake Barnes in *Fiesta*.

A Farewell to Arms

SUMMARY During the First World War Lieutenant Frederic Henry, an American serving in the Italian Army, returns from leave to his unit at Gorizia near the Austrian front. His friend Lieutenant Rinaldi is ecstatic about the beautiful English nurses who have arrived at the hospital. Henry lets Rinaldi take him to see Catherine Barkley, one of the nurses. She turns out to be pretty but still obviously affected by the death of her fiancé the previous year. Rinaldi talks to Miss Barkley's friend, a prim young Scottish nurse named Miss Ferguson. Henry visits Catherine again and kisses her as they walk through the hospital garden together. When they next meet she makes fierce protestations of love; Henry pretends to respond, but really sees the romance in cynical terms as an alternative to the tedium of war.

Henry is called to the front to take part in an Italian attack. Just after he has been briefed about arrangements for transporting the wounded, his dugout is hit by a trench mortar. When he regains consciousness Henry discovers that one of the drivers, Passini, is dead and that he himself has been wounded in the head and legs. After an emergency operation he is taken on a painful ambulance journey back to the field hospital. He is then moved to a hospital in Milan, where Catherine has also been posted. Seeing her for the first time after so eventful a gap, Henry suddenly realizes that he is in love with her. The x-rays show that several lumps of mortar are still embedded in his knee, but the cheerful Dr Valentini performs a successful operation. Henry's romance with Catherine, after its cynical start, has now blossomed: she visits him each night in his hospital room.

Away from the stresses and dangers of war, he spends an idyllic summer with Catherine. He is eager for them to marry but she refuses; if she were married she would have to resign her job and return to England until the end of the war. That autumn Catherine announces that she is pregnant: both are overjoyed. However, Henry has to return to the front almost immediately, and they say a sad goodbye outside the Milan railway station.

Henry arrives back at the front to find that little has changed, except that the combatants have grown more cynical than ever. Rinaldi greets him enthusiastically but complains that Henry's romance erects a barrier between them. That evening in the mess Rinaldi gets noisily drunk while the company's priest remains silent and embarrassed. Afterwards the priest talks to Henry about his desperate hopes that the war will end.

The Austrians attack and after several days' indecisive bombardment and skirmishing the Italian Army retreats. Henry and his men rest at Gorizia that night and join the column of retreating vehicles the next day. He fears that there will soon be an aerial bombardment and so he leads his vehicles up a series of rural sideroads away from the main body of the army. They take food from a local farmhouse. Soon, however, one of the cars sticks in the muddy road and two of the soldiers try to desert: Henry shoots one but the other manages to get away. The rest change to the remaining vehicle but the road comes to an end and they have to proceed on foot. One of the ambulance drivers, Aymo, is shot by an unseen sniper. This makes another driver run away in fear, and only Henry and Piani are left to make their way back to the dispirited army.

The battle police are singling out officers from the retreating columns and accusing them of deserting their men; some are shot. When he is stopped Henry is scared that he will be mistaken for a spy because of his foreign accent. He escapes by jumping into the river and floating away under the cover of a log. After a tiring and hazardous walk, he is able to board a freight train which takes him to Milan. But when he presents himself at the hospital he learns that Catherine and her friend Miss Ferguson have been moved to Stresa. Borrowing some civilian clothes, Henry follows Catherine there. She is overjoyed to see him but Miss Ferguson, regarding him as her friend's seducer, receives him angrily. After his recent hectic adventures, Henry can at last relax: being quietly happy with Catherine, fishing on the lake by the hotel, or playing billiards with a fellow-guest, Count Greffi. But one night the barman comes to Henry's room to warn that the military police are on their way to arrest him for desertion. He and Catherine sneak out of the hotel and row across the lake to Switzerland. The Swiss authorities are suspicious but issue them with visas when they learn that their passports are in order and that they are well supplied with money.

At last Henry and Catherine feel they can be unreservedly happy together, able to forget the war and await the birth of their child in peace. They spend the autumn in a small chalet near Montreux, seeing few people and spending all their time contentedly together, and move to Lausanne in the winter in order to be near the hospital. When Catherine's pains begin Henry rushes her to the hospital, but more than twelve hours pass without her giving birth. The doctor reluctantly decides to perform a Caesarean operation. The baby is stillborn and Catherine begins to haemorrhage. She dies. Henry walks back to his hotel in the rain.

CRITICAL COMMENTARY In his first important novel, *Fiesta*, Hemingway has dealt obliquely with the First World War. Jake Barnes' account of the lives of American and English expatriates in the Paris of the 1920s revealed the cynicism and disillusionment that the conflict had bred in an entire generation of young people. In this next novel, *A Farewell to Arms*, Hemingway dealt with the war directly. There are obvious autobiographical origins: like his hero Lieutenant Henry, Hemingway himself served in the Italian Army and was badly wounded in the legs. By confronting these horrors Hemingway was apparently able to purge himself of some of their effect; at any rate, the novel expresses a more mature and optimistic view of life than its predecessor. The ending of *A Farewell to Arms*, with the death of Catherine and her baby in the hospital and the hero's lonely return to his hotel room, clearly makes it a tragic novel; but it has progressed beyond the complete disillusion that lay behind the gaiety of *Fiesta*.

The reader who is familiar with Hemingway's earlier work will also immediately recognize a striking technical advance in *A Farewell to Arms*. Hemingway's chosen training ground as a writer was the short story; he produced several dozen (some of them very distinguished) before he turned his hand to writing a full-length novel. Not surprisingly, he had great difficulty giving pace and direction to *Fiesta*: the book makes false starts and gets sidetracked, jerks and falters. But *A Farewell to Arms* makes it clear that Hemingway, for all the vaunted 'modernity' of his style and his themes, is also a fine storyteller in the traditional mould. The story of Lieutenant Henry's romance with the English nurse is handled with assurance, smoothly unfolding from their first meeting in the hospital garden to Catherine's death in Switzerland.

Moreover, Hemingway shows surprising skill in keeping a balance between the personal drama that occupies the foreground of the action and the larger drama of the war that is the novel's background. He is helped here by the manner in which his prose style has changed. It is still as terse and as consciously simple as ever but it has developed unexpected subtlety. It not only expresses the deliberately hard-boiled and cynical outlook of the hero, but also describes in panoramic terms military scenes like the retreat of the Italian Army from Gorizia. In *Fiesta* Hemingway had worked hard to convey the atmosphere of Paris in the 1920s; here he is even more successful in bringing the locales to life. His descriptions of wartime Italy and of Switzerland in winter are never just 'settings' in the conventional sense of the term: they are living parts of the novel, almost characters. From the first assured sentence Hemingway establishes his powerful and precise sense of place: 'In the late summer of that year we lived in a house in a village that looked across the river and the plain to the mountains.'

As the title implies, the novel sets out to offer a statement about war, but Hemingway's attitude is in fact surprisingly ambivalent. He has of course little time for clichés about patriotism and military glory, for these quickly lose any meaning in the face of harsh reality. In a significant scene (Chapter 27) Frederic Henry talks to an ardent Italian patriot and then comments to the reader:

> I was always embarrassed by the words sacred, glorious and sacrifice and the expression in vain ... There were many words that you could not stand to hear and finally only the names of the places had dignity. Certain numbers were the same way and certain dates and these with the names of the places were all you could say and have them mean anything. Abstract words such as glory, honor, courage, or hallow were obscene beside the concrete names of villages, the numbers of roads, the names of rivers, the numbers of regiments and the dates.

This implies a dislike of war, but nothing so extreme as the revulsion found in, say, the poetry of Wilfred Owen. Hemingway turns (typically enough) in contempt from phoney abstractions but he still finds something to revere in the humble factual details of the fighting. Throughout his life he was fascinated by violent situations: boxing, bullfighting, hunting. He found something exhilarating about danger and something particularly admirable about the ability to show grace under pressure, to endure suffering and still carry out one's task.

For all this admiration of military virtues, the book describes a movement away from the world of war to the world of romantic love. Henry is finally sickened by the cruelty and the sheer muddle of the fighting. His own wound reminds him of the omnipresence of death and he yearns for a more satisfying and less lonely life. He finds this in his romance with Catherine. To begin with, he is callous and casual – the typically cynical Hemingway hero – but, after the wound has sobered him, his attitude grows serious. Love, as he says, is the only way in which man can overcome his loneliness.

To some extent Henry deludes himself about the power of love. By fleeing the battlefield and making his 'separate peace', as he calls it, he cannot evade death completely. The end of the novel proves that. But even before Catherine dies Henry has glimpsed the inevitability of death and suffering:

> If people bring so much courage to this world the world has to kill them to break them, so of course it kills them. The world breaks every one and afterward many are strong at the broken places. But those that will not break it kills. It kills the very good and the very brave impartially. If you are none of these you can be sure it will kill you too but there will be no special hurry.

This statement comes as near as anything in the novel to encapsulating the view of life that Hemingway elaborated throughout his career as a writer. It implies the essential tragedy of existence and also the need to meet that tragedy with dignity and stoical endurance.

For Whom the Bell Tolls

SUMMARY Robert Jordan, an American fighting for the Republicans in the Spanish Civil War, is sent behind Fascist lines to destroy a bridge. Anselmo, an old and trustworthy guide, takes him to a local guerilla camp. Its leader is Pablo, a distinguished soldier who has begun to lose his nerve. The other members of the group whom Jordan meets are the gipsy Rafael, amiable but feckless, and Pablo's wife Pilar, an ugly woman who is far braver than her husband. Jordan is particularly struck by Maria, a shy young girl with a cropped head. He learns that she has recently been rescued from the Fascists and is still recovering from the ill treatment she suffered at their hands.

Pablo is suspicious of the mission. After reflection he announces that he will not help: the destruction of the bridge would bring the guerillas no profit but only danger. Pilar villifies him as a coward and finally manages to overrule him. Jordan still does not trust Pablo, but rejects Rafael's suggestion that the leader should be killed.

That night Jordan sleeps outside the guerillas' cave in his sleepingbag. He is joined by Maria who, despite her shyness, had earlier shown that she found him attractive. As they lie together she explains that the Fascists killed her parents and raped her. The next morning enemy planes pass overhead. Jordan sends Anselmo to watch for unusual troop movements on the nearby road. He hears from another member of the group that the nearest town is already alive with rumours that the Republicans are about to attack and that the Fascists have strengthened the guard on the bridge. Pilar takes Jordan and Maria to see El Sordo, another guerilla leader whose help they will need. On the way she tells the American how the revolution came to her hometown of Avila. At El Sordo's camp Pilar exchanges badinage with Joaquin, a young man who wanted to be a bullfighter before the war, while Jordan confers with the leader. Sordo agrees to help with the bridge but worries about where to take his men afterwards. On the way back Pilar questions Maria and Jordan about their romance. She encourages them and even discreetly walks ahead so that they can be alone together. Although Jordan is rapidly falling in love his thoughts are soon drawn back to the difficulty of his mission.

As she prepares supper in the cave that night Pilar talks of her life as mistress to a famous bullfighter. Meanwhile, Anselmo sits in the snow watching the road and the bridge until Jordan comes out to fetch him. By the time they get back to the cave Pablo is already drunk and quarrelsome, grumbling at the folly of the assault on the bridge. When he goes out to tend the horses the group decides to kill him, but Pablo returns unexpectedly and claims to be in favour of the mission. The evening passes slowly in the drowsy and overheated atmosphere of the cave, and the guerillas talk nervously about death in battle.

Jordan sleeps outside again and is again joined by Maria during the night. He is woken in the morning by the sound of a Fascist cavalry officer approaching the cave; he quickly shoots the man and alerts the other guerillas. They conceal the body while Jordan sets up the Lewis gun in case any more soldiers come. But the cavalry patrol to which the dead man belonged stumbles on Sordo's camp instead. Sordo and his men put up a brave fight but are killed when the Fascist bombers arrive. Late that night Anselmo comes accidentally on the scene of the battle and finds that the Fascists have cut off the heads of their dead enemies. But Anselmo brings even more disquieting news to Pablo's camp: from his account Jordan can gather that the Fascists are prepared for the imminent Republican attack. He sends a young guerilla named Andres with a message of warning for the Republican commander, General Golz.

Andres is delayed by an endless series of bureaucratic checks and his message arrives too late. Jordan, meanwhile, has received another shock: during the night Pablo has absconded with the detonators. But to everyone's surprise Pablo returns in the morning. He had intended to leave the band for good but changed his mind; he has managed to recruit some new guerillas for the expedition.

They make their way to the bridge and separate into two groups, each of which will attack a guard post when the sound of bombs signals the beginning of the Republican offensive. Pablo goes with the men he recruited during the night, while Jordan takes Anselmo and Agustin. When they receive the signal, he and Anselmo easily kill the guards and place the dynamite under the bridge, but Anselmo is killed in the explosion by a flying piece of metal. When the group gathers again in the hills Jordan discovers that all of Pablo's new followers have been killed. He suspects that the guerilla leader simply recruited and then murdered them for their horses. They begin to make their retreat under enemy fire. Although the rest are unscathed, Jordan is shot from his horse and breaks his leg as he falls. He cannot continue but insists that the rest of the band, including Maria, go on without him. With difficulty he says goodbye to her and makes her accept the need to part. Left alone in the forest he wonders whether he should kill himself before his wound grows too painful. But a troop of Fascist cavalry soon appears and Jordan, barely conscious, waits patiently for its officer to come within range.

CRITICAL COMMENTARY   Published in 1940, Hemingway's *For Whom the Bell Tolls* is at once the longest and the most ambitious of his novels; it is also widely regarded as his masterpiece. It is dominated by the familiar Hemingway themes of love, war and death, but where an earlier work like *A Farewell to Arms* finds war to be a meaningless muddle and love the most fragile of blossoms, it strikes a confident and affirmative note. *For Whom the Bell Tolls* completes Hemingway's gradual conversion from his youthful nihilism to a new belief in himself and in mankind. In *Writers in Crisis* (1947) Maxwell Geismar, after commenting on the 'total renunciation of all social frameworks' in Hemingway's early work, goes on to welcome the later novel as showing its author's 'return to humanity'.

This change was catalysed by the Spanish Civil War of the 1930s, that unsuccessful struggle by the motley supporters of the Republic – democrats, Communists and anarchists – against the Fascist armies of General Franco. If Hemingway and his generation grew up under the shadow of the First World War, their political attitudes were forged in the crucible of the Spanish war. To contemporaries it seemed the harbinger of a conflict imminent in European affairs: the fight between freedom and tyranny. Young people from England and America, especially intellectuals and writers, flocked to join the Republican side. From England the poet W. H. Auden and the writer George Orwell went to fight. (Orwell's book *Homage to Catalonia* is still one of the best and most vivid accounts of the war.) After the Republican defeat the volunteers returned, either disillusioned by the internecine feuding between the Communists and the anarchists that had done so much to damage their cause, or strengthened in a belief in the need to oppose Fascism and defend liberty.

Hemingway himself attended the war as an observer, sending back valuable journalistic despatches. The experience left him with something that he had been seeking for a long time: the sense of a cause that he could believe in. His earlier novels are self-absorbed: their heroes fight lonely struggles for their own happiness, ignoring the affairs of the world around them. But *For Whom the Bell Tolls* is suffused with a sense of involvement in the lives and sufferings of others. Its hero, Robert Jordan, is willing to die for the eventual happiness of the Spanish people. This spirit is summed up in the famous sermon by John Donne, the seventeenth-century poet and divine, from which the novel's title is derived:

> No man is an *Iland*, intire of it selfe; every man is a peece of the *Continent*, a part of the *maine*; if a *Clod* bee washed away by the *Sea*, *Europe* is the less, as well as if a *Promontorie* were, as well as if a *Mannor* of thy *friends* or of *thine owne* were; any mans *death* diminishes *me*, because I am involved in *Mankinde*; And therefore never send to know for whom the *bell* tolls; It tolls for *thee*.

Hemingway's commitment is a matter of broad humanitarian concern rather than partisan loyalty. His novel has no specific political axe to grind. Its hero, Robert Jordan, is committed enough to the Republican cause to give his life for it, but his political ideals are of the most general kind. Indeed, his Marxist friend Karkov thinks him politically naïve and uneducated. Moreover, the book manages to give a remarkably objective account of the two sides in the struggle. The Republicans are certainly not whitewashed. Their ranks include someone like Pablo, who cheerfully shoots his own comrades for the sake of their horses, and who orders a disgusting massacre of the Fascist sympathizers at Avila. Nor is the reader asked to see the enemy as monsters or bogeymen. They include the young sentry at the bridge whose death makes Anselmo weep and the humane and sensible Lieutenant Berrendo. (Ironically, it is Berrendo whom Robert Jordan is planning to shoot as the novel ends.)

When *For Whom the Bell Tolls* was first published supporters of both Spanish sides found much to criticize in the novel. Later critics, while not regretting Hemingway's failure to take a partisan stance, have sometimes felt his attitude to the war to be vague and undefined. It is, Maxwell Geismar complains, 'romantic and immature': 'beyond the broad outlines of the Spanish Civil War, we are given relatively little of the impact of the struggle in either sociological or personal terms.' Yet surely the root of Hemingway's concern is his love of Spain, its landscape and its people. For all his obvious Americanness he always felt great affection for Europe; he used Italy as the scene of *A Farewell to Arms* and Paris as the setting for *Fiesta*. But his love affair with Spain was particularly intense. The novel begins and ends with a reference to the landscape – in each case the pine-needled floor of the forest – and the sheer beauty of the country is continually stressed. The action is designed to celebrate the characteristic virtues that Hemingway discerned in the Spanish people. Pilar, wife of the treacherous Pablo, is earthy, kind and sensible, as her treatment of Maria shows. Anselmo, for whom Robert Jordan comes to feel a special respect, is courtly, dignified and sensitive. The effect is to suggest that Jordan is fighting for the Republicans not so much out of a political sense as an instinctive love of Spain itself.

Yet although *For Whom the Bell Tolls* shows the emergence of a new spirit in Hemingway's work, its underlying tone is still tragic. The hero inherits a legacy of violence: his father committed suicide while his grandfather was a distinguished soldier in that terrible conflict, the American Civil War. He himself dies at the end of the book. Indeed, it sometimes seems that Hemingway welcomed his discovery of a worthwhile cause because it could give significance to an otherwise meaningless death: it was something to die for. The final scene, where the wounded Robert Jordan prepares to meet the Fascist cavalry, reminds the reader that to Hemingway the ultimate purpose of any code of values was to help the individual meet his death in a resigned and graceful manner.

The Old Man and the Sea

SUMMARY Santiago is an old man who fishes off the coast of

Havana for his living. Even at the best of times it is a hard, unremunerative life, but for eighty-four days now the old man has not caught a fish. The young boy Manolin who usually helps him has left: his parents insisted that the boy should work with a more profitable boat. Manolin, however, worships the old man and waits to greet him as he sails into the harbour after yet another day's unsuccessful fishing. Ignoring the mocking remarks of the other fishermen, the old man takes down his sail, shoulders his harpoon and his lines and goes to his home. This is a poor one-room dwelling decorated with religious pictures and a photograph of his dead wife. The boy insists on being allowed to buy some sardines for the old man to use as bait the next day.

They go through a fiction by which the old man pretends to delay eating his supper; in fact, as they both know, he cannot afford anything to eat. He settles down to read an old newspaper while the boy goes out to fetch the sardines. On Manolin's return the man is asleep, so old and weathered that he looks lifeless. The boy steals out again and brings a simple meal for them both from the local hotel. As they eat they ardently discuss baseball, for both are admirers of Joe DiMaggio. When it is dark the old man goes to sleep, rolling up his trousers to make a pillow. Now he is old he no longer dreams of people but of places. He sees African beaches with lions patrolling up and down.

He wakes early the next morning, rouses the boy and takes him down to the beach where they drink coffee together before setting out in their separate boats. As the old man rows out of the harbour it is still dark and he can only hear, not see, the other fishing boats in the water near him. But he soon leaves these behind, for he has resolved to go far out to sea in a desperate attempt to break his run of bad luck and catch a fish. He loves the sea, accepting its hardships and cruelties as one might accept the fickleness of a woman he loved.

By the time dawn comes up he has already baited several lines with sardines and sunk them at various depths. He sits in the boat waiting and praying for good luck. He moves to where he can see a bird circling over the water and finds a fast-moving school of flying fish pursued by dolphins. All he catches is a small tuna fish that he can use for bait. As he rows or waits he talks aloud to himself, a habit he has developed since the boy stopped coming with him.

At last he feels a gentle tug on the supple stick that supports one of his lines, and knows instantly that a fish is cautiously feeding on the bait. By delicately pulling the line he can judge the fish to be very big. After an agony of suspense, the fish at last swallows the hook. It immediately proves its strength and intelligence, for instead of jerking at the line in panic it begins to swim steadily away, towing the boat in its wake. The fisherman bides his time, hoping that the fish does not decide to dive. The strange journey continues throughout the day and when night comes the old man can see the lights of Havana receding in the distance. Since he has to hold the line over his shoulder, he is now extremely uncomfortable and wishes the boy were there to help him. As he goes he thinks about the fish, admiring its courage and intelligence, and beginning to feel a strange affection for it. Another fish bites one of the other lines but the old man lets it go in order to concentrate on the big struggle.

The fish is still there the next morning and begins to jerk at the line. The old man finds it difficult to cope, for in addition to his tiredness he now has a bad cramp in his left hand. He eats some raw fish to give himself energy and remembers the trial of strength he once won against a Negro in Casablanca. The fish at last jumps and the old man gets his first opportunity to see it: it is beautiful – longer than the old man's boat. After midday the man's hand loses its cramp and he is able to catch a dolphin, which he eats that evening to keep up his strength. In the night he is woken from a doze by the fish jerking and jumping. He pays out more line, but makes the fish work hard to gain each extra inch. His hands are now raw and bleeding, so he bathes them in the soothing water.

On the third day the fish begins to circle, a sure sign that the end of the contest is at hand. The old man is now groggy with tiredness and desperately afraid that his strength will fail before he can kill the fish. As it circles he draws in the line, bringing his prey nearer and nearer to the boat. At last the fish comes within range and the old man harpoons it, striking the heart cleanly. The fish jumps out of the water in its death throes, but is soon dead and lashed to the boat. Tired but fulfilled, the old man heads for home.

His troubles are not over, however, for the sharks soon scent the blood of the dead fish and come in pursuit. He kills the first one without trouble, but the beast sinks with the precious harpoon still in it. When more sharks attack, the old man is forced to resort to progressively makeshift means of repelling them: first his knife lashed to a pole, then a club, and finally the tiller of the boat itself. By the time he comes into the harbour next morning he is exhausted from the fighting. The dead fish is completely mutilated; both its beauty and its valuable meat are gone. Sadly the old man takes down his mast, collects his damaged fishing tackle and stumbles back to his shack in a stupor of tiredness. The boy brings him coffee and comforts him at being beaten by the sharks. In the harbour the other fishermen marvel at the catch. The old man falls asleep and dreams about the lions again.

CRITICAL COMMENTARY Even to his most ardent admirers Hemingway's later career was a disappointment. In his youth he had been a fertile writer, always developing and experimenting. But after the publication of *For Whom the Bell Tolls* in 1940, his most ambitious and most assured work, there was a long silence. His next novel, *Across the River and Into the Trees* (1950), showed him at his weakest and most mannered. With the appearance of *The Old Man and the Sea* in 1952, however, the rising tide of criticism of Hemingway's work was at least temporarily quelled. The award of the Nobel Prize the following year reaffirmed his importance amongst twentieth-century novelists.

Yet *The Old Man and the Sea* itself remains a difficult work to judge. It has been seen both as the fitting climax to a distinguished career and as the final evidence of the author's decline. To some critics the account of the old fisherman's battle to catch the giant fish has seemed grand and tragic, to others merely inflated and sentimental.

Throughout his career Hemingway was famous for the simplicity of his literary style. He broke irrevocably with ornate and 'literary' mannerisms, and cultivated short sentences, simple words and colloquial idioms. In the early work this simplicity often seems the clipped and deliberately inexpressive utterance of a man trying to conceal his own pain and despair; it lends itself to quiet irony and deliberate understatement. The simplicity of *The Old Man and the Sea* is of a very different order, for here Hemingway is aiming at a Biblical grandeur. 'He was an old man who fished alone in a skiff in the Gulf Stream . . .' – so the story begins and the reader at once senses that he is being offered something very like a parable. The story cultivates a careful surface realism – it gives a minute and particular account of all the old man's thoughts and actions – but also aims at a universality of meaning and reference. Santiago and Manolin are usually called 'the old man' and 'the boy', since they are intended to be typical or universal figures.

This approach is fitting, for in *The Old Man and the Sea* Hemingway is directly confronting one of the oldest and grandest of literary themes: the relation between man and nature. As he conceived the story he was obviously aware in particular of Melville's *Moby Dick*, that great American classic which also describes a hunt at sea lasting for three days. But in *Moby Dick* the emphasis is on the malevolence of nature and on Captain Ahab's monomaniacal hatred of the white whale. In Hemingway's story the old man feels a sense of union with nature. This is implied in the way he is described at the beginning of the novel, for Hemingway continually draws his images from nature. Santiago's eyes 'were the same colour as the sea and were cheerful and undefeated'; while his hope of catching a fish was 'freshening as when the breeze rises'. The point is spelt out directly in the scene where the old man rows out of the harbour on his epic voyage. He always uses the feminine article to refer to the sea, Hemingway explains, unlike the younger fishermen who use the masculine article:

> They spoke of her as a contestant or a place or even an enemy. But the old man always thought of her as feminine and as something that gave or withheld great favours, and if she did wild or wicked things it was because she could not help them.

Given this underlying sense of union, hunting becomes not an expression of antagonism but a way of cultivating an even deeper intimacy. The greater part of the book is occupied by the account of the development of the man's attitude to the fish on his line. At first he welcomes it as an end to his run of bad luck and as a source of much-needed income. Then he comes to respect its strength and intelligence, for they make the fish a worthy foe. When he finally sees it he is moved by its beauty. Finally, he comes to love the fish and to lament its death even as he kills it.

For all this, the essentials of the world in which the story takes place remain as grimly tragic as Hemingway's earlier fiction would lead one to expect. The destruction of the dead fish by the rapacious sharks is clearly intended to be emblematic. The fish's death after its epic struggle with the old man represents a moment of glory, but this is quickly lost amidst sordidness and greed. The fish is hardly dead before its beauty is defiled. The story ends with the tourists watching the fish's tailbone swilling about amongst the refuse in Havana harbour. As usual in Hemingway's fiction, the only positive values are stoic endurance and acceptance. The old man suffers the physical ordeal of the hunt as uncomplainingly as he had suffered the earlier run of bad luck.

FURTHER READING Although there is not yet a collected edition of Hemingway's work, most of his novels are readily available. The majority of his work has been issued in paper-backs; *Fiesta* (*The Sun Also Rises*) is included in the Penguin *Essential Hemingway* (1964). The standard biography is Carlos Baker's *Ernest Hemingway: A Life Story* (1969). Charles A. Fenton's *The Apprenticeship of Ernest Hemingway: The Early Years* (1954) also gives a useful account of his early life. These books are supplemented by Hemingway's own reminiscences of his days in Paris, *A Moveable Feast* (1964), and A. E. Hotchner's *Papa Hemingway: A Personal Memoir* (1966).

Philip Young's *Ernest Hemingway* (1952) and Carlos Baker's *Hemingway: The Writer as Artist* (1956) are both useful general studies of the fiction. Baker has also edited a collection of essays by various hands, *Hemingway and His Critics* (1961); more essays are included in *Ernest Hemingway: The Man and His Work* (1950), edited by John K. M. McCaffery. Harry Levin's essay, 'Observations on the Style of Ernest Hemingway', in his book *Contexts of Criticism* (1957) mediates intelligently between the extremes of praise and damnation that Hemingway's fiction so often attracted.

Thomas Wolfe

The career of Thomas Wolfe is one of the most extravagant legends in modern American letters; it captured in micro-cosm all the energy and defeat of that 'Lost Generation' of writers to which he belonged. Born and brought up in Asheville, North Carolina, Wolfe gained his first real taste of the intellectual life as a graduate student at Harvard. His first novel, *Look Homeward, Angel* (1929), was immediately acclaimed by Hemingway, Scott Fitzgerald and Sinclair Lewis. (He repaid the last kindness by caricaturing Lewis as Lloyd McHarg in *You Can't Go Home Again*.) After this success Wolfe threw himself into the role of Great American Writer with relish. He travelled widely in Europe, enjoyed a much-publicized love affair with the stage designer Aileen Bernstein, became an increasingly heavy drinker, and continued to pour out a ceaseless stream of writing. His second novel, the gargantuan *Of Time and the River*, was published in 1935. Where Scott Fitzgerald was the gilded youth of the age, Wolfe was its boy genius – exuberant, egocentric and unflinchingly confident of his talents. After his early death in 1938, two further novels were assembled from his manuscripts: *The Web and the Rock* (1939) and *You Can't Go Home Again* (1940).

'All serious work is autobiographical,' Wolfe pronounced in the preface to *Look Homeward, Angel*. The general proposition is dubious but its relevance to Wolfe's own case is beyond dispute. His novels constitute a minute and voluminous spiritual diary, charting his odyssey from Asheville to Harvard to Europe. This is recorded in a flamboyant declamatory style which Maxwell Geismar has called 'a kind of syllabic Mississippi, the Wolfian phrases flowing and boiling every which way, often beautiful, often penetrating, and like the Mississippi too, often stagnant'. Anxious to recount every detail of his life and always eager for rhetorical effect, Wolfe almost entirely neglects form and structure. All his novels were heavily edited – the first two by Maxwell Perkins, the last by Edward C. Aswell – but they still remain bulky, shapeless and undisciplined.

It is these defects that have been responsible for the rapid decline in Wolfe's reputation since his death. In his influential *Love and Death in the American Novel* (1950) Leslie Fiedler declared that: 'Wolfe's work finds its place . . . not even in the children's library . . . but in the high school department, on the shelf of masturbatory dreams.' Yet such criticism is as exaggerated as the earlier adulation of Wolfe's fiction. For all his egocentricity Wolfe was a relentlessly curious and accurate observer of the world around him: the details of American life are recorded in tones that vary from loving relish to biting satire. 'His aim,' suggested the critic John Peale Bishop, 'was to set down America as far as it can belong to the experience of one man.' Despite the formlessness of his individual novels, his total *oeuvre* forms a moving and quintessentially American saga: it is, as Walter Allen notes in *Tradition and Dream* (1964), an unfulfilled pilgrimage which is at once flight and search. Wolfe's heroes, Eugene Gant and George Webber, continually flee the confines of their present existence in pursuit of new horizons, new experiences. Yet the end of their quest is unattainable: like their creator they are left nostalgically yearning for an ideal security and stability that is forever eluding them. Indeed, Wolfe had already written his own epitaph when he exclaimed in his first novel: 'O God! O God! We have been an exile in another land and a stranger in our own.'

Look Homeward, Angel

SUMMARY Shortly after the end of the Civil War Oliver Gant, a stonemason, settles in Altamont, North Carolina. He is an impulsive man, given to extravagant rhetoric and brooding melancholy. Soon after his arrival he marries Eliza Pentland, the shrewd daughter of a powerful local family. The Gants have many children – Steve, Daisy, Helen, Grover, Ben and Luke – but over the years they come to hate each other. Gant becomes an increasingly violent alcoholic: he is only narrowly prevented from attacking Eliza the night before their last child, Eugene, is born.

When Eugene is still young his mother takes him and the other children to Tennessee, where she hopes the family might settle. Grover dies during the visit and Eliza returns grief-stricken to Altamont. Gant has sunk deeper into alcoholism; only Helen can handle him during his drunken rages. Eugene grows up a quiet and bookish child, set apart from the other boys at the village school. In his spare time he is sent out delivering papers under the direction of Luke, a nervous but businesslike young man. Eugene resents the job, but only his brother Ben is sensitive enough to notice this and remonstrates with his parents.

In the face of Gant's opposition Eliza buys a building, Dixieland, on the edge of town and turns it into a boarding house. Now at the high school, Eugene has turned into a shy, physically awkward youth given to dreaming and introspection. An essay competition brings his literary talents to the attention of the headmaster and Eugene is transferred to a private school where he can receive special tuition. The teacher Mr Leonard is a dull pedantic man, but his wife Margaret Leonard becomes Eugene's intellectual mentor, suggesting books for him to read and encouraging him in his literary ambitions.

Eugene's home life continues to be unhappy and chaotic. His older brother Steve, recently married to a rich woman, has developed into an unpleasant and quarrelsome drunk. Helen earns her living as a variety singer touring the Southern circuits. Luke is studying to be an electrical engineer, though his real talents lie in business and salesmanship. Now old and ill, Gant has grown more melancholy and embittered than ever.

Eugene is sent back to work delivering newspapers. Although he still hates the job, he is fascinated by the 'niggertown' area where he works. One day he almost sleeps with a black prostitute, but his courage fails him. At the outbreak of the First World War he is transported by heroic fervour, dreaming of dying gallantly on the battlefield. During a visit to Charlestown he has his first love affair with a waitress named Louise. Helen marries Hugh Barton, the son of a genteel local family, but continues her close relationship with her father.

Eugene has dreamt of going to Harvard but his parents insist on sending him to the State University. During his first year he does little work and furthers his sexual initiation by a visit to a local brothel. This experience makes him guilty and scared that he has venereal disease, but he is reassured by his brother Ben and the local doctor, McGuire. During his vacation at Dixieland he falls passionately in love with Laura James, an older girl staying in the boarding house. But soon after Laura returns to her home in Virginia Eugene hears that she has married another man. He is distracted by grief and enraged at the way his mother and the boarders mock his disappointed love. Only Ben comforts him. In an attempt to forget about Laura, Eugene has a brief affair with Miss Brown, another of his mother's boarders.

The atmosphere at the university is overshadowed by the war. During his next holiday at home he gets helplessly drunk for the first time in his life. The rest of the family, scared that he will become an alcoholic like his father and Steve, nag him endlessly. At last Eugene rebels, denouncing the way his family have always made him feel an outsider. He decides to go to Virginia in the faint hope of seeing Laura again. He spends several miserable months there, working as a labourer and living in terrible poverty.

Shortly after he returns to university he is summoned home by the news that Ben is dying of pneumonia. His brother's death upsets him deeply, for Ben was the only member of his family to whom he felt any real attachment. At college he does well academically, earning a reputation as an eccentric genius. When they attend his graduation ceremony Gant and Eliza are proud to hear the way their son is praised by his teachers. On his return home Eugene finds the atmosphere almost unbearably oppressive: his father, tended by Helen, grows more and more ill while his mother is increasingly absorbed in her property investments. At last he persuades his mother to give him the money to go to Harvard as a graduate student; he sets out confident and hungry for new experience.

CRITICAL COMMENTARY It is by now a well-established axiom of criticism that most first novels are, to a greater or lesser degree, autobiographical in impulse. The apprentice novelist almost inevitably turns to his own experience for inspiration: he has much about himself and his past that he needs to express and assimilate before he can approach other subjects with a more detached eye. In this respect *Look Homeward, Angel* belongs to a familiar type of modern novel: it is yet another *Bildungsroman* or 'portrait of the artist as a young man'.

What does make *Look Homeward, Angel* unusual is the exact and literal nature of its autobiography. It records the early life of Thomas Wolfe in minute detail, from his childhood in Asheville through his years at the University of North

Carolina to the eve of his departure to become a graduate student at Harvard. Only the smallest concessions are made to the conventions of fiction. Asheville becomes 'Altamont', Chapel Hill becomes 'Pulpit Hill' and so forth. In fact, Wolfe did not even trouble to alter the real-life names of some of his minor characters.

The tendency of recent criticism has been to dwell on the disadvantages of this method, to view it as evidence of overweening arrogance and undisciplined romanticism. But the reader who approaches Wolfe with an impartial mind is likely to be struck first by the advantages of this reliance on personal experience. It gives the novel the quality of vivid reportage. Here, for example, is a fairly typical passage describing the domestic routine of the Gant family:

> By breakfast, save for sporadic laments, Gant was in something approaching good humour. They fed hugely: he stoked their plates for them with great slabs of fried steak, grits fried in egg, hot biscuits, jam, fried apples. He departed for his shop about the time the boys, their throats still convulsively swallowing hot food and coffee, rushed from the house at the warning signal of the mellow-tolling final nine-o'clock school bell.

It is obviously no coincidence that Eugene Gant, the hero of the book, should later express a preference for the physical gusto of eighteenth-century fiction over the sentimental pieties of the Victorian novel.

Wolfe's gift for capturing the immediacy of experience is not limited to such cosy scenes. The account of Ben Gant's death, for example, is handled with savage and merciless accuracy; the critic Walter Allen has suggested that Wolfe's greatest strength is 'his ability to face the horror and the evil of life and to render it without flinching, stoically to accept it even though it is "inexplicable".' Wolfe also shows himself to be an expert in the minutiae of American smalltown life. He turns this skill to satiric purposes in the description of the local high school's ludicrous 'Shakespearean pageant'. This, of course, is the element in Wolfe's work that so impressed Sinclair Lewis, that other literary expert on small-town America. (With his love of mimicry, Lewis also appreciated those passages where Wolfe parodies the cheap fiction on which the young Eugene's literary taste is nourished.)

Yet these are local effects and a 500-page novel cannot simply be built on local effects. It needs an over-arching theme and a selective use of imagination and reminiscence. It is here, as so many recent critics have pointed out, that Wolfe fails. At one point he remarks that Eugene Gant loved exams because of 'the delight of emptying out abundantly on paper his stored knowledge'. Unfortunately Wolfe approached fiction in the same spirit. Everything that happened to Thomas Wolfe is poured out in endless detail in the belief that it must be important simply because it happened to Thomas Wolfe.

The effect is not merely repetitive but also curiously adolescent. Eugene's revulsion from Altamont and his desire to escape into a better world are made credible enough. Yet the reader is asked to accept them not as the predictable reactions of a sensitive adolescent, but as the stirrings of a genius who represents the spirit of the race. Beneath all the flamboyant rhetoric Wolfe is inarticulate: his hero's yearnings remain vague and ill-defined. Indeed Wolfe himself is uneasily aware of this deficiency. As Eugene is about to set out on his quest at the end of the novel there is a momentary glimpse of his final bafflement and failure: 'And then the voyages, the search for the happy land. In his moment of terrible vision he saw, in the tortuous ways of a thousand alien places, his foiled quest of himself.'

FURTHER READING Inevitably, the story of Thomas Wolfe's life has been written many times: the most reliable account is by Andrew Turnbull (1968). Other useful biographical material can be found in J. S. Terry's *Thomas Wolfe's Letters to his Mother* (1948) and Elizabeth Nowell's *The Letters of Thomas Wolfe* (1956; abridged edition by Daniel George, 1958). *The Portable Thomas Wolfe* (1950) contains an excellent introduction by Maxwell Geismar; the relevant sections of Alfred Kazin's *On Native Grounds* (1942) and Walter Allen's *Tradition and Dream* (1964) also contain useful general discussions. The English novelist Pamela Hansford Johnson has written a full-length study of Wolfe (1948).

John Dos Passos

In *Exile's Return* (1961) his friend Malcolm Cowley paid tribute to Dos Passos as 'the greatest traveller in a generation of ambulant writers'. Born in 1896, the son of a Chicago lawyer and the grandson of a Portuguese immigrant, Dos Passos was already familiar with Europe before he entered the exclusive Choate School and then, in 1912, Harvard University. After leaving Harvard he studied architecture in Spain, enlisting in the French ambulance brigade when America entered the First World War. One of his colleagues in the brigade was the poet e e cummings. After 1918 Dos Passos remained in Paris, working as a journalist and mingling with the usual crowd of expatriate artists and demobbed soldiers.

Apart from a graceful travel book about Spain, *Rosinante to the Road Again* (1922), Dos Passos' early work was unpromising. His first novel, *One Man's Initiation . . . 1917* (1920), shows a dilletante-ish outlook, no doubt encouraged by the atmosphere of pre-war Harvard, while his second novel, *Three Soldiers* (1921), flirts unsuccessfully with social realism. *Three Soldiers*, however, did bring Dos Passos' name to the attention of the literary world: in 1922 the fashionable magazine *Vanity Fair*, implicitly preferring the novel to Scott Fitzgerald's *This Side of Paradise*, described it as 'probably the most substantial work yet produced by the younger generation'.

Dos Passos' distinctive style and preoccupations emerged in his fourth novel, *Manhattan Transfer* (1925). The book is an elaborate experiment in realism, attempting to capture the variety of life in New York through a series of multiple narratives. Its brutal realism caused *Manhattan Transfer* to be denounced as 'an explosion in a cesspool' by the influential elder generation critic Paul Elmer More, but the novel was praised by Sinclair Lewis, the literary lion of the early 1920s, in a review, 'Manhattan at Last!' published in the *Saturday Review of Literature*.

The technique of *Manhattan Transfer* recurs in *The 42nd Parallel* (1930), *Nineteen Nineteen* (1932) and *The Big Money* (1936). When these were collected as *USA* in 1937 they could be seen as an attempt to give a panoramic portrait of American life from the turn of the century to the beginning of the 1920s. After *USA*, his most substantial claim to recognition, Dos Passos' work declined in quality though not in quantity. Of his later fiction the trilogy *District of Columbia* (1952) is interesting for the predictable shift from youthful radicalism to middle-aged conservatism that it shows. Dos Passos died in 1970.

Dos Passos' later decline has done much to obscure the real importance of *Manhattan Transfer* and *USA*. Once exciting and controversial, they are now more likely to be read out of a sense of historical obligation than real interest. Because they have influenced so few later novelists, Dos Passos' experiments with narrative technique may seem 'something of a museum piece' (as Geoffrey Moore remarks in his anthology, *American Literature* [1964]). Dos Passos' machine-like prose and his concentration on masses rather than individuals may seem curiously heartless: Edmund Wilson has charged that 'his disapproval of capitalistic society becomes a distaste for all the human beings who compose it.' For all this, Dos Passos' best work still comes to life for the modern reader. *USA*, in particular, remains one of the most illuminating comments on its era, and a grand reminder of the possibilities of the American novel. In *On Native Grounds* (1942) Alfred Kazin paid the novel a sensible and judicious tribute; it is, he suggests, 'a national epic, the first great national epic of its kind in the modern American novel'.

USA

Trilogy consisting of *The 42nd Parallel, Nineteen Nineteen, The Big Money*

SUMMARY Part One: *The 42nd Parallel* Fainy McCreary (Mac) grows up in the poor section of a large American city at the turn of the century. His mother dies when he is young, and soon afterwards his father loses his job. Mac's Uncle Tim takes him, his sister Milly and his father to Chicago. After leaving school Mac works in his uncle's printing business. But Tim is a radical and his support of a local strike loses him so much custom that he goes bankrupt.

Mac gets a job selling books on commission for Doc Bingham, a colourful trickster who pretends to be a pious gentleman. They travel to Michigan together selling books on the way, but are soon separated. Mac meets Ike, an affable young hobo. Ike is a socialist, convinced that the free institutions on which America was founded have been undermined by big business interests. The two young men strike up a firm friendship and travel around America together, riding illegally on goods trains, taking temporary jobs and spending their money on girls. After they have been accidentally separated Mac goes to San Francisco and settles down as a printer. He falls in love with Maisie but they quarrel when she learns about Mac's socialist convictions. Maisie is furious when Mac gives up his job to go and help a miners' strike in Nevada.

During the strike Mac joins a friend, Fred Hoff, in printing a newspaper for the workers. However, he soon gets a letter from Maisie saying that she is pregnant. After some hesitation Mac returns and marries her. They settle down in San Francisco and then in Los Angeles. A daughter Rose is born. Mac feels tied down by responsibilities and increasingly guilty about abandoning political activity. After prolonged quarrelling with Maisie he runs off to join the Mexican revolution.

Janey is brought up in Georgetown. During her childhood she hates her father and worships her older brother Joe. In adolescence she falls in love with Joe's friend Alec and is heartbroken when he is killed in a motorcycle accident. After leaving school Janey goes out to work as a stenographer and becomes friendly with Jerry Burnham, an attractive but dissolute young man who works in the same office. When she visits her dying father she realizes how much she still loves him despite her youthful resentments. Soon afterwards Jerry tries to seduce her but because of her strict upbringing Janey resists his advances. She does feel great affection for him, however, and is sad when he goes to Europe as a foreign correspondent at the outbreak of the First World War. Her brother Joe, now a sailor, comes to visit her and she is disturbed to find that he seems coarse and uneducated. Janey herself is growing more sophisticated and less scared of men.

J. Ward Moorehouse is born in Delaware. Although he does well at school, his family is not rich enough to send him to university. He goes to work for an estate agent and is soon offered a good job in Ocean City. There Moorehouse meets a fashionable society girl, Annabelle Strang, and falls in love with her. When she discovers that she is pregnant, they get married. But even during the honeymoon Moorehouse is disturbed to see Annabelle flirting with other men. He soon has concrete evidence of her infidelity and leaves her. He moves to Pittsburgh, full of ambitions for starting his career anew and becoming a big businessman.

Eleanor Stoddard comes from a poor section of Chicago, but from an early age she reacts against the coarseness of her background. When she is visiting the local art gallery one day she meets Eveline Hutchins, and the two soon become firm friends. They mix in Bohemian circles and Eleanor becomes less prudish than she had been as an adolescent. The two young women decide to open an interior decorating business together. It does well and they are soon invited to New York to design the scenery for a Broadway play.

At this time J. Ward Moorehouse is leading a depressing life as a reporter in Pittsburgh; the work is poorly paid and he has few friends. By chance, however, he is offered a new position in the advertising department of a local metal firm. He works desperately hard, still hoping that he will one day be an important businessman. Gertrude Staple, a rich man's daughter, falls in love with him but her parents disapprove. The couple cannot marry until after the death of Gertrude's father. Moorehouse is already beginning to succeed in business and Gertrude's inherited money helps him further. He decides to start a public relations agency specializing in the relations between employers and employees.

Eleanor Stoddard is swept off her feet by New York and decides to settle there. She soon gets a commission to decorate Moorehouse's new house in New York. They like each other and strike up a platonic friendship. At the same time Janey also encounters Moorehouse: she is hired as his secretary and is soon devoted to him.

In Mexico Mac enjoys a happy-go-lucky life. He has a mistress, Concha, and spends his days drinking with other American expatriates. George Barrow, a labour leader who is also an associate of Moorehouse, visits Mexico and Mac shows him the sights of the city. In the evening they get drunk and visit a brothel. Soon afterwards, Mac is able to buy a small bookshop. When Zapata's revolution begins Mac at first joins in the general panic and sells the shop; he even plans to desert Concha and flee to America. But on second thoughts he decides to remain.

In New York Janey continues to enjoy working for Moorehouse; in fact, she is unconsciously falling in love with him. She lives in the suburbs with Gladys Compton, a young Jewish girl who also works for Moorehouse, but later moves into the city and associates with a more Bohemian crowd. She is jealous of her employer's close friendship with Eleanor Stoddard. One day Mrs Moorehouse storms into the office and accuses her husband of adultery with Eleanor. When Janey's brother Joe returns from sea to visit her, she is again struck by his coarse manners; indeed, she is even ashamed to introduce him to her friends. Just after Joe's departure America's entry into the First World War is announced.

Moorehouse and his circle are transported with patriotic fervour; Eleanor even resolves to go to Europe with the Red Cross.

Charley Anderson's mother keeps a cheap boarding house in a small North Dakota town and brings her son up according to the strictest religious principles. But Charley gets a taste of a freer way of life one summer when he works at a garage in a nearby city with his older brother Jim. On his return home he finds small-town life boring and heads back to the city, working in a fairground and leading a carefree existence. He falls in love with Emiscah but is frustrated when she refuses to sleep with him. He soon discovers that she has been sleeping with his best friend, Ed, and is pregnant by him. At first Charley agrees to marry her; but after she has an abortion he changes his mind and deserts her. Soon after moving to Chicago Charley becomes interested in the trade union movement. He is arrested at a union meeting and loses his job as a result. As the rumours that America will enter the war grow, Charley tramps around the country doing casual labouring jobs. When America's entry is finally announced Charley is in New York; he immediately joins the ambulance brigade.

SUMMARY Part Two: *Nineteen Nineteen* Joe Williams* deserts in disgust from the navy and signs up on a merchant ship bound for England. Because he has no passport he is temporarily interned on his arrival at Liverpool. Once released, he tours the city on a drunken spree with his shipmates; they are arrested and shipped back to America. In New York Joe becomes involved with Della, a respectable and conventional girl, and begins for the first time in his life to think about settling down. But he cannot find work on shore and is forced to sign up for another voyage. During a brief stop in Washington he sees his sister Janey* and is awed by her newly acquired sophistication. When his ship's tour of French ports is complete, Joe hurries back to New York and

---

* Denotes that the character has appeared in a previous part of the trilogy.

marries Della. But he sets off to sea again almost immediately after the wedding.

Richard Ellsworth Savage comes from a genteel background, but has a poor and unhappy childhood after his father deserts the family. At Harvard University he dreams of being a writer and publishes poems in undergraduate magazines. At the outbreak of the First World War he enlists in the ambulance brigade and is sent to France.

Eveline Hutchins* comes from a solidly respectable Chicago family. Passionately interested in art from an early age, she enlists at the local art school. However, she finds life in Chicago boring until she chances to meet Eleanor Stoddard,* who shares her artistic tastes. On her way back from a trip to Europe Eveline begins a romance with Dirk McArthur which continues in Chicago until her parents find out; they take her away to Santa Fé for a holiday. She returns to discover that Dirk, whom she once thought glamorous and daring, now seems just a drunken and cynical rake. Eveline and Eleanor open an interior decorating business together and are invited to New York to design the scenery for a play. However, Eveline is soon summoned home to tend her sick father. She goes with him to Santa Fé and has an affair with a local artist, Jose O'Riely. Back in New York again, she is soon involved in another romance, this time with Don Stevens, a young radical who is bitterly opposed to America's entry into the war. Eveline herself is intensely patriotic and welcomes the chance to go to Paris and work in a new branch of Eleanor's business. She finds life in the wartorn city, with its continual air raids, exciting as well as scaring.

Joe Williams is in Bordeaux when America enters the war. He tries to return home to Della, but after a series of setbacks and distractions arrives to find that she is being unfaithful to him. He leaves her immediately and goes to see Janey, who is in New York. Joe finds his sister's cool reception of him disappointing and does not even mention his marriage.

Richard Ellsworth Savage, in France with the ambulance brigade, has mixed attitudes to the war. His own life is

pleasant enough – he is glad of the opportunity to see foreign
countries – but he is more and more disillusioned about the
cause for which the war is being fought. He is posted to
Italy and immediately falls in love with its beautiful landscape and its antiquities. His superior officers find out about
his pacifist views, however, and Richard is sent back to
America in disgrace.

Eveline is now sharing a flat in Paris with Eleanor. She
has made friends with Jerry Burnham,* who is deeply discontented with his work as foreign correspondent. J. W.
Moorehouse* visits Paris to boost the morale of the Red
Cross workers and Eleanor is tremendously excited to see
him again. Eveline, however, does not like Moorehouse and
this adds to a growing estrangement between the two young
women. Eveline finally moves into a flat of her own.

Joe Williams is now down and out in New York. He gets
a job on a boat bound for France and Spain. The war hardly
affects his life and he continues his usual round of hard
unrewarding labour punctuated by bouts of drinking and
whoring. On Armistice Day he is in St Nazaire. During the
drunken celebrations Joe is killed in a fight with a French
officer.

Anne Elizabeth Trent (nicknamed 'Daughter') grows up
in a prosperous family living in Dallas; but when she goes
to a Pennsylvanian finishing school the other girls mock her
Southern accent and manners. She runs away, refuses to
return and insists on being allowed to go to New York. She
arrives there excited and scared, to be greeted by Ada
Washburn, a friend from Dallas. Anne Elizabeth finds the
city a lonely and depressing place until she meets Edwin
Vinal, a young intellectual involved in radical politics.
Despite her Southern conservatism she is attracted to Edwin
and they become engaged. His opposition to her plans of
being a journalist estrange them and Anne Elizabeth begins
to flirt with another young radical, the fiery and dissolute
Webb Cruthers. She joins in his political activities more out
of a love of adventure than because of any ideological conviction. When she is arrested in a demonstration it takes

all her family's influence to get her out of trouble. The out-break of war again excites her adventurous spirit and she applies to be sent abroad with the Red Cross. But her young brother, recently enrolled in the Air Force, is killed during a training flight and Anne Elizabeth is forced to stay at home and comfort her parents. To their annoyance she insists on going to do relief work in France at the end of the war.

The armistice overjoys Eveline Hutchins, who now lives alone in Paris. J. W. Moorehouse is also in the city and Eveline finds her initial dislike of him yielding to uncon-fessed attraction. When he returns from the front line Jerry Burnham, Eveline's former lover, is jealous of her relation-ship with Moorehouse. Although Eveline and Eleanor now usually see little of each other they decide to take a holiday together at Nice. After Eleanor has returned to Paris, Moorehouse arrives and his tentative romance with Eveline begins to blossom. But soon after arriving back in Paris Eveline learns that Eleanor is sleeping with Moorehouse. The discovery confuses and upsets her, projecting her into a brief affair with Paul Johnson, an innocent young American soldier. Eveline discovers that she is pregnant.

After returning to America in disgrace, Richard Ellsworth Savage is drafted into the Army and sent back again to France. At first he is more doubtful than ever about the war, but he gradually adjusts to life in his regiment and earns the respect of his fellow-officers. He encounters Moorehouse and Eleanor Stoddard in Paris at the time of the armistice. Army work takes him to Rome, where he meets Anne Elizabeth Trent. Their brief affair is interrupted by Richard's return to Paris. Moorehouse and his circle have been impressed by him and offer him a job. Richard's happiness at finding so comfortable a niche in life is qualified when Anne Elizabeth arrives in Paris, pregnant and pleading that he marry her. Richard refuses. Anne Elizabeth becomes reckless with desperation and, after meeting a drunken French pilot in a bar, challenges him to take her up in his plane. The Frenchman is drunk enough to accept but too drunk to fly properly: they crash and are killed.

Ben Compton comes from a poor Jewish family in Brooklyn. He works hard and does well at school. Originally he dreams of becoming a rich businessman, but he soon is converted to radicalism and decides to devote his life to political agitation. His views appall his parents and Ben goes to live with a fellow radical, Helen Mauer. He gets a reputation as a brilliant speaker and leader; this earns him a six-month jail sentence. On his release he studies law, hoping that this skill can be used in the service of socialism. When war is declared he registers as a conscientious objector. He is sentenced to twenty years in prison for his radical activities but is released on appeal. Just after the armistice has been signed Ben's appeal is rejected; he goes to prison.

In Paris Richard Ellsworth Savage is recovering from the shock of Anne Elizabeth's death and adjusting to his job with J. W. Moorehouse. Eleanor, with whom he is increasingly friendly, insists that he attend her reception party for the newly-wed Eveline and Paul Johnson. It is an embarrassing occasion because the couple are clearly unhappy together. Richard leaves early, reflecting with pleasure on the new affluence that allows him to take taxis.

SUMMARY Part Three: *The Big Money* At the end of the First World War Lieutenant Charley Anderson* sails back to America on the same boat as Eveline* and Paul Johnson.* Charley is effusively greeted as a returning hero by his family in Minnesota but soon quarrels with his older brother Jim.* Their relations reach snapping point when Charley refuses to join Jim in his car sales business. After his mother's death Charley leaves for New York, anxious to start in the aviation business and make a fortune. The city, however, has few jobs and Charley is soon dispirited. His only friends are the Johnsons; he begins a tentative affair with Eveline. After doing various sorts of menial labour, Charley meets his old wartime friend Joe Askew and they start an aeroplane factory together.

Mary French grows up admiring but seeing very little of her father, a hard-working doctor in a poor mining district.

Mary's mother, who continually criticizes Dr French as a failure, insists that the family move to the fashionable Colorado Springs. While Mary is at Vassar College she hears that her parents have got divorced. Her own life shows an increasing political commitment, stirred by the First World War and strengthened by the speeches of George Barrow,* the labour leader. On a visit to Colorado Springs Mary finds her father desperately overworked and drinking heavily; he dies in a 'flu epidemic. Anxious to tackle social problems, Mary leaves Vassar and becomes a social worker. She finds this unsatisfactory and moves to Pittsburgh in an attempt to see how the poor of America really live.

She gets a job as a newspaper reporter but is sacked by the right-wing editor, Mr Healy, when she writes a sympathetic account of a local steel strike. She goes to work for the union and is soon entirely committed to its cause. She becomes deeply depressed when her friend Gus is sent to jail for radical activities; so she leaves Pittsburgh and takes a job as George Barrow's secretary in Washington. The lonely middle-aged unionist flirts with her and they begin a casual affair. But Mary soon becomes disenchanted with Barrow, finding his politics too conservative; they quarrel and part. Living in New York with her friend Ada Cohn, Mary discovers that she is pregnant. Barrow wants to marry her, but Mary refuses and has an abortion.

Margo Dowling's father is a drunkard whose progressive deterioration makes her childhood unhappy. When Mr Dowling deserts his family Margo's stepmother Agnes takes her to New York. Margo leads a cheerless life until Agnes becomes the mistress of Frank Mandeville, a vaudeville actor. Margo adulates Frank and loves the theatrical world. Soon, however, Frank begins to fail in his career; he drinks heavily and even sexually assaults Margo. To escape her home Margo elopes with a young Cuban boy, Tony, to Havana.

Charley Anderson's and Joe Askew's aircraft business is beginning to succeed. But Charley's personal life is unhappy. He is jilted by Doris Humphries, a flighty young socialite, and begins to drink heavily. At last in an attempt to start his career anew, he accepts an offer of a job with a firm in Detroit.

Margo has a miserable time in Havana, neglected by her husband and despised by his relatives. The discovery that she is pregnant makes her feel completely trapped; but the baby is born blind and dies after a few days. There is now nothing to keep her in Havana, so she deserts Tony and returns to live in New York with Agnes and Frank. Soon she begins to succeed as a vaudeville actress, shrewdly cultivating the attentions of Jerry Herman, the casting director, and Tad Whittlesea, a rich young admirer. She goes on a yachting trip with Tad and his friends. But when the boat is moored off Jacksonville Margo meets Tony in a local bar; he looks depressed and has become overtly homosexual in his manners. He insists on talking to Margo and scares off her companions. She stays behind in Jacksonville to tend Tony when he falls ill. But as soon as he is well again Tony runs off with all her money, leaving her stranded.

In Detroit Charley Anderson flirts with the boss's daughter but soon transfers his attentions to the equally rich Gladys Wheatley. They marry and move into an expensive new house built for them by Gladys' father. But Charley is soon unhappy and unsettled again. He crashes on a practice flight with his old friend Bill Cernak; Bill is killed and Charley spends several months in hospital. He comes out in a state of depression and is advised to take a holiday in Florida. There he meets Margo Dowling and takes her to Miami, where she gets a job in a night club. He returns to New York and leads a dissolute life: gambling on the stock exchange, drinking heavily and sleeping with prostitutes. Gladys divorces him.

Margo returns to New York and begins to see Charley regularly. She allows him to win money for her on the stock market and cautiously builds up a comfortable bank balance. Her regular income comes from working as a model in a fashionable shop. A young photographer Sam Margolies sees her and is impressed by her looks. Tony turns up again, this time addicted to drugs. Margo borrows money from Charley to send her husband for a cure. Charley takes Margo down to Florida for a holiday. But instead of resting quietly he drinks even more. One night he crashes his car into a railway crossing and dies several days later in hospital.

Agnes arrives to console Margo but finds her as cool and self-possessed as ever. She is being advised in her financial affairs by the powerful Judge Homer Cassidy. Tony, temporarily cured of his drug addiction, joins them and helps run the expensive house that Margo has inherited from Charley. The trio drive to Los Angeles, hoping to make their fortune in films. Only Margo, however, gets jobs and these are only very small parts. At last she meets Sam Margolies, now a motion picture magnate. He turns her into one of his big stars and proposes to her. When the troublesome Tony is killed in a bar-room brawl Margo is free to accept Margolies' offer.

Mary French works as a radical agitator in New York. When Ben Compton,* a young Jewish radical, is released from prison she puts him up at her flat. They fall in love, but his intense and narrow dedication to his political work estranges them. Mary goes to Boston to help the defence in the Sacco-Vanzetti case and meets Jerry Burnham,* a drunken and cynical journalist covering the trial for his newspaper.

Richard Ellsworth Savage* works hard in the advertising firm opened by the tycoon J. W. Moorehouse* at the end of the war. Richard is friendly with Eveline Johnson, who is now in the process of divorcing her husband Paul. Together they attend a party to celebrate the engagement of Eleanor Stoddard,* now a successful designer, to an exiled Russian prince. Although he is depressed at still being a bachelor and has taken to drinking heavily, Richard is good at his work. He lands an important contract for the firm and takes over the business when Moorehouse falls ill. Once unsettled, with radical views and literary ambitions, Richard has become a model businessman.

Mary French, back in New York working in support of a

miners' strike, has an affair with the radical leader Don Stevens.* Her mother has remarried but Mary finds her stepfather pompous and hypocritical. Mary is desperately overworked and, when Don Stevens jilts her, she has a nervous breakdown. On her recovery she goes to a party given by Eveline Johnson, where she meets George Barrow again and glimpses Margo Dowling, now a famous film star. Although she is still tense and overtired Mary insists on returning to work the next day. At the office she learns that a fellow-radical has been killed by the police, and that Eveline Johnson committed suicide during the night. Mary grimly goes on with her work.

CRITICAL COMMENTARY The books which compose *USA* originally appeared as separate novels: *The 42nd Parallel* in 1930, *Nineteen Nineteen* in 1932, and *The Big Money* in 1936. Only in 1937 were they published together under a joint title. Yet the claim that they comprise one book is not a publisher's convenience or a writer's afterthought; the unity of *USA* was clearly central to Dos Passos' conception from the start. For all its appearance of sprawling divergence the trilogy is not what Henry James liked to call a 'loose baggy monster'. Its details are carefully controlled; its structure is elaborately planned.

The title provides a clue to the book's unity. Perhaps because their country attained identity and self-awareness so recently, American novelists are continually attracted to the idea of achieving a distinctively 'American' note in their writing, or tackling a distinctively 'American' subject. Their titles often encourage the reader to view their books as comments on the culture that produced them: Dreiser labelled the life and death of Clyde Griffiths *An American Tragedy*, while Norman Mailer called one of his recent novels *An American Dream*. Dos Passos' choice of *USA* as the title of his trilogy implies the same claim, though in an even more ambitious form. The book is intended as nothing less than a history of the American people from the turn of the century to the 1920s. While obviously not a history book in the scholarly and technical sense, it takes history as its subject in the same way that the novels of Tolstoy or George Eliot or Stendhal do. This, Dos Passos claims, is how international and national events impressed themselves on individual lives and characters; this is what history seemed like to those who lived through it. As Alfred Kazin has suggested, *USA* is a 'national epic', whose real hero is not this or that particular person but a larger abstract concept: America, or even History itself.

Dos Passos' choice of the years 1900–1920 is significant. At the time he wrote, this was neither the distant past nor the immediate present: it was the era in which he himself had grown up and which had formed his own sense of how the world worked. So he was at once conveniently distanced from, and involved in his subject, a fertile position for the artist to occupy. The first volume, *The 42nd Parallel*, deals with the years immediately preceding the First World War. It shows a secure middle class enjoying an Edwardian elegance and luxury, and a working class at last beginning to protest its deprivations. The second volume, *Nineteen Nineteen*, examines the war and its aftermath (though the battleground itself is never actually described). The mood alternates between patriotic fervour and political turmoil, public glory and inner confusion. The financial boom of *The Big Money* smashes the hopes of radical agitators. Yet by the end of the book the business world is already showing those cracks which led to the Depression, while its hectic and desperate pace exacts an intolerable personal price from its members.

Once the scope and purpose of *USA* is grasped, its otherwise bewildering narrative technique becomes comprehensible, and to a large extent justifiable. Carlyle's dictum that 'history is the essence of innumerable biographies' may irritate the historical determinists, but it does indicate the problem confronting the novelist who wants to show history in action. The life of no one individual adequately represents the life of the age: he will be middle-class or working-class, right-wing or left-wing, a businessman or a poet, a success or a failure. The writer must create a large and disparate group of characters, too disparate to be assimilated into conventional notions of plot: many of them would not normally meet each other let alone significantly affect each other's lives. But even this would fail to spell out the precise relations between the individual and history, for few people are close to (or even aware of) the major public events which can mould their lives. The novelist will need to find some more tangible method of recording major historical events.

To tackle these problems Dos Passos uses not one narrative method but several. These are deliberately juxtaposed to create a form of multiple perspective by which the same thing – social trend, historical figure, public event or private life – is seen from differing angles. Out of this process a sense of the corporate life of the age, at once variegated and unified, emerges. The first and simplest narrative device is the 'Newsreel', with which each book and each individual section usually begins. This is a collage of documents about the period, mingled and excerpted to give the reader a sense of the atmosphere of the times. A headline announcing a battle in the First World War is followed by a fragment of a popular song; a passage from a gossip column is followed by an account of a miners' strike. The second device is what Dos Passos calls the 'Camera Eye', short exercises in stream-of-consciousness narration. These are not ordered or objective commentaries, but vivid and immediate re-creations of how a particular event might impinge on the mind of a spectator.

Neither of these devices is entirely successful. The 'Newsreel' sequences, at first a novelty, quickly become repetitive, while the 'Camera Eye' sections always smack too much of the deliberately 'literary' experiment. Much more successful and more vital to the trilogy's real achievement are the short biographies of important historical figures. Dos Passos provides, for example, a succinct summary of the career of Woodrow Wilson, America's President during the First World War and the architect of the Treaty of Versailles.

On other occasions he selects historical figures because they represent important tendencies in the culture. *The 42nd Parallel* implicitly contrasts the careers of Eugene Debs, the radical imprisoned during the war, and Andrew Carnegie, the pious millionaire. The two later books deal with a variety of representative Americans: J. Pierpoint Morgan the banker, Henry Ford the motor car magnate, Thorstein Veblen the philosophical radical, Isadora Duncan the dancer, Rudolph Valentino the matinée idol, Frank Lloyd Wright the architect, and William Randolph Hearst the newspaper owner.

Most of *USA* is taken up by some two dozen fictional narratives, the lives of people like Mac or Eveline Hutchins or Charley Anderson. These are not handled as separate vignettes, each one ending before the next begins, but as parallel stories. The narrative shifts from the life of, say, Richard Ellsworth Savage to Margo Dowling like a tape-recorder shifting between tracks. To start with, the reader is likely to find this device frustrating and confusing. Many of the individual lives seem formless and meandering: Dos Passos' people move aimlessly from bar to bar, city to city, and romance to romance. They disappear from the book in a disconcertingly casual manner. J. Ward Moorehouse, a major character in *The 42nd Parallel*, has been demoted to a minor character by the end of the trilogy; while Joe Williams is suddenly struck down in a bar-room brawl half-way through *Nineteen Nineteen*. Moreover, the lives of the various individuals fail to overlap according to the best traditions of plotting. They meet each other, but rarely to important effect; and the reader never supposes that the conclusion of the story will knit the various threads of their lives into one climactic scene.

Yet by the end of the trilogy a valid and impressive structure has emerged. Dos Passos' choice of people to study is far from random: they are characteristic expressions of life at a particular moment in history. In *The 42nd Parallel* the lives of Mac and J. Ward Moorehouse show respectively the conversion of an itinerant workman into a committed radical and of a poor boy into a business tycoon. *The Big Money* presents typical cases in postwar American culture: the war hero failing to adjust to civilian life (Charley Anderson), the young radical aesthete gradually assimilating the gospel of business (Richard Ellsworth Savage), and a girl from a poor background becoming a Hollywood film star (Margo Dowling). Moreover, the various lives invite comparison and contrast. The cases of Anne Elizabeth Trent, Eveline Hutchins and Mary French show the different ways that sexually liberated women can react to unwanted pregnancies.

Setting out to offer a synoptic view of America, Dos Passos reaches conclusions strikingly similar to those of other 'Lost Generation' writers like Scott Fitzgerald and Hemingway. The keynote of *USA* is disappointment and frustration; as Alfred Kazin has suggested, the trilogy is 'one of the saddest books ever written by an American'. Hemingway and Fitzgerald dealt largely in personal terms, but Dos Passos' language is political. His book is at root a history of the defeat of American radicalism by big business. The commercial attitudes of men like Moorehouse and his protegé Richard Ellsworth Savage finally crush the hopes of radicals like Mac and Mary French almost out of existence. This political concern looks toward the work of later writers like John Steinbeck, but the underlying experiences with which Dos Passos deals are strangely familiar to readers of *The Great Gatsby* or *Fiesta*. Like those novels *USA* is preoccupied with failure: its characters ring the changes of disintegration, from heavy drinking and casual sex to suicide and mental breakdown.

FURTHER READING   It is too early for there to be a standard biography of John Dos Passos. He himself wrote a memoir of his youth, *The Best Times* (1966). This has recently been supplemented by Townsend Ludington's *The Fourteenth Chronicle: Letters and Diaries of John Dos Passos* (1974). The growth of the novelist's political attitudes is traced by Melvin Landsberg in *Dos Passos, Path to 'USA': A Political Biography,*

1912–1936 (1974). Most of the best criticism, however, belongs to the 1930s: Granville Hicks, 'John Dos Passos', *The Bookman* (1932); Bernard De Voto, 'John Dos Passos: Anatomist of Our Time', *The Saturday Review of Literature* (1936); Delmore Schwartz, 'John Dos Passos and the Whole Truth', *Southern Review* (1938). Maxwell Geismar's *Writers in Crisis* (1947) and Alfred Kazin's *On Native Grounds* (1942) also contain useful estimates of Dos Passos' achievement.

6 Moderns and Contemporaries

Modern literature offers both the excitement and the frustration of a journey without maps. The supportive paraphernalia of definitive biographies and major critical books is often missing, and in its absence the student can enjoy the freedom of discovering and judging for himself. But although the literary history of the present age cannot yet be written adequately, the American novelists represented in this section can still be placed in a tentative historical framework.

The two earliest writers considered here, William Faulkner and John Steinbeck, are close in time to the Lost Generation but significantly different in spirit. Faulkner is distinguished from men like Hemingway and Scott Fitzgerald by the idiosyncratic (and sometimes wayward) nature of his own genius. With his deep involvement in Southern culture Faulkner ploughed a brave and rather lonely furrow; his work is now beginning to seem one of the main achievements of twentieth-century fiction. Steinbeck differs from the Lost Generation in a simpler way. Deeply influenced by the Depression, he abandoned wistful romanticism for a gritty naturalism with undercurrents of radical protest; he became, in fact, the heir to that earlier tradition pioneered by Norris and Dreiser.

Critics have often succumbed to the temptation of presenting Faulkner and Steinbeck as opposing models between whom subsequent writers have had to choose. The American novelist, so this argument goes, may write either in the romance tradition epitomized by Faulkner or the realist tradition represented by Steinbeck. There is certainly evidence to support this view. There has been, for example, a whole school of Southern writers using Faulkner's mode of Gothic romance: Paul Bowles, Truman Capote, William Styron and Flannery O'Connor. And one can certainly see the influence of *The Grapes of Wrath* on Norman Mailer's *The Naked and the Dead*. Yet this interpretation simplifies contemporary American fiction to the point of distortion. It leaves a major figure like J. D. Salinger dangling in limbo: what does he owe to either Faulkner or Steinbeck? Is he realist or romancer? And it neglects that increasingly significant group of novelists – Vladimir Nabokov, John Barth, Thomas Pynchon, Kurt Vonnegut Jr – whose playful technical experiments owe as much to foreign influences like Joyce and Borges as they do to native traditions.

One of the most important trends in postwar American fiction has been the emergence of the so-called 'ethnic novel'. In earlier sections of this book the importance of regionalism in American culture has been continually stressed: the differences between a Southerner like Poe and a New Englander like Hawthorne are all-important. In our own time ethnic distinctions have come to occupy the place formerly taken by regionalism. This was first apparent with the growth of a substantial group of American Jewish novelists: Saul Bellow, Herbert Gold, Bernard Malamud and more recently, Philip Roth. For all their obvious personal differences, these men have much in common: they write about the anxieties of urban man, alternating between exuberant picaresque comedy and wry sadness. A parallel school of Negro fiction has developed. Just as he has begun to assert a political voice, the American black has developed a literary identity. The seminal book here is Richard Wright's *Native Son* (1940). Ralph Ellison's *Invisible Man* remains the finest achievement of this school, although the novels of James Baldwin also deserve mention. Like the Jewish novelists, black writers concentrate on urban man; but for obvious sociological reasons they sound a deeper and more urgent note of discontent.

In general, as Saul Bellow has noted, 'the tone of complaint prevails.' Jewish anxiety and black discontent can be seen as versions of that sense of alienation so prevalent in the modern literature of most countries. In fact, alienation has been particularly striking and particularly extreme in America, where a succession of historical events – the Depression, the Cold War and the Vietnam War – have combined to isolate the artist from the country to which he supposedly belongs. He feels little kinship with that vast 'silent majority' or 'middle America' which politicians delight in praising. The writer's reaction, of course, can take many forms: he may withdraw into his own private world, engage in active political protest, or simply view his country with wry amusement. But most contemporary fiction is united by a common assumption: no reconciliation or even mediation between the self and society is possible, for the individual can join the community only at the price of spiritual extinction. The typical American heroes – J. D. Salinger's Holden Caulfield, Ralph Ellison's 'invisible man', Saul Bellow's Herzog – remain rebels, oddballs and loners to the end.

William Faulkner

Born into a generation of writers who suffered from a sense of rootlessness and cultivated a polished cosmopolitanism, William Faulkner (1897–1962) is an anomaly. His family ancestry stretches far back into the history of the South; his great-grandfather Colonel William Falkner (as the family name was then spelt) was the author of a popular novel, *The White Rose of Memphis*. After briefly attending the University of Mississippi, Faulkner worked as a bookshop assistant in New York and a journalist in New Orleans, where he became a close friend of the writer Sherwood Anderson. He then returned to Oxford, Mississippi ('my little postage stamp of native soil') and lived there for the rest of his life. This move, made when most intellectuals of his generation were heading for Paris, has almost the air of a defiant gesture: Faulkner had decided to risk being called 'provincial' at a time when the term was a polite synonym for 'hick'.

This sense of local attachment, including as much hatred as involuntary love, is the central inspiration of Faulkner's fiction. As Maxwell Geismar has remarked in *Writers in Crisis* (1947), he 'not merely represents, but is the deep South as no other American novelist may quite claim to be.' Faulkner chronicled the life of Mississippi in much the same spirit that Thomas Hardy chronicled the life of the English West Country, turning Oxford into the fictional 'Jefferson' and inventing 'Yoknapatawpha County'. 'I found out,' he commented, 'that not only each book had to have a design, but the whole output or sum of an artist's work had to have a design.' Characters and places recur from novel to novel until Faulkner's *oeuvre* begins to seem a continuous saga of Southern life: the record of an anguished backwater, peopled by poor white farmers, get-rich-quick politicians, exploited Negro servants and decaying aristocrats haunted by memories of past glory.

Despite this overall unity, Faulkner's novels show significant differences in quality. A consensus of current critical opinion has chosen the years 1929 to 1936 as his best period. He produced five novels that have passed into the repertory of modern classics: *The Sound and the Fury* (1929), *As I Lay Dying* (1930), *Sanctuary* (1931), *Light in August* (1932) and *Absalom, Absalom!* (1936). At the time of their publication these books were received with indifference or hostility. Moralists were repelled by their pessimism and their violence, while literary critics found their technique baffling, obscure and capricious. In the early 1940s, however, the tide of opinion began to turn and today Faulkner is usually regarded as the most important American novelist of this century. His status received formal recognition with the award of the Nobel Prize for Literature in 1950.

It cannot be denied that the newcomer to Faulkner's work will find him an intimidating writer. Dealing with a way of life alien to most readers, Faulkner also chooses to don a bewildering variety of masks: he is by turns the simplest of backwoodsmen, the most anguished of modern intellectuals, the most daring of literary experimentalists and the most traditional of moralists. But although Faulkner's novels demand hard work from the reader they are also richly rewarding. The sense of local attachment is not parochialism but Faulkner's own personal route to fundamental and timeless literary themes. The complex experiments with narrative technique are not mere *tours de force* but legitimate vehicles for complex statements. Faulkner was never a very reliable critic of his own work, but in his Nobel Prize speech he gave an important reminder of his ultimate purpose as a writer. He aimed, he said, to illumine 'the old verities and truths of the heart, the old universal truths lacking which any story is ephemeral and doomed – love and honour and pity and pride and compassion and sacrifice'.

The Sound and the Fury

SUMMARY The Compsons are an aristocratic Southern family, once rich but now decaying and impoverished. The father is an alcoholic, while Mrs Compson becomes more and more querulous in the face of her family's misfortunes. Their daughter Candace (Caddy) becomes pregnant by a local boy and marries a prosperous banker to provide a father for the child; but he soon discovers the truth and divorces her. Meanwhile her brother Quentin, a sensitive young man at Harvard University, commits suicide. Of the remaining children, Benjy is an idiot, gelded after he made a sexual assault on a young girl in the neighbourhood and finally committed to the State asylum, while Jason grows up bitter and neurotic. The final seal is set on Jason's bitterness when his niece, Caddy's daughter Quentin, for whom the family has been caring, steals his savings and elopes with a travelling showman. This story is narrated in four separate sections, each one dealing with the events of a single day and concentrating on a single character.

Benjy's narrative, 7 April 1928: Benjy spends most of his thirty-third birthday being led around by his keeper, the young black servant Luster. They watch golfers playing on ground that once belonged to the Compson family and then wander over the course looking for a lost twenty-five cent piece that Luster had hoped to spend on the travelling show that night. On their way home Benjy sees his niece Quentin playing on the swing with a man. In the family kitchen Dilsey, a family servant, reproves Luster for making Benjy cry by mocking him. Over dinner that evening Benjy watches as Jason and Quentin argue. As he falls asleep he sees someone emerge from Quentin's bedroom window and climb down a tree.

For most of the day Benjy's mind is flooded with confused and fragmentary memories, usually of his own childhood and of his sister Caddy, whom he adores uncritically: 1) One evening near Christmas he insists on waiting out in the cold yard with his keeper Versh for Caddy to come home. 2) He plays near the water with Caddy and her brother Quentin. Caddy gets her clothes wet and takes her dress off to dry. When they arrive home the children are made to eat in the kitchen with the servants and can hear their mother crying in the living room. Later Caddy climbs a tree in the yard to look in the living room window but is caught and scolded by Dilsey. The children learn afterwards that this was the evening of their grandmother's death. 3) Wandering round the yard in the twilight, Benjy surprises Caddy kissing her boyfriend. 4) Benjy is inconsolable when Caddy leaves the house to get married. He breaks out of the yard and chases after some schoolchildren under the impression that Caddy is amongst them. 5) In infancy Benjy's name is changed. He was originally christened Maury after his maternal uncle, but Mrs Compson objects to this when she discovers that her son is mentally defective. 6) Benjy loves fire, and on one occasion burns his hand on the live coals. Mrs Compson is merely annoyed at his crying but Dilsey comforts him. 7) One evening Caddy returns home silent and upset (in fact, she has just lost her virginity). Benjy senses that something is wrong and hurls himself at her crying wildly.

Quentin's narrative, 2 June 1910: On the day of his suicide Quentin is awakened in his Harvard rooms by the ticking of a watch he inherited from his grandfather. He smashes the watch in frustration, cutting his hand in the process. After dressing carefully in his best suit, he packs his possessions and writes letters to his father and his roommate, Shreve. He breakfasts in a leisurely fashion and then goes to an ironmonger's shop to buy two heavy flat-irons. On a streetcar journey through Boston he thinks of his sister Caddy, recently married to Herbert Head. He is deeply disturbed by his sister's sex life and finds both her earlier affair with Dalton Ames and her subsequent marriage to Head distasteful. His own unhappy position at Harvard makes Quentin find ironic the fact that the Compsons sold land rightfully belonging to Benjy to pay the university fees. He meets Deacon, a black who delights in serving Southern students, and gives him the letter for Shreve with instructions that it should not be delivered until the next day.

As he takes another streetcar journey Quentin remembers his painful interview with Herbert, an arrogant and pompous young man whom he resented at first sight. He gets off the streetcar and walks through the countryside until he comes to a small village shop. There he befriends a shy young girl and buys her some buns. The child, apparently lost, follows Quentin around. Finally he is accosted by a posse led by the child's brother, who thinks that Quentin has tried to abduct the girl. He submits to being arrested and is being taken to the marshal's office when he meets a group of friends from Harvard – Shreve, Spoade, Gerald, and Gerald's mother, Mrs Bland. They manage to clear up the misunderstanding and secure Quentin's release. He joins them on a picnic. Soon, however, he is overwhelmed by memories of a humiliating interview with Dalton Ames, when he failed to defend the Compson honour. These thoughts so possess him that he starts a fight when Gerald begins talking loosely about women. Shreve separates the combatants, and Quentin heads back to his Harvard rooms.

He cleans his clothes of the blood spilt during the fight, waits until evening and then goes out to drown himself.

Jason's narrative, 6 April 1928: When he learns that his teenage niece Quentin has been playing truant from school Jason reacts in his usual angry and embittered fashion: he threatens the girl and is only narrowly prevented by Dilsey from whipping her. He drives Quentin to school and then goes on to his own menial job in the town's general shop. There he reads a letter from Caddy which asks what has become of all the cheques sent to Quentin over the years. (In fact Jason has been embezzling the money and now has a substantial hoard hidden away.) During the morning he reflects bitterly on the way his family has failed him: how weak was his drunken father, how the Compsons spent their last money sending Quentin to Harvard, and how Caddy's divorce ruined Jason's chance of a good job in Herbert Head's bank. After his father's funeral Jason had met his sister Caddy secretly and accepted a bribe to arrange a meeting with young Quentin; but Jason cheated his sister.

At lunch Jason talks to his mother about family finances, carefully concealing his own peccadilloes. As he sits in the store that afternoon he sees his niece pass the door with a man from the travelling show. Incensed, he gives chase in his car but fails to find them. He returns more angry than ever, to find that his shares have lost money on the stock market. Back at home that evening he teases Luster by burning two free tickets to the show rather than give them to him. The family eat a sullen meal, with Mrs Compson being querulous and Jason insulting Quentin. After dinner Quentin locks herself in her room to study.

Dilsey's narrative, 8 April 1928: The Compsons' old black servant rouses Luster to get wood for the fire and cooks breakfast for the family. Jason comes down grumbling that somebody broke one of his bedroom windows in the night. When Quentin fails to answer her morning call Jason unlocks her room and finds that she has disappeared. Rushing back to his own room, he finds that his hoarded savings have also gone. He informs the local police and demands that they search for Quentin. Dilsey takes Benjy to an Easter service and returns inspired by the fundamentalist fervour of the preacher.

Meanwhile Jason, having failed to get satisfaction from the police, hunts for Quentin and the money. He finds the new location of the travelling show, but Quentin and her lover are not there. He returns home in black despair. As he arrives in the town square he is in time to stop the rearing of the horses on Benjy's carriage. Once the noise is stilled and the drive resumed, Benjy relapses into a vacuously happy state.

In an Appendix Faulkner traces the history of the Compson family from its beginnings to the present. He adds several details about the characters in the novel. After being divorced by Herbert Head, Caddy had several more unsuccessful marriages and then became the mistress of a German general. In 1945 Jason at last sold the family home, discharged the servants, sent Benjy to the state asylum and began to succeed as a local tradesman.

CRITICAL COMMENTARY *The Sound and the Fury* was Faulkner's own favourite amongst his novels. 'I have the most tenderness for that book,' he told an audience of students at the University of Nagano. Earlier, in a Preface to the Modern Library edition of *Sanctuary* (1932), he spoke of 'having written my guts into *The Sound and the Fury*'. Modern criticism has concurred with this preference. Today *The Sound and the Fury* is widely acknowledged to be Faulkner's finest achievement – and hence one of the finest achievements of modern American literature.

Yet at the time of the novel's publication in 1929 its critical reception was discouraging; as he confessed in the *Sanctuary* preface, Faulkner 'believed then that I would never be published again. I had stopped thinking of myself in publishing terms.' The most frequently voiced objection was the baffling obscurity of Faulkner's narrative technique. Indeed, when the novel was published as part of Malcolm Cowley's *The Portable Faulkner* in 1946, the editor and publisher persuaded Faulkner to add an Appendix elucidating much of the plot. The author had, after all, a simple enough story to tell. He wanted to recount the traumatic and unhappy lives of the four Compson children – Caddy, Quentin, Jason and Benjy – and suggest the ways in which their separate tragedies echoed the general decline of the old Southern aristocratic families. Why, then, should he break this straightforward family chronicle into a series of cryptic interior monologues that proceed in defiance of the usual conventions of plot, chronology, and even, sometimes, syntax?

Even today, when readers approach Faulkner's work with much greater sympathy and respect than they used to, this question remains valid. Merely to point to the novel's 'classic status' or to murmur complimentary phrases about its 'dazzling technique' is to shirk an important critical issue. In his later life Faulkner proved almost embarrassingly ready to talk about his fiction, and what he said should always be taken with a grain of salt; but his account of how *The Sound and the Fury* germinated in his mind sheds important light on the book's structure. It began as a simple idea for a short story: a group of young children are sent out of the house to play on the evening of their grandmother's death. (This situation, of course, is one of the chief memories that haunt Benjy in the first section of the novel.) To enforce the contrast between the children's innocence and the harshness of adult life Faulkner decided to narrate his story from a child's point of view. He did not develop this situation by incorporating it into a simple linear plot; he circled round and round it, looking at it from different points of view, allowing new depth and meaning to be revealed with each new perspective. First Benjy communes with his memories, then Quentin, and then Jason; finally an impersonal narrator takes up the tale and concentrates on Dilsey's actions.

> And that's how the book grew. That is, I wrote the same story four times. None of them were right, but I had anguished so much that I could not throw any of it away and start over, so I

printed it in four sections. That was not a deliberate *tour de force* at all, the book just grew that way. That I was still trying to tell one story which moved me very much and each time I failed . . .

For all its calculated modesty, this is a lucid description of organic structure. The novel was not built according to a preordained or superimposed pattern: it just 'grew that way'.

Faulkner stressed a sense of failure when talking about the novel but what is more likely to strike the reader is his success in identifying with very different personalities. Benjy, the idiot son of the Compson family, is at once the simplest and the most moving of the characters. His idiocy gives him a quality of total innocence: his very inability to understand or interpret events makes him a strangely accurate reporter. Yet he is so vulnerable as to be almost a sacrificial victim: he is cheated of his land so that Quentin can go to Harvard, gelded and finally committed to the state asylum. Quentin, of course, belongs to a type familiar in modern fiction: the sensitive intellectual trying to come to terms with an oppressive heritage. His life at Harvard makes him progressively discontented with the traditions of the South; yet in his desperate preoccupation with Caddy's virginity he is a walking parody of the strictest Southern notions of honour. Jason, as Faulkner conceded, is the closest thing to the villain of the novel: a cheat, a racist and a family tyrant. But as Jason tells his story he becomes a curiously sympathetic figure. Faulkner does not indulge in moralizing and Jason comes to seem like Quentin or Benjy, a victim of circumstances that he cannot control and can only partially comprehend.

Faulkner took his title for the novel from Macbeth's nihilistic speech about life's futility; and the fate of the Compson family would seem to fulfil this pessimistic note. Yet the decision to add a fourth section to the novel, concentrating on the black servant Dilsey, introduces a note of qualified optimism. Alone amongst the characters in the novel Dilsey retains an ability, not to enjoy life or even to ask much from it, but to survive and help others to survive.

As she goes about her depressing round of chores – gathering firewood, cooking breakfast, comforting the querulous Mrs Compson and the tearful Benjy – Dilsey radiates an atmosphere of warmth and stability. In the final sentence of his 1946 Appendix Faulkner paid a cryptic but moving tribute to Dilsey and her fellow blacks: 'They endured.' In his Nobel Prize speech Faulkner returned, though in more confident and assertive vein, to this notion of endurance. He believed, he said, 'that man will not merely endure: he will prevail . . . because he has a soul, a spirit capable of compassion and sacrifice and endurance.'

As I Lay Dying

SUMMARY   The Bundren family are poor Southern whites, scraping a meagre living from barren farmland. When Addie Bundren, the mother, realizes that she is dying she expresses a wish to be buried in nearby Jefferson, where her family originally lived. Anse, the usually easygoing father, galvanizes his children into complying with the request. But the Bundrens' pilgrimage is hampered by a series of comic and grotesque disasters, and it is nine days before Addie's body is finally laid to rest. This story is told through a series of monologues by the major characters.

Darl and Jewel walk home together through the fields to where their brother Cash is making a coffin with careful and precise craftsmanship. In the kitchen Cora Tull finishes baking some cakes; as she works, she worries about the family economy and consoles herself with religious platitudes. Addie lies in the bedroom listening to the sound of Cash at work. Anse discusses the imminent journey to Jefferson with his sons, and persuades Darl and Jewel to take the wagon out on a last-minute job to raise extra money. This angers Cora, for she knows that Darl would feel guilty if his mother died in his absence.

Anse and Vernon Tull sit outside the house discussing the dying woman. Dr Peabody soon arrives, but Addie dies almost immediately; her last gesture is to raise herself to look at the coffin outside her window. Anse views his wife's body with mixed feelings. He grieves, of course, but he also reflects that Addie's death will allow him to buy the set of false teeth he desperately needs. The youngest son, Vardaman, always strange in his behaviour, is rendered more confused than ever by his mother's death. As the family sit down to a supper cooked by Dewey Dell, a storm blows up.

From her house nearby Cora has seen Dr Peabody visit the Bundrens, so she insists that her husband drive her over. On his arrival Vernon Tull helps Anse and Cash to complete the coffin; they work through the night in lashing rain, with Cash refusing to compromise his impeccable standards of craftsmanship. In the morning the storm subsides, allowing Dr Peabody to leave and Whitfield, a local clergyman, to come to conduct prayers over Addie's body. Darl and Jewel have not yet returned, so the Bundrens settle down to wait for them before embarking on the journey to Jefferson.

They have to wait three days, for Darl and Jewel have been stranded by the storm. The coffin is hastily loaded and the pilgrimage begun. Jewel insists on riding the horse which is his main joy in life rather than join the others in the wagon. The Bundrens soon run into trouble when they find that a bridge has been washed away by the flooded river. They put up for the night in Samson's barn, insisting on staying to watch over the coffin. Samson and his wife Rachel are hospitable at first, but are soon revolted by the smell of Addie's putrefying corpse. The next day the Bundrens attempt to cross the river by a ford, but their wagon is over-turned and can only be recovered with difficulty. Cash breaks his leg in the accident.

The narrative is interrupted by a monologue spoken by the dead Addie. She remembers how Anse courted her and took her from Jefferson to his lonely farm. As the years passed she came to feel more and more estranged from her husband. This monologue is followed by one from the pious and self-righteous Whitfield.

The Bundrens stop at Armstid's farm to give Cash relief from the pain of his broken leg. Anse rides over to a neighbour, Snopes, to buy some new mules. On his return he reluctantly confesses that he has stolen money from Cash and mortgaged Jewel's beloved horse to complete the deal. The Bundrens set off again for Jefferson, followed by a buzzard. As they pass through Mottson they cause a sensation; the townspeople are revolted by the smell of Addie's body. Anse buys some cement and makes a primitive cast for Cash's leg. Meanwhile, unknown to the rest of the family, Dewey Dell is trying to procure an abortion at a local chemist shop. That night the Bundrens again sleep in a barn; there is a fire and the coffin is only just rescued from the flames.

At last they arrive in Jefferson and bury Addie. They realize that Darl, long a sensitive and neurotic youth, started the fire in the barn, and so they arrange for him to be committed to the state asylum. Cash gets his leg, now badly inflamed by the cement cast, treated by Dr Peabody. Dewey Dell goes to a chemist in search of an abortion. The assistant tricks her with worthless medicine and insists that she sleep with him. Anse Bundren goes off mysteriously by himself and then returns to his family with a gramophone, a new set of teeth and a new wife.

CRITICAL COMMENTARY   After the intense and convoluted power of *The Sound and the Fury*, *As I Lay Dying* seems almost a lucid and nonchalant book. It also seems slight where its predecessor was great; but it is the sort of 'slight' novel that only a master of the form could write. Faulkner deploys his usual themes of violence, death, madness and endurance to create not a tragedy but a comedy of the grotesque.

Summarized crudely, the action of *As I Lay Dying* can sound earnest and harrowing. The mother of a family of desperately poor farmers dies and with her dying breath expresses a wish to be buried in her hometown near the graves of her parents. Against all the odds, the family piously carry out this act of homage to their dead relative. One of the sons lovingly fashions a coffin and they then set out on a joint pilgrimage. The journey confronts them with

William Faulkner 291

elemental disasters – the Bundrens literally have to pass through water and fire – before the body of Addie is finally laid to rest.

In practice, however, the reader does not feel that he is witnessing the performance of a timeless and moving ritual. He sees a group of incompetent sub-literates hauling a rotting corpse through the backroads of Mississippi. *As I Lay Dying* is about life's stubborn refusal to fit into those smooth and majestic patterns in which writers delight. The Bundrens continually fail to live up to the grand roles that fate assigns to them. Anse Bundren, left alone to contemplate the body of his wife, finds himself distracted from his grief by the thought that Addie's death makes him able to afford a set of false teeth.

Nor is the pilgrimage to Jefferson the solemn act of piety that it might at first sight appear. In a sense the Bundrens are acting not out of respect for the dead, but out of a desire to exorcise the fractious and assertive spirit of the dead Addie. Moreover, they are roused from their customary lethargy into undertaking the journey for a variety of reasons that range from the bizarre to the pathetic. Anse wants to get his new teeth and (as the family later learn) his new wife. Jewel welcomes the opportunity to ride the horse which is his one interest in life, while Dewey Dell wants to get an abortion.

As the Bundrens proceed on their way, the funeral procession turns into a bizarre travelling circus. They are followed by buzzards, shunned by their neighbours and viewed with disgust when they pass through towns. The Bundrens undergo very real suffering – Cash breaks a leg and Dewey Dell is raped by the Jefferson chemist – but even their agonies have an accidental effect of clownishness. Of all the family only Darl cares deeply about the nominal aim of their pilgrimage, and can comprehend the magnitude of the tragedy in which he is involved. Yet even he has no adequate response to the situation: his knowledge merely drives him to madness and the state asylum.

As is common in Faulkner's fiction, the story is told not

by an impersonal, omniscient narrator but through a series of monologues and soliloquies by the major characters. These range from the passionate and moving speech by Addie about the bitterness of her life with Anse Bundren to the rambling interjections of Vardaman, the idiot son. However, Faulkner's use of this technique is considerably less complex than it had been in *The Sound and the Fury*. The interior life of the characters is rarely complicated (indeed, part of the book's point is how impoverished the Bundrens' emotions are), and the story is never difficult to follow in the way that Benjy Compson's narrative is.

In one respect at least, *As I Lay Dying* is an important indication of the direction which much of Faulkner's later fiction was to take. When he started out as a writer he tended, for obvious personal reasons, to concentrate on the life of the decaying Southern aristocracy. Some of his most memorable families – the Sartorises, the Compsons, the Sutpens – move amidst tattered but still magnificent remnants of past glory; they are haunted by ghosts of the Civil War and the days of slave plantations. But in *As I Lay Dying* Faulkner turned his attention to the poor whites, impoverished farmers scraping a meagre living out of the soil. Such people were to fascinate him more and more, if only because they came to play an increasingly important part in Southern life. In three of his most interesting later novels – *The Hamlet* (1940), *The Town* (1957) and *The Mansion* (1960) – he recounted the fortunes of the Snopes family, a group very like the Bundrens who came finally to supplant the older Southern aristocracy.

Sanctuary

SUMMARY   Walking aimlessly through the Southern country-side, the lawyer Horace Benbow is accosted by Popeye, a shabbily dressed man with a sinister and impassive manner. Popeye forces Benbow to accompany him to Old Frenchman Place, a lonely and dilapidated farmhouse. When Benbow meets Popeye's associates – Lee Goodwin, his mistress Ruby

Lamar, Tommy and a deaf old man – he realizes that they are running an illicit whisky still. After dining with the group, the lawyer gets drunk and confesses that he has recently left his wife and home in Kinston in an attempt to break away from his boring, conventional life. Later that night the kindly Tommy takes Benbow from the farmhouse and arranges for him to get a ride into town.

The next day Benbow visits his great aunt Miss Jenny and his prim sister Narcissa in Jefferson. At their house he also meets Narcissa's latest escort, an arrogant young man named Gowan Stevens. After leaving Narcissa's house Gowan goes to a dance at the local university with Temple Drake, the spoilt and adventurous daughter of a local Judge. Gowan spends the night getting drunk and, when he sees Temple the next morning, insists on driving her out to Goodwin's house to get more moonshine whisky. Temple finds the house and its inhabitants, especially the impassive Popeye, extremely disquieting. When Gowan gets too drunk to leave, Temple has to endure a nerve-racking night in the house; only Ruby's protection stops her being raped by the members of the gang. The next morning Temple awakes to find that Gowan, scared by the atmosphere in the house, has run off and left her stranded. She wanders frantically around the place, looking for a way to escape; but she is cornered and sexually assaulted by Popeye. Shortly afterwards Ruby is alarmed to see Popeye driving away from the house with Temple. Her fears are increased when Goodwin comes in and tells her to contact the local sheriff.

Benbow has now settled in Jefferson, living in the old family house that has been empty for years. The body of Tommy, shot through the head, is brought into the town and Goodwin is charged with the murder. Benbow volunteers to defend Goodwin and, to his sister's annoyance, even thinks of inviting Ruby and her child to stay in his house. Goodwin refuses to say anything to Benbow, assuming that his innocence will be obvious to the court. Ruby finally tells the lawyer about Temple's stay at Old Frenchman Place.

Meanwhile, Popeye has taken Temple to a Memphis

brothel run by Reba Rivers. The girl lies in her room recovering from the loss of her virginity; although obviously horrified by her ordeal she is also strangely passive and acquiescent. Benbow, disgusted by the way Gowan Stevens betrayed Temple, begins a fruitless search for her. At last he gets a clue from the pompous Senator Clarence Snopes, who has visited Rivers' brothel and seen Temple. Benbow visits Memphis and explains the situation to Reba Rivers; she agrees to let the lawyer talk to Temple.

Left alone again in her room Temple decides to escape from Popeye's control. After destroying the rich clothes he has given her she runs out of the house – but is met by Popeye on the doorstep. He takes her to a sinister local nightclub. An associate named Red arrives and Temple draws him aside for a private discussion. It becomes apparent that she is desperately in love with him: she kisses him passionately, warns him that Popeye is planning to kill him, and urges him to run away with her. But Popeye is obviously suspicious and the plan fails. On her return to the dancefloor Temple is hustled out of the club by Popeye's tough hirelings; later that evening Red is shot to death. After Red's extravagant and bizarre funeral Reba Rivers and her friends discuss the matter. Apparently Popeye is impotent and had hired Red to make love to Temple while he watched.

In Jefferson Goodwin's trial for the murder of Tommy opens with a striking success for the defence. Benbow gets Ruby to testify that Popeye and Temple were present at Old Frenchman Place at the time of Tommy's death. The lawyer is jubilant, but his clients are frightened that Popeye will find a way to revenge himself. The next morning Temple appears in court unexpectedly and gives false evidence, attributing Popeye's actions to Goodwin. She alleges that Goodwin killed Tommy and then assaulted her; because he was impotent he used a corncob pipe to violate her. At the end of her testimony Temple is led from the court by her father, Judge Temple. Goodwin is found guilty.

Benbow is badly shaken by the verdict. His sense of horror reaches a climax when, walking aimlessly through the streets of Jefferson that evening, he sees an angry mob take Goodwin from the jail and burn him to death. The lawyer flees to his wife and home in Kinston. Later that year Popeye, on his way to visit his mother, is arrested for the murder of a policeman. He is innocent of the crime, but can hardly produce an alibi, for the policeman had been killed at the very time when Popeye was killing Red. Apparently Popeye's mother had kept a shabby boarding-house after being abandoned by her husband. Her son, a weak child from birth, grew up into a strange and self-contained youth given to uncontrollable outbursts of violence. Throughout his trial Popeye maintains an aloof and superior attitude to the court, hardly deigning to defend himself. He is found guilty and hanged.

CRITICAL COMMENTARY Faulkner himself always spoke of *Sanctuary* as a simple potboiler. It was, he confessed in a preface to the Modern Library edition of 1932, 'a cheap idea . . . deliberately conceived to make money'. At the time he wrote *Sanctuary* he had already published five novels; two of them, *The Sound and the Fury* and *As I Lay Dying*, were obvious masterpieces. Yet his fiction had received little critical attention and had made practically no money: he had been forced to write *As I Lay Dying* in his spare time while working as a boiler attendant at the University of Mississippi. It is hardly surprising that he should have decided to set aside serious literary interests and aim for the bestseller lists. *Sanctuary* fulfilled its commercial goal admirably: it was the first of Faulkner's novels to be a financial success and was later turned into a Hollywood film.

Faulkner adjusted his talents to the marketplace by a series of simple and ruthless decisions. His customary method of telling a story through interior monologues and flashbacks had proved too baffling for literary critics, let alone the readers of bestsellers. So he abandoned such experiments for a straightforward impersonal narrative with an obvious beginning, middle and end. He bastardized his instinctive love of Gothic melodrama and violence into the clichés of the sensational shocker. The story centres on Popeye's rape and corruption of Temple Drake, the innocent college girl. Popeye is made into a sinister psychopathic killer and Temple into an amoral thrill-seeker who seems almost to welcome her progressive depravity. Determined to get as much commercial mileage as possible out of his material, Faulkner manages to incorporate into the plot a Memphis brothel, a gangster funeral, an execution scene and a lynching party.

Inevitably *Sanctuary* has become something of an embarrassment to Faulkner's admirers: in *Writers in Crisis* (1947) Maxwell Geismar calls it Faulkner's 'worst work'. It is, after all, disquieting to see the best American novelist of this century donning the mask of Mickey Spillane. Moreover, the reader of *Sanctuary* is not left with the impression that Faulkner is writing reluctantly, against the grain. Indeed, the novelist seems to be pandering to the vulgarest aspects of his sensibility with cheerful relish. The revelation about the corncob pipe and the reference to Popeye's habit of mutilating animals, for example, merely seem gratuitously nasty. The novel is frequently far more shocking than its commercial purpose requires.

It is obviously not very difficult to build up a damning case against *Sanctuary*. But there are real virtues embedded beneath the book's deliberate commercialism and unintentional vulgarity. Faulkner's career suggests that he, like so many serious modern novelists, was always fascinated by the detective story. During his stay in Hollywood he collaborated on the screenplay of Raymond Chandler's novel *The Big Sleep*, and he published an excellent collection of short detective stories, *Knight's Gambit* (1949). In *Sanctuary* the death of Tommy and the sexual assault on Temple Drake are handled like the central mysteries of a detective novel. In his attempts to defend his client Horace Benbow is drawn unwittingly into the role of detective: unravelling the truth of what happened at Old Frenchman Place, hunting for the missing Temple Drake and pitting himself against the mindless criminal Popeye. This process is skillfully handled: it gives a sense of form and plot to a novel which otherwise seems to jump from one set-piece of horror to another.

Benbow himself is the book's most interesting character. An intellectual lawyer living a domestic life in Kinston, he is moved by obscure motives of guilt and compassion to venture out from his 'sanctuary' into a more complex and violent world. But when Benbow finds himself cast in the role of detective, he also finds that his weapons of goodness and sensitivity are inadequate to resist evil. The book may use the conventional thriller situation of good versus evil, but it comes to some disquieting and unconventional conclusions. Benbow fails in his fumbling attempts to prove Goodwin's innocence and Popeye's guilt; indeed, he has to stand by while his client is burnt to death by a lynch-mob. Popeye, the villain of the piece, is finally caught and hanged; but he dies through a miscarriage of justice as shocking as the one which had killed Goodwin.

Absalom, Absalom!

SUMMARY Quentin Compson (see *The Sound and the Fury*), a young Southerner brought up in Jefferson, Mississippi and now about to leave for Harvard University, is summonsed to visit Rosa Coldfield, an old lonely spinster. When Quentin arrives he finds that, for obscure and complex reasons, Miss Coldfield wants to tell him the story of her family past:

One Sunday morning in 1833, just as the local gentry were going to church, Colonel Thomas Sutpen rode into Jefferson. He was a complete stranger (indeed, nobody could discover any clue to his origins) and was secretive about his present plans. All the townspeople knew was that Sutpen rode a fine horse, carried two pistols and exuded an air of indomitable determination. Shortly afterwards Sutpen bought a nearby plot of land, which he named Sutpen's Hundred, and brought a train of wild Negroes and a French architect into Jefferson. He spent the next two years living rough while the architect and the slaves built a magnificent house on his property. When the mansion was completed but unfurnished, Sutpen moved in and spent several more years leading a solitary life. He then suddenly disappeared from Jefferson, to return with several cartloads of extravagant furnishings. He befriended Goodhue Coldfield, a stern Methodist tradesman, and proposed to his daughter Ellen. But by this time the townspeople were so suspicious and resentful of Sutpen that they organized a posse and arrested him. With Coldfield's help Sutpen was released and went ahead with his marriage to Ellen, though most of the neighbouring gentry refused to attend the ceremony. In the next few years Sutpen had two children, Henry and Judith, by his wife, as well as a mulatto daughter, Clytemnestra (Clytie), by one of his slaves.

Mr Compson, Quentin's father, adds to Rosa Coldfield's account of the Sutpen history:

At the University of Mississippi Henry Sutpen made friends with the elegant Charles Bon and invited him to visit Sutpen's Hundred. Judith and Charles Bon fell in love. Colonel Sutpen opposed the match and Henry, siding with Bon, abjured his birthright. At the outbreak of the Civil War Colonel Sutpen led the local Confederate regiment; Charles and Henry enlisted in a different regiment. When the two young men returned to visit Sutpen's Hundred near the end of the war, Henry shot Charles dead at the gate of the house. Apparently, Charles Bon had been married already and had a son by his Negro wife. Mr Compson believes that this explains why Colonel Sutpen objected to Bon and also why Henry turned so violently against his friend.

Rosa Coldfield takes up the story again, telling Quentin about the fortunes of the Coldfields and the Sutpens during the Civil War:

Ellen Coldfield died, leaving Judith and Clytie alone to manage Sutpen's Hundred. Rosa herself stayed in the town with her father; but he, in disgust at the war, boarded himself up in his room to block out the sight of the wartorn countryside and died of starvation. When Wash Jones, a poor white squatter on Sutpen's land, came to tell Rosa the news of Charles Bon's death she packed her bags and went over to Sutpen's Hundred. She found that Henry had disappeared; Clytie, Judith and Wash Jones buried Bon's body secretly. For the remainder of the war the three women scraped out a meagre existence. When Colonel Sutpen returned from the war he made a brave effort to repair the house and reclaim the ruined plantation. He also proposed to Rosa, but the engagement was broken off a few months later and she returned to her father's old house in Jefferson, where she has lived ever since.

Shortly after his arrival at Harvard Quentin receives a letter from his father bringing the news that Rosa Coldfield is dead. His preoccupation with the Sutpen history leads him to talk to his roommate, Shreve McCannon. (See *The Sound and the Fury*. In the earlier novel Shreve's surname had been given as MacKenzie.) Quentin also adds an account of Thomas Sutpen's later life:

After his effort to reclaim and rebuild Sutpen's Hundred failed Sutpen took to drinking heavily and began an affair with Wash Jones' granddaughter Milly. When he learnt of this, the usually submissive Jones killed Sutpen. After their father's death Judith and Clytie sought out Charles Bon's son, Charles Etienne de Saint Valery Bon, and brought him to live with them. But the young Charles repudiated white society and married a Negress, by whom he had a son, Jim Bond.

Quentin has also learnt from his father some clues about Thomas Sutpen's early life; Sutpen had confided these glimpses of his past to Quentin's grandfather, General Compson:

Born into a poor farming family in the West Virginia mountains, Sutpen had grown up determined to become rich and powerful. He accomplished this by emigrating to the West Indies, where he became a sugar plantation owner. He married Eulalia Bon but repudiated her when he discovered that she had negro blood. Sutpen's son by this marriage was Charles Bon.

Talking late into the night in their Harvard room Quentin and Shreve offer a speculative reconstruction of the history of Bon's life:

Bon was brought up in ignorance of his father's name and sent to the University of Mississippi. Soon after meeting Henry Sutpen, he realized with horror that Henry was his half-brother. He visited Sutpen's Hundred out of a desire to see the father who had so ruthlessly disowned him. But instead of being welcomed, or even recognized, as Sutpen's son he was treated merely as a casual guest. When Bon found himself falling in love with his half-sister Judith, his dilemma increased. At last Thomas Sutpen realized who Bon was, opposed the marriage and explained the grounds of his objection to Henry. Caught between his horror of incest and his uncritical admiration of Bon, Henry spent the years of the Civil War desperately trying to persuade Bon not to marry Judith. When all arguments failed, Henry finally steeled himself to kill his best friend.

At the end of their long and involved conversation Quentin reveals to Shreve the final chapter of the Sutpen saga:

Just before Quentin left for Harvard, Miss Coldfield insisted that he accompany her to Sutpen's Hundred. There in the decaying house they found Henry Sutpen, old and sick, returned home to die near the scene of his crime. Quentin and Miss Coldfield tried to summon medical help but Henry forestalled them by burning the house to the ground, immolating himself in the process.

CRITICAL COMMENTARY Those early readers of Faulkner who had been baffled or irritated by the complexities of *The Sound and the Fury* could take little comfort from *Absalom, Absalom!* The critic Clifton Fadiman wittily expressed a common objection to the novel: 'One may sum up both style and substance by saying that every person in *Absalom, Absalom!* comes to no good end, and they all take a hell of a time coming even that far.' Faulkner's treatment of his subject, Mr Fadiman went on to suggest, 'may be called Anti-Narrative, a set of complex devices used to keep the story from being told'. It is not difficult to see Mr Fadiman's point. At first sight Faulkner appears to have taken a lurid chapter of Southern history and broken it up into a series of baffling cryptograms.

Yet in essence *Absalom, Absalom!* has a very simple subject: a man whose desperate ambition to found a dynasty is defeated by tragic and grotesque ironies. Born into a poor family, Thomas Sutpen sets out with iron determination to become a patriarch and an aristocrat. In the West Indies he almost succeeds. But he discovers that his wife has negro blood, so he abandons his family and goes to Mississippi to start anew. Soon he again has a plantation, a wife and a son. Yet the grand design is shattered by the outbreak of the Civil War and the appearance of Charles Bon at Sutpen's Hundred. A last frantic effort to begin again leads only to a sordid death at the hands of Wash Jones. All Thomas Sutpen has left behind him is a ruined house, a crew of embittered spinsters and a group of enfranchised slaves.

This story fascinated Faulkner because it was, in micro-cosm, the history of the South during the Civil War period – the years when the Southern states were transformed from a grand feudal culture into an embittered backwater. More-over, the events of the novel provide Faulkner with abundant opportunities for those striking images in which his fiction always excels: Sutpen riding into Jefferson with his two pistols and his retinue of wild Negroes, for example, or Goodhue Coldfield boarding himself up in his room to shut out the sight of the Civil War. Out of the figure of Sutpen himself Faulkner creates one of the few convincing tragic heroes in modern literature.

But why does Faulkner not tell his story in its proper chronological sequence? Why does he present it as a bewildering sequence of flashbacks, second- and third-hand memories and conjectural reconstructions? The answer, of course, lies in the fact that *Absalom, Absalom!* is not designed as a historical novel in the conventional sense of the term. In Faulkner's view history is at once remote enough to be almost impossible to reconstruct and close enough to have a pervasive influence on the life of the present. Thomas Sutpen, for all his failure to establish a dynasty, left a complex legacy for future generations, a landscape 'peopled with garrulous outraged baffled ghosts'. *Absalom, Absalom!* takes as its subject Thomas Sutpen the ghost as well as Thomas Sutpen the man.

At the beginning of the book Rosa Coldfield tells the young Quentin Compson the story of her past relations with Sutpen. She never offers an adequate explanation of her motives, but it is soon clear to the reader that Miss Coldfield is making a final attempt to exorcise the memory of a man whom she certainly hated and probably also loved. Quentin himself quickly ceases to be a passive listener and becomes an actor in the drama himself. Like a detective, he probes and hunts for information about the Sutpen family, gleaning memories from his father and working out hypotheses with his room-mate Shreve McCannon.

For Shreve these conversations are largely an academic exercise. Born in Canada, knowing and caring little about the South, he can view the Sutpens with the detachment of an anthropologist. Their grotesque antics confirm his impression that Southerners are a strange breed, and he is content to draw the most flippant of morals from the story: 'So it takes two niggers to get rid of one Sutpen, dont it?' But for Quentin this excavation of the past has a very different significance: it is ultimately an attempt to come to terms with his Southern heritage and hence with himself. Such quests do not have neat and simple endings. At the novel's conclusion Quentin is left with the ghost of Thomas Sutpen more vivid than ever in his mind, and with his ambivalent feelings about his native land not resolved but intensified. Shreve asks him: 'Why do you hate the South?'

'I dont hate it,' Quentin said, quickly, at once, immediately;
'I dont hate it,' he said. *I dont hate it* he thought, panting in the cold air, the iron New England dark; *I dont. I dont! I dont hate it! I dont hate it!*

FURTHER READING The standard account of the novelist's
life is Joseph Blotner's two-volume *Faulkner: A Biography*
(1974). *Faulkner in the University: Class Conferences at the
University of Virginia, 1957–1958* (1959), by F. L. Gwynn and
Joseph Blotner, contains many valuable and some dangerously misleading remarks by Faulkner himself about his
own work. F. J. Hoffman and O. W. Vickery have edited a
useful anthology of early criticism, *William Faulkner: Two
Decades of Criticism* (1951; revised as *Three Decades of Criticism*
in 1960). The volume includes essays by Sartre, F. R. Leavis,
Malcolm Cowley and Robert Penn Warren. Alfred Kazin's
On Native Grounds (1942) and Maxwell Geismar's *Writers in
Crisis* (1947) both contain useful sections on Faulkner's
fiction. The best general studies are by Irving Howe (1952)
and Cleanth Brooks (1963).

John Steinbeck

John Steinbeck (1902–1968) was born and brought up in
Salinas, California. He attended Stanford University
between 1919 and 1925 but on the whole his education was
unconventional. He worked at a variety of menial jobs:
ranch hand, trainee carpenter, painter, labourer and
chemist. This experience of working-class life, together with
his commitment to California, established the characteristic
tone of his fiction. His fourth book, *Tortilla Flat* (1935), won
him a popularity which rarely deserted him throughout his
career. It was followed by *In Dubious Battle* (1936), about
California fruit pickers, the tragic *Of Mice and Men* (1937)
and a volume of short stories, *The Long Valley* (1938). His
most famous work of these years, however, was *The Grapes
of Wrath* (1939), a grim but moving saga of displaced
Oklahoma farmers during the Depression.

Steinbeck's subsequent career was less fruitful and his
later work less widely praised. He tried to extend his range
as a writer beyond his early preoccupation with the life of
California's rural workers. He wrote a war novel, *The Moon*

is Down (1942), an account of marine life, *The Sea of Cortez* (with Edward F. Ricketts, 1941), and several books of journalism. Later he published a comic novel, *The Short Reign of Pippin IV* (1957), and a novel about New England, *The Winter of Our Discontent* (1961). But when he returned to his earlier subjects in *Cannery Row* (1944), *The Wayward Bus* (1947) and *East of Eden* (1952), critics were quick to note a decline in power. In 1962, also the year he published *Travels with Charley in Search of America*, Steinbeck was given the Nobel Prize.

The award of this prize was unfortunate, for over-praise is one of the quickest ways of provoking criticism. Steinbeck's fiction has continued to be popular with general readers in both England and America, but amongst academics and intellectuals it now enjoys very little reputation indeed. Steinbeck's sentimentality, his simplistic view of social problems and his lack of technical sophistication are stressed. All these criticisms are true, especially of the later work, but they distract attention from the very real merits of his early fiction. In an age when so many Americans have turned away from their native country as a source of inspiration, Steinbeck is an important exception. A commitment to his native California, especially to its rural poor, shines through his best work. Moreover, he has always avoided fashionable experimentation and cultivated the traditional arts of narrative. The result is an exact and topical realism, given a timeless quality by its presentation of human suffering and human dignity.

Of Mice and Men

SUMMARY After a hard day walking in the California sun George and Lennie stop to rest by a shaded pool. Inseparable companions for many years, they are both itinerant farm workers, poorly paid, and little better than tramps. George is a small, alert man, while his friend Lennie is large and muscular but mentally defective. For all his strength Lennie is very gentle, and as he sits by the pool he begins to fondle a pet mouse. George takes the mouse away and scolds his friend: Lennie should not have pets since he always manages to kill them accidentally.

They light a fire and eat a simple supper of beans. George grumbles that Lennie is just a burden to him, losing him jobs and preventing him from living a decent life. Apparently the pair have just been forced to leave a nearby town because Lennie was accused of assaulting a girl. Lennie is contrite and the two are soon reconciled. George entertains them by telling a familiar story of the life they one day plan to lead: they will buy a small plot of land and settle down as smallholders.

The next morning George and Lennie arrive at a ranch where they can get work. Candy, an old man, shows them to the poorly furnished bunk house where the workers live. When the owner appears George tries to do all the talking, lest Lennie's idiocy create a bad impression. Curley, the nervous and arrogant son of the owner, arrives and begins baiting Lennie; George intervenes and stops trouble developing. He plays cards with Candy and learns that Curley recently married a pretty but flirtatious girl. Curley's wife enters and greets the newcomers with self-conscious coquetry. George warns Lennie to avoid both Curley and his wife.

George becomes friendly with Slim, a quiet, shrewd man known to be an expert worker. When Slim learns of Lennie's fondness for animals he gives him a puppy; the big man is delighted. George talks freely to Slim about his relationship with Lennie, even mentioning the accusation of assault. By this time Lennie has won the respect of the other hands by his strength and dedication as a worker. Candy, the janitor of the hut, brings in his old dog. Carlson, one of the farmhands, insists that the animal is too weak to be of use and should be put down. Candy is too timid to protest and watches helplessly as the dog is taken out and shot.

Candy asks to be included in George's scheme of becoming a smallholder. The old man is desperately scared that he will outlive his use, like his dog, and be sacked. George and Lennie readily agree when they learn that Candy could contribute his savings, three hundred dollars, to the price of the land.

Curley lives in a state of continual suspicion that his wife is playing him false. One day he enters the hut and sees a foolish grin on Lennie's face. Assuming this to be mockery, Curley flies into a rage and attacks the big man. Lennie seizes his opponent's hand and crushes it in his own massive fist. Slim is appalled at Lennie's violence, but is quick-witted enough to make the half-conscious Curley agree to say that his hand was hurt in an accident with a machine.

One day when most of the other workers are in the nearby town Lennie visits the harness room where Crook, the Negro stablehand, lives. Crook is not allowed in the main bunk house and leads a lonely, embittered life. He is far from pleased at the visit, but Lennie's innocent idiocy overcomes his hostility. The two chat casually and Lennie mentions the scheme for buying a smallholding. Candy comes in and Crook jeers at them for being unrealistic; he claims that all farmhands dream of owning land but none ever succeed. Curley's wife enters and treats Crook with insolent disdain.

Lennie has accidentally killed the puppy given him by Slim. He sits in the barn debating whether or not to hide the corpse and worrying that George will not let him tend the rabbits on their smallholding. Curley's wife joins him and begins to talk freely about herself. She used to cherish dreams of becoming a film star and only married Curley in a rash moment; now she has grown to hate and despise her husband. She flirts with Lennie, inviting him to stroke her hair. His response frightens her and, in his clumsy attempts to stop her screaming, Lennie kills her. He runs away in panic, leaving the body lying in the hay.

Candy and George find the body and reluctantly agree that a search for Lennie should be organized. Curley, how-ever, tries to turn it into a lynching party: he brandishes his gun and vows that he will shoot Lennie on sight. George slips away and finds Lennie in some nearby brush. As the big man dreamily talks about the smallholding they will own one day, George takes out a revolver and kills him.

Curley is exultant at Lennie's death but George, who simply committed the deed to save his friend from further suffering, walks sadly back to the ranch with Slim.

CRITICAL COMMENTARY Despite its brevity Steinbeck's *Of Mice and Men* is not a slight work. Since its first publication in 1937 it has established itself as a minor classic. To some readers, indeed, it has seemed more satisfying than some of Steinbeck's more ambitious but more flawed work, novels like *The Grapes of Wrath* and *The Winter of Our Discontent*. The reasons for its success are not difficult to see. In his portrayal of George and Lennie Steinbeck treats the lives of poor and inarticulate people with compassion; as the story of their friendship and its violent end unfolds, the two ranchhands are invested with tragic dignity. This story, moreover, is told in an appropriately simple and straightforward manner. The narrative is allowed to develop to its climax – George's merciful killing of Lennie – without extraneous action or description. One can easily see how Steinbeck was able to convert the novel into a successful play.

Many of the book's virtues are those of naturalistic fiction, the style of writing pioneered at the turn of the century by Dreiser and Norris. Like them, Steinbeck rejects the assumption that novels should deal with the affluent and the articulate. He shows a familiarity with the life of the working classes which owes something to personal experience, for he himself worked as a California labourer in his youth. In *McTeague*, a crucial novel in the development of naturalism, Frank Norris had made his hero stupid and brutish. Steinbeck takes this interest to its logical extreme by making one of his main characters, Lennie, mentally defective.

Moreover, Steinbeck has the naturalist's passionate interest in social justice. He was profoundly influenced by the Depression, which drew attention to existing social problems as well as creating new ones, and this concern always finds expression in his writings. In *Of Mice and Men* he stresses the desperate insecurity of the ranchhands' lives and the hopelessness of their ambition to possess land of their own. He even contrives to give in passing a telling vignette of racial prejudice. Crook's enforced isolation from the rest of the hands is not treated at any great length, but it shows an awareness of racial tension unusual in the fiction of the 1930s.

At the same time, however, Steinbeck's interest continually moves beyond the somewhat narrow confines of naturalistic fiction. That school too often restricted itself to showing the effects of a particular milieu on individual lives: it gave little sense of those universal emotions found in all societies. It is just these experiences that interest Steinbeck in *Of Mice and Men*. One notes, for example, the stress on private dreams and fantasies. George and Lennie compensate for the insecurity of their lives by elaborate but unrealistic plans of buying their own smallholding. This cherished fantasy is embellished with minute detail – Lennie is forever thinking about the rabbits he would tend on the farm – and repeated to each other at night like a soothing bedtime story. This dream captivates Candy as well and even, however briefly, the cynical Crook.

At root the main theme of the story is the oldest and most universal source of tragedy: man's inevitable isolation from his fellows. Crook and Candy are both desperately lonely; even Curley's wife seems to be yearning for a sense of companionship to ease the tedium of her life. The friendship of George and Lennie is thus a rare and special achievement in a world of solitaries. Slim remarks on it as a curiosity, for itinerant workers usually travel alone. Yet despite this celebration of the love and understanding that exists between the two friends, the end of the novel again asserts man's ultimate loneliness. Even the sincerest attempts to make contact with other people can fail: poor Lennie, approaching all living things with warm affection, is fated to harm them. He accidentally kills his pets and then, by the same blundering, suffocates Curley's wife. In the final scene George is brought to understand a lesson that the killing of Candy's dog had earlier suggested: for all his kind intentions, man still has to act with apparent callousness towards his fellows.

George kills his best friend, not out of anger or malice but out of a desire to save him from further suffering.

Despite its status as a classic, *Of Mice and Men* has not escaped criticism. Some readers have found it deliberately sentimental. In *On Native Grounds* (1942) Alfred Kazin, who is far from unappreciative of Steinbeck's merits, suggests that the story of Lennie and George does not attain the grandeur of real tragedy: its tone is rather of an obvious pathos, a too calculated 'ambush of the heartstrings'. He also feels that the deliberate simplicity of style militates against the seriousness of its themes. Lennie and George, for example, need to be fully realized as complex individuals, and yet they remain merely cartoon figures. It is difficult not to admit the justice of these strictures, but they should not distract attention from the book's merits – its vivid portrayal of American ranch life, and its preoccupation with some of the oldest tragic themes of literature.

The Grapes of Wrath

SUMMARY When Tom Joad is released from prison he heads back to his family's farm in Oklahoma. On the way he meets Jim Casy, a young man who used to be a revivalist preacher but has lost his faith. The two arrive to find the Joad farm deserted. In recent years many of the small farmers have been evicted by the local banks, who realize that farming can only be made profitable if it is conducted on a large scale. Muley Graves comes along and tells Tom that his family are staying with their Uncle John several miles away. They plan to go to California, attracted by stories of the state's fertile land and high wages. Muley's own family have already migrated west but he has refused to leave. He stubbornly stays near his old farm, resisting the new owners' attempts to drive him away.

The next morning Tom and Casy walk to Uncle John's farm. There they find the elder Tom Joad (Pa) tinkering with his old van and Ma indoors cooking. Tom also greets Grandma and Grandpa, his brothers Noah, Al and young

Winfield, his sisters Ruthie and Rose of Sharon, and Rose's husband Connie. The family are preparing for departure – selling their farm equipment, loading the lorry, killing the pig and salting meat for the journey. Casy asks to join the journey and the Joads agree.

The Joads' van joins the steady stream of migrant traffic – dispossessed farmers and unemployed labourers – on the long road to California. At their first camping place they meet the Wilsons, a friendly couple from Kansas. Grandpa dies of a stroke and the Joads, unable to afford a proper funeral but too proud to apply for a pauper burial, simply bury the body by the roadside. Al works on with Wilsons' car to make it run better and the two groups travel together. As they go they console themselves with dreams of the luxurious life that awaits them in California. Ma gradually supplants Pa as head of the family, desperately striving to preserve its unity under the stresses of travel. At the next campsite the Joads meet a man returning from California. Hungry and emaciated, he warns the migrants that farm-workers are badly paid and cruelly exploited in California.

The long journey continues, with travel eventually becoming a permanent way of life. The migrants begin to feel a sense of community with each other, and laws and customs spontaneously develop. At last the Joads cross into California. Their joy is curtailed when they meet more dis-illusioned farmworkers returning east. Noah, always a strange and silent man, suddenly announces that he will go no further: he plans to stay by the river and fish. A police-man appears and tells the Joads to move on, treating them with contempt. Sairy Wilson is too ill to move, so she and her husband are left behind.

After a gruelling drive through the desert the family at last sees the fertile fruit-growing valleys. But Grandma died during the journey and this time the Joads have to apply for a pauper burial. They then join the immigrant popula-tion of dispossessed farmers, at once hated and exploited by the wealthy local landowners. When a man arrives at the campsite offering work, a young man named Floyd protests at the pitifully low wages. A deputy sheriff threatens to arrest Floyd but the young man fights back. Surprisingly, the usually quiet Jim Casy joins the brawl and knocks the lawman out. Casy is arrested when police reinforcements arrive. As rumours that the locals are planning to attack the campsite grow, the Joads move out. Connie deserts the family.

They go to a Government camp, whose comfortable conditions and relaxed atmosphere help them regain a sense of dignity. Yet none of the family except Tom is able to find work, and their savings dwindle even further. The committee of immigrants who administer the camp hear rumours of a plan to break up their Saturday-night dance. Most of the locals resent the camp: they plan to infiltrate the dance, start a fight to give the police an excuse to move in and make arrests. The immigrants band together and foil this plot; on the night of the dance they manage to spot the infiltrators and eject them before any trouble starts.

The Joads reluctantly leave and head north in search of work. Finally they are hired to pick peaches. But the pay is low and the family soon realize that they have been employed as blackleg labour. To his surprise Tom learns that the leader of the peach-pickers' strike is Jim Casy, now out of jail. The two friends talk and Tom learns that Casy has now entirely abandoned Christianity in favour of radicalism. Their conversation is abruptly ended when the pickets are attacked by a group of local vigilantes wielding pick handles. Casy is killed in the scuffle and Tom, maddened with anger, lashes out blindly at one of his attackers.

The next day Tom learns that his victim is dead and that a police hunt has started. Under cover of night the Joads leave and get work further north picking cotton. Tom hides in a nearby wood, supplied with food by the other members of the family. After a while he tires of hiding and decides to take up the political crusade that Casy had started.

The Joad family is now much depleted, despite all Ma's efforts to keep it together: only Pa, Ma, Al, Ruthie, Winfield and the pregnant Rose of Sharon are left. Al gets engaged to

Aggie Wainwright and drifts away from the family. The rain and cold weather come and the seasonal labour disappears. The immigrants are reduced to desperation. They live in waterlogged tents, falling ill of fever and malnutrition; to support themselves they have to beg or steal.

Rose, once healthy and active, is already feverish and emaciated when she goes into labour. Her baby is stillborn. The family abandons its waterlogged car and walks through the sodden countryside in search of shelter. At last they find a barn whose only inhabitants are a young boy and his father. The man has not eaten for a week and will obviously die of starvation unless he is helped immediately. Rose bravely decides to nurse him at her breast.

CRITICAL COMMENTARY Published in 1939, John Steinbeck's *The Grapes of Wrath* is one of the classic documents of the Depression. It belongs with the early paintings of the American artist Ben Shahn and the 'Dust Bowl Ballads' of the folksinger Woody Guthrie. Steinbeck's description of the Joads' frustrated pilgrimage across America from the barren farmland of Oklahoma to the fruit orchards of California captures the mood of a whole chapter in American history. He aims to convey the harsh realities of the Depression not just by facts and objective descriptions but by an imaginative reconstruction which convinces and moves the reader. He shows how an almost endless accumulation of suffering changes the Joads' initial puzzlement to discontent, from discontent to hopelessness, and from hopelessness to that terrible wrath mentioned in the book's title: an angry certainty of the injustice of the system that has pauperized and enslaved them. The result is, with little doubt, Steinbeck's finest achievement, an epic account which can still move the modern reader.

Despite its concern for a particular historical moment, the novel uses a traditional device of American fiction. Like those classics of the nineteenth century, Melville's *Moby Dick* and Twain's *Huckleberry Finn*, *The Grapes of Wrath* is about a journey. In fact (as Steinbeck obviously felt) the idea of the journey is central to American culture. After all, the country was originally colonized as a result of the Pilgrim Fathers' voyage across the Atlantic, and its frontiers were expanded by those great moves westward in the nineteenth century.

The Joads' enforced pilgrimage from Oklahoma to California is an ironic recapitulation of these earlier American journeys. Like the original settlers, the Joads uproot themselves to escape tyranny and go off in search of a better land. It is a blind, reflex action, like the lonely pilgrimage of the turtle which Tom sees near the beginning of the book. The Joads' entry into California is reminiscent of the Israelites' arrival in the Promised Land. They go through a desert and a river (like the Jordan) in which they stop to cleanse themselves of the dust of travel. Yet the effect of these allusions to the Bible is ironic, for California is anything but the Promised Land. Despite the fertility of the country itself, the state is already corrupt and tyrannical. The present settlers – landowners, shopkeepers and policemen – have a hypocritical attitude towards the immigrants. On the one hand they abuse people like the Joads by calling them 'Okies'; on the other hand they are only too willing to exploit their labour as much as possible.

Steinbeck's fiction usually describes its characters from the outside rather than delving into the subtleties of individual psychology. The epic scope of *The Grapes of Wrath* accentuates this tendency to make his people into types rather than individuals. The Joad family are presented as emblems of suffering humanity, modern types of the Everyman of medieval morality drama. Their reactions to events are always simple – anger, discontent, hopelessness – and spring from universal causes.

Grandma and Grandpa represent the older generation of Oklahoma farmers, steeped in local tradition and deeply rooted in the land they have cultivated. Their death on the road to California suggests how travel divorces the Joad family from its settled customs and traditions. The birth of Rose of Sharon's dead baby makes a similar point: cut off from their past, the Joads do not have any real future in the

Californian system. Meanwhile, the fate of the adult members of the Joad family shows other tensions. Noah, Connie, Al and Tom have all disappeared by the end of the book; only Ma, Pa, Ruthie, Winfield and Rose are left. Ma, who gradually takes over the role of leader from the dispirited Pa, resists this break-up fiercely. To her, the family itself is the only stable value left in a changing world. But even this cannot be preserved.

The characterization of Jim Casy shows in an extreme form Steinbeck's tendency to present people as types. On the surface, Casy is simply a predictable product of his times. Trained as a preacher in that evangelical tradition peculiar to rural America, Casy finds that his faith fails him. Witnessing the suffering of his fellow men on the route to California, he develops a new faith – this time a political one. He becomes a radical activist, organizing strikes against the tyrannical bosses. He dies, but Tom Joad takes over the crusade. Jim Casy is also conceived as a modern Christ-figure. His initials are 'J.C.' and he dies paraphrasing the words of Christ on the cross: 'You don' know what you're a-doin'.' In the modern age, Steinbeck implies, Christ would have turned to political activism in the service of mankind.

But what of Steinbeck's own political views? He obviously shares Casy's and Tom's belief in union organization as the solution to the immigrants' problems. But apart from this, Steinbeck s attitudes seem traditional – very like the inherited values of the Okie farmers themselves, in fact. He dislikes machines, as his moving description of the tractor raping the Joads' land makes clear, and feels farming should be the product of a harmonious relationship between man and the soil. He is suspicious of large abstract organizations, like the banks that take over the small farmers' land at the opening of the book. He prefers small units of people: communities like the Government camp, the wayside camp-sites and, above all, the family. His code of belief, in fact, is humanistic and humanitarian. It is based on the insistence that people are more important than things. The flesh-and-blood needs of the dispossessed Okie farmers are more important than banks, profit margins, or abstract theories of economy.

FURTHER READING There is little important secondary material about John Steinbeck. He died too recently for the academic work on editions and biographies to have begun, while he remains too unfashionable to provoke many useful articles. The progress of his reputation is charted by E. W. Tedlock, Jr and C. V. Wicker in *Steinbeck and His Critics: A Record of Twenty-Five Years* (1957). Harry T. Moore's *The Novels of John Steinbeck* (1939) is a useful early estimate. Peter Lisca (1958), Warren French (1961) and F. W. Watt (1962) have contributed more recent studies. The paperback edition of his works is published by Pan.

Norman Mailer

Brought up in Brooklyn and educated at Harvard, Norman Mailer (born 1923) served with the American Army in the Pacific during the Second World War. This experience provided the basis for his first (and still most famous) novel, *The Naked and the Dead* (1948). The book's frank sexual descriptions and its use of 'obscene' language earned it a temporary *succès de scandale*; but it has also gained a lasting reputation as the most important novel to emerge from the last war. It was a hard novel for a young writer to follow up, and it may have been inevitable that his next two novels, *Barbary Shore* (1951) and *The Deer Park* (1955), should have been found disappointing by critics and reviewers. Perhaps because of these reverses Mailer temporarily abandoned fiction, returning to the genre only recently to write *An American Dream* (1965) and *Why Are We in Vietnam?* (1967). His main energies have been devoted to non-fictional essays and journalism, and in this area he has produced at least two masterpieces: *The Presidential Papers of Norman Mailer* (1963), a collection of essays nominally addressed to President Kennedy, and *The Armies of the Night* (1968), an account of the 1967 Pentagon march in protest against the Vietnam war.

Together with Allen Ginsberg, Norman Mailer is now America's prime example of the artist as ebullient and rebellious public figure; in Walter Allen's phrase he has become 'the voice of what might be called the permanent opposition in America'. His turbulent private life has received wide publicity, and he makes frequent lecture and television appearances pronouncing on a large range of topical issues. Like many modern writers Mailer has obviously realized that, in his life as well as his work, the artist needs to communicate with his audience through a variety of masks. In *The Armies of the Night*, commenting on one of his television appearances, he writes with typical self-irony about his many public images:

> For a warrior, presumptive general, ex-political candidate,
> embattled aging enfant terrible of the literary world, wise father
> of six children, radical intellectual, existential philosopher,
> hard-working author, champion of obscenity, husband of four
> battling sweet wives, amiable bar drinker, and much
> exaggerated street fighter, party giver, hostess insulter – he had
> on screen . . . a fatal taint, a last remaining speck of the one
> personality he found absolutely insupportable – the nice Jewish
> boy from Brooklyn.

The main impulse behind Mailer's writing can be summed up by the title of a poem by his friend and contemporary Robert Lowell: 'We Are Here to Preserve Disorder'. Mailer is fascinated by the heterogeneity of his own country; he is forever analysing its different ethnic groups and regional types. At times, like Walt Whitman before him, he seems to be trying to subsume all the contradictions of America into his own literary personality. Thus, for example, in his *Presidential Papers* he undertakes to explain the significance of Floyd Patterson the heavyweight boxer to President Kennedy, and in *The Armies of the Night* he identifies with the police and National Guard as well as with the protestors. Probably no other living writer gives the reader so vivid an impression of the turbulence and vitality of contemporary America.

The Naked and the Dead

SUMMARY During the Second World War a regiment of American troops under the command of Major General Cummings is sent to capture the Pacific island of Anopopei from the Japanese. The night before their arrival the atmosphere on the troop ship is tense. The members of Sergeant Croft's squad alternate between boredom and anxiety. Wilson and Gallagher play a desultory game of poker with the Sergeant, while Red wanders sleeplessly around the deck. Sergeant Brown talks with Stanley, an ambitious young GI anxious for promotion. Sergeant Julio Martinez, the squad's Mexican scout, lies in his bunk sweating with fear.

Shortly before dawn the naval bombardment of the island begins. Croft, a tough professional soldier who delights in combat and killing, briefs his men and leads them into the landing vessels. As they approach the shore the Sergeant watches the youthful and nervous Hennessey and wonders if the man will be killed in the forthcoming fight. After landing, the troops dig themselves into foxholes and wait nervously, venting their tensions in petty quarrelling. When the Japanese mount a mortar attack Hennessey loses his nerve and is killed as he runs frantically along the beach.

During the next few days the troops push forward into the interior of Anopopei; the jungle, which continually separates the various companies, poses greater problems than the Japanese. Cummings conducts the advance in a leisurely fashion, building roads and creating supply lines as he goes, for he realizes that the Japanese are reserving their strength for a later battle. Croft, who is working on a beach detail, is angered at the poor quality of the new men added to his squad: Wyman, Roth and Goldstein are all nervous and inexperienced soldiers. In the officers' mess Lieutenant Hearn, a liberal-minded young Harvard graduate, is disgusted by the coarseness and conservatism of his fellow officers, Hobart, Dalleson and Conn. He insults Conn and is only saved from an embarrassing incident by the intervention of Cummings, whose favourite he is.

By now the American soldiers are close to the Japanese General Toyaku's lines. In Croft's squad the tensions have increased: Red, Wilson and Gallagher are resentful of being asked to work with Jews like Roth and Goldstein, and also of the fact that Stanley has been promoted to Corporal. During a heavy rainstorm the Japanese mount an attack and Cummings counters with his usual dexterity. Croft's squad is sent into action, hauling heavy guns along slippery roads and through dense undergrowth. They meet the Japanese troops near a river; Croft, with his delight in killing, marshals his men into repelling the attack.

Despite his guilt and uneasiness in the role of officer, Hearn is drawn into an increasingly intimate relationship with Cummings; he is attracted by his superior's intelligence but repelled by his cold and arrogant conservatism. Meanwhile, Croft's squad encounters a group of Japanese during a patrol. The Sergeant kills all except one with a well-aimed hand grenade and then, despite Gallagher's protests, shoots the survivor in cold blood. The men get drunk on illicit whisky and stumble through the jungle in search of souvenirs from Japanese corpses. Shortly afterwards the mail boat arrives and Gallagher learns that his wife has died in childbirth.

Cummings watches the American advance grinding to a halt and vents his frustration by bullying and humiliating his former favourite, Hearn. At last the General works out a new strategy: he will send a reconaissance patrol round the south side of the island to attack the enemy from behind, while a major frontal assault is initiated. Croft's squad is chosen for the task and Hearn is put in command. Hearn has mixed feelings, pleasure at being away from Cummings and anxiety about the danger of the mission; Croft is annoyed at no longer being in command of the squad. The men are scared by the thought of the combat to come.

When they land on the south side of the island the men are at first awed by the beauty of the scenery, but they are soon tired and irritated by the difficulties of forcing a path through the jungle. Their tempers fray, while Hearn and Croft jostle for effective command over the squad. On the second day of their mission, they start out already enervated by the heat and quickly fall into a Japanese ambush. In the confusion they retreat without realizing that Wilson has been left behind wounded. Croft heads a party to rescue him and then deputes Brown, Stanley, Goldstein and Ridges to take the wounded man back to the beach. Brown, whose nerves have begun to break, is desperately anxious to fulfill his task properly.

Hearn feels the mission should be abandoned but Croft is in favour of continuing. They send Martinez out during the night to look for Japanese patrols; but although the scout sees large numbers of the enemy (indeed, he has to kill a Japanese soldier), Croft persuades him to conceal this from Hearn. When the squad advances the next morning Hearn is killed by a Japanese sniper. Against growing protests Croft insists that the squad continue to advance; he forces the tired and dispirited soldiers to climb over difficult mountainous terrain. The group with Wilson meet similar difficulties: Stanley and Brown collapse with fatigue, leaving Ridges and Goldstein to carry the wounded man.

Cummings has temporarily left the island to get naval support for his attack. In his absence the unimaginative Dalleson feels nervous and unselfconfident. To his surprise, however, he finds that the American assault meets with little resistance; by the time the General returns the operation is virtually complete. In the jubilation at the victory the fate of Croft's squad is forgotten.

Wilson dies during the journey to the beach and his body is washed away in a flooded river. Ridges and Goldstein, once antagonistic but now made intimate by their mutual ordeal, stumble on to the shore to await the boat which will collect them. Croft still tries to get his squad to push ahead. Red tries to rebel against the orders but is cowed when the

Sergeant threatens to shoot him. Soon afterwards the men stumble into a hornets' nest; they panic and begin to retreat. Croft realizes that he cannot persuade them to return again, and allows them to make their way to the beach, where they are picked up by the navy.

CRITICAL COMMENTARY   It used to be a critical commonplace that the Second World War, unlike the First, had produced little or no important literature. But this judgement now needs revision. English readers can point to Evelyn Waugh's *Sword of Honour* trilogy (1952–1961), Richard Hughes' *The Fox in the Attic* (1961) and the relevant volumes of Anthony Powell's *roman à fleuve*, *The Music of Time* (1951–1975). In America the war inspired at least three major novels: Joseph Heller's *Catch-22* (1961), Kurt Vonnegut Jr's *Slaughterhouse-Five* (1969) and Mailer's *The Naked and the Dead*.

Of this American trio *The Naked and the Dead* is the earliest and probably the best. It is also significantly different in tone from its successors. *Catch-22* and *Slaughterhouse-Five* are both 'anti-war' novels, albeit of an extremely sophisticated sort. Heller and Vonnegut write out of personal bitterness and personal suffering, using irony and satire to deride the stupidity of military bureaucracy and the larger lunacy of war itself. While Mailer is obviously neither sentimental nor idealistic about war, his writing lacks this undercurrent of protest and satire. He is fascinated by military strategy in a way that is entirely alien to Heller and Vonnegut. The book is prefaced by a map of the imaginary island of Anopopei and Mailer's descriptions of the battles strike a note of exciting reportage rather than ironic discontent. (In this respect, Mailer is showing in his first novel those journalistic skills that he later put to very different use in his account of the Pentagon march in *The Armies of the Night* and the Chicago riots in *Miami and the Siege of Chicago* [1968].) He also shows a lurking respect for the old military virtues: courage and endurance. Throughout the novel, in fact, Mailer reveals a spiritual kinship with Hemingway's *A Farewell to Arms*; and Mailer's essays on literature frequently refer to Hemingway's work with great respect.

At the time of *The Naked and the Dead*'s first appearance critical debate centred not on Mailer's attitude to war but on his use of obscenity – that is, his frank reproduction of the troops' conversation. Despite its utter lack of eroticism the book enjoyed a vogue as a pornographic classic. In *Miami and the Siege of Chicago* Mailer describes a meeting with a policeman who remarked happily about *The Naked and the Dead*: 'Brother, does *that* have bad language in it.' The novel also entered that long and distinguished list of modern classics which puritans have wished to ban or suppress, a list that includes Joyce's *Ulysses*, Lawrence's *Lady Chatterley's Lover*, Dreiser's *An American Tragedy* and Nabokov's *Lolita*. In defence Mailer could cite the realist's obvious justification: that is how real-life soldiers talk. No doubt he also enjoyed shocking his public. But in *The Armies of the Night* he produces a central statement about his attitude to 'bad language':

> There was no villainy in obscenity for him, just – paradoxically, characteristically – his love for America. . . . He had come to love what editorial writers were fond of calling the democratic principle with its faith in the common man. He found that principle and that man in the Army, but what none of the editorial writers ever mentioned was that that noble common man was obscene as an old goat, and his obscenity was what saved him. The sanity of said common democratic man was in his humour, his humour was in his obscenity.

This passage also points to one of the driving forces behind *The Naked and the Dead*: Mailer's love of American culture, in its sordid and everyday as well as its picturesque and noble aspects. At the heart of the book's achievement is Mailer's ability to sympathize with – and hence to create from within – entirely different types of American people. The nervous Jew Goldstein, the intelligent and power-hungry General Cummings, the pious and stolid Ridges – all these are depicted with vivid understanding. Particularly successful, of course, is the portrait of Hearn, the young Harvard liberal who finds his beliefs wavering in the face of Cummings' persuasive conservatism. Taken as a whole, *The Naked and the Dead* presents a statement not so much about the Second World War as about the tensions and conflicts of American society. In a recent review the critic Nat Hentoff hailed Mailer as 'the best writer in America'; this is a bold declaration, but surely few readers would disagree if Mr Hentoff had said that Mailer is 'the best writer *about* America'.

J. D. Salinger

At one point in *The Catcher in the Rye* Holden Caulfield remarks: 'What really knocks me out is a book that, when you're all done reading it, you wish the author that wrote it was a terrific friend of yours and you could call him up on the phone whenever you felt like it.' J. D. Salinger himself obviously does not share this attitude. In an age and country where writers delight in making extravagant public appearances – 'wearing funny hats', to use James Dickey's phrase – he has lived a deliberately reclusive life. No photos or biographical details appear on the dustjackets of his books, and he has consistently refused to be interviewed or to let his works be reprinted in anthologies. He recently defended this policy of reticence: 'It is my rather subversive opinion that a writer's feelings of anonymity-obscurity are the second-most valuable property on loan to him during his working years.' Virtually all that is known about Salinger's life is that he was born in New York in 1919 of a Jewish father and Irish mother, and now lives in New Hampshire with his second wife and two children.

Yet even without the usual paraphernalia of personal publicity Salinger's prominence has been assured since the appearance of his first (and still his only full-length) novel, *The Catcher in the Rye*, in 1951. With its distaste for the blandness and 'phoniness' of urban middle-class culture the novel perfectly caught the mood of young Americans of the day. High-school and college students idolized and imitated

Holden Caulfield much as their earlier counterparts had aped Hemingway's Jake Barnes or Scott Fitzgerald's Blanche Amory.

Subsequently Salinger published *Nine Stories* (sometimes titled *For Esmé – with Love and Squalor*; 1953). Since then he has been working on what he calls 'a narrative series . . . about a family of settlers in twentieth-century New York, the Glasses.' Any echoes of Galsworthy's Forsyte saga that this description may conjure up are entirely misleading. Salinger's narrative of the Glass family has so far been confined to a handful of cryptic and tantalizing fragments. Seymour Glass, the eldest child, is described on the day of his suicide in 'A Perfect Day for Bananafish' in *Nine Stories*. Other members of the family appear in *Franny and Zooey* (1961), and *Raise High the Roof Beam, Carpenters* and *Seymour: An Introduction* (1963), a total of four long short stories originally published in the *New Yorker*. Their theme is essentially an expansion of the basic situation of *The Catcher in the Rye*: the effort of the sensitive and intelligent individual to come to terms with the complacent ad-mass culture that surrounds him. That quality of sensitive innocence which Holden Caulfield retained beneath his rebellious mannerisms has developed into a note of religious mysticism.

At the moment Salinger's critical reputation varies wildly: he has been hailed as a great novelist and dismissed as a passing fad. *The Catcher in the Rye* is viewed by some as an established classic and by others as a dated piece of sentimentality. Salinger's later work has been greeted as the fertile preliminaries to some future masterpiece along the lines of Proust's *À la Recherche du Temps Perdu* and cited as evidence of a dwindling and fading talent.

The Catcher in the Rye

SUMMARY Holden Caulfield is a sixteen-year-old American boy, cynical and rebellious but deeply sensitive. He is expelled from Pencey Prep, the exclusive school to which his parents have sent him, for his failure to work. One Saturday he returns early from an abortive fencing match (he managed to lose all the team's equipment on the underground), and stands in the school grounds trying to inculcate a sense of sadness about leaving. He then goes to say goodbye to his history teacher, Mr Spencer, who is ill at home. The interview is embarrassing, for Mr Spencer is anxious to justify himself for failing Holden in his history exams; he insists on rehearsing the boy's mistakes. Holden gets increasingly annoyed and takes advantage of the earliest opportunity to leave.

He goes to his room and reads until he is interrupted by Ackley, an insensitive youth who lives in the same dormitory. They are joined by Stradlater, Holden's handsome and good-natured room-mate. Stradlater is going out on a date that evening and wants Holden to write an English composition for him. Holden agrees but is jealous when he learns that Stradlater is going out with Jane Gallagher, a girl whom he himself had almost fallen in love with the previous summer. After a desultory evening in the nearby town Holden returns to his room and writes Stradlater's composition. He finds himself thinking of Allie, his young brother who died several years before. When Stradlater comes back Holden's jealousy about Jane Gallagher returns: he provokes a fight which he loses badly.

On impulse he decides to run away from school without waiting for the end of term. He takes the train to New York, travelling part of the way with the mother of one of his classmates; he tells her extravagant and untrue stories about how popular her son is. On arrival in New York he checks in at a hotel, rather than going to his parents' flat to tell them about his expulsion. He is annoyed that it is too late at night to phone his younger sister Phoebe.

He spends a restless night. In the bar he is refused alcohol because of his age and flirts unsuccessfully with a group of girls from out of town. In his room he finds himself thinking about Jane Gallagher again and resolves to go out. He pays a brief lonely visit to a nightclub. Back at the hotel he is accosted by the liftman, who offers to send a prostitute to his room. Holden accepts but when the girl, Sunny, arrives he does not feel like sleeping with her. She is puzzled and angered, even though he insists on paying. Left alone, he sits in bed smoking and brooding until the liftman and Sunny return to extort more money from him. Holden objects but the man hits him and rifles his wallet. Holden goes to bed miserably.

In the morning he phones to make a date with Sally Hayes; he does not like the girl much, but is lonely and desperate for company. He breakfasts near Grand Central station. During the meal he falls into conversation with two nuns and, on a sudden impulse, insists on giving them a charitable donation from his own dwindling reserve of money. He goes over to Broadway to buy theatre tickets for his date with Sally and a record for his sister Phoebe. He wanders around Central Park on the off-chance of meeting his sister, but is unlucky.

Despite his mixed feelings about Sally, he is pleased to see her at the theatre that afternoon. During the interval, however, she is joined by a sophisticated young college boy and Holden gets increasingly annoyed at their affectedly intellectual conversation. When the play is over he takes Sally skating. As they drink coffee afterwards he launches into an inarticulate tirade against conventional people. He ends up by proposing that she run away and live with him in the country. When she will not take his suggestion seriously, they quarrel and part in anger. Holden goes to a bar to meet an old school friend, Carl Luce, an intelligent but supercilious young man. He is angered by Luce's air of amused condescension and starts another quarrel. He sits in the bar alone getting drunk, before making an incoherent apologetic phone call to Sally. Wandering around Central Park he drops the record that he had bought for Phoebe.

Anxious to see his sister, Holden takes the risk of creeping into his parents' flat. Phoebe is awake and tells him that his parents are out for the evening. They chat together, and Holden feels relaxed and cheered by her company. He phones Mr Antolini, a former English teacher, and makes arrangements to stay the night at his house. Holden's parents return unexpectedly but he is able to sneak out of the flat unseen. Antolini and his wife greet him sympathetically, but the teacher warns Holden that he is a dangerously confused and directionless young boy. In the middle of the night Holden wakes to find Antolini stroking his hair. Assuming the man to be making a homosexual advance, he storms out of the house angrily and spends the rest of the night in the waiting room of Grand Central station.

The next morning he walks through the city feeling tired, hung-over and nervous. At last he resolves to leave and seek some rural hideaway where he can live in peace and quiet. But before departing he wants to say goodbye to Phoebe, so he leaves a note at her school asking her to lunch with him. When she hears of his plan she is desperately insistent on being allowed to come as well. To placate her Holden takes Phoebe to the zoo; for all his confusion and anxiety he still finds a strange pleasure in her company.

In a brief concluding chapter Holden gives a summary account of the end to his weekend as a runaway. He finally goes back to his parents and is sent to a psychiatric hospital. There he is visited by his elder brother, D.B., once a promising novelist but now a Hollywood scriptwriter.

CRITICAL COMMENTARY 'The central and controlling image of recent fiction is that of the rebel-victim.' Few American novels bear out Ihab Hassan's generalization more strikingly than *The Catcher in the Rye*. Salinger transforms an apparently simple account of a high-school dropout's weekend excursion in New York into a poignant expression of modern alienation. For all his confused immaturity Holden Caulfield is an ideal iconoclast: he rejects the simple-minded *esprit de corps* of Pencey Prep, the classic American success story embodied in his brother's career as a Hollywood scriptwriter and the pseudo-intellectualism of chic middle-class New Yorkers.

Holden's witty and cynical impiety does not stem from

either rational thought or simple bloody-mindedness. It is the result of an honest sensitivity – a type of holy innocence that recurs as one of the central values in Salinger's later fiction. Holden's absolute refusal to accept the 'phoney' so alienates him from the established way of life that he can identify only with the oddballs and losers. He sympathizes with the prostitute who comes to his hotel room and even with the pimp who beats him up. He admires the childlike vulnerability and wisdom of Phoebe and obviously more than half envies his dead brother, Allie. Unable to envisage any place for himself in society (the most he can manage is an extravagant fantasy about a cabin in the woods) he becomes society's victim. His only refuge, as the novel's closing pages reveal, is the mental hospital.

From this account it is obvious that Holden Caulfield is a twentieth-century version of those loner heroes so beloved by American novelists. Most critics have been struck by the parallels with Twain's *Huckleberry Finn* in particular. In each case a young boy narrates, in conversational idiom, his flight from society. Holden, of course, flees into the heart of New York rather than the world of nature. But even in the city he dreams that familiar dream which has so long haunted the American imagination – the simple country life ennobled by honest manual labour and the joys of romantic love.

Yet at the time when *The Catcher in the Rye* first appeared readers were struck more by its topicality than its traditionality. It was linked with other rebellious works of the 1950s like Kingsley Amis' *Lucky Jim* and John Osborne's *Look Back in Anger*. Psychologists found in *The Catcher in the Rye* an embodiment of Erik Erikson's theory of the adolescent 'identity crisis', while sociologists saw it as an illustration of David Reisman's conception of American society as a 'lonely crowd'. On a simpler level, millions of young people recognized in Holden Caulfield an image of themselves. The book became a cult. As Lawrence Lipton has testified in *The Holy Barbarians* (1960), it exerted a crucial influence on the Beat

Generation. (In this connection it is interesting to note that Salinger, like the Beats, has subsequently trod the path toward mystical religion.)

The book's very pertinence as a sign of its times has tended to obscure the question of its literary value. Viewed as a work of art, rather than a social or psychological document, *The Catcher in the Rye* raises considerable problems. It is, of course, a superb technical feat. Its rendition of New York life is a triumph of realistic observation: the atmosphere of shabby hotels or of Central Park on a winter day is brilliantly conveyed. Moreover, Salinger shows a mastery of Holden's rhythm and idiom of speech that can at times rival Twain's use of Huck Finn as narrator. Yet the very invocation of *Huckleberry Finn* serves to underline the weaknesses of *The Catcher in the Rye*. The essence of Twain's achievement is that, while appearing to reproduce the artless narrative of a fourteen-year-old boy, he in fact manages to establish a mature and detached attitude to his hero. Salinger, by contrast, seems to identify almost completely with Holden; the result is a book which often shares the immaturities of its hero.

Some critics have been troubled by the novel's streak of sentimentality and morbidity. Holden Caulfield's compassion for other people – one can see it in his encounter with the nuns in Grand Central station – and his innocent love of his sister can be genuinely moving. Yet the total effect is exaggerated; as Alfred Kazin has complained, it is 'too obviously touching'. In a similar fashion, Holden's almost obsessive preoccupation with his dead brother is presented without critical detachment. In fact, Frank Kermode suggests that the novel has a 'built-in death wish'. Other readers have felt that the book asks them to accept Holden on his own evaluation as the last sensitive person alive. The portraits of the insensitive adults are very convincing; but is it really credible that in all his wanderings Holden should encounter nobody, whether peer or adult, who is intelligently sympathetic towards his problems? As Philip Roth has pointed out, this note of spiritual elitism has come to sound increasingly loud in Salinger's work: 'this place and time is seen as unworthy of those few precious people who have been set down in it only to be maddened and destroyed.'

Ralph Ellison

Unlike so much black fiction, *Invisible Man* is not an autobiography. While his hero is a Southerner, Ellison himself was born and raised in the state of Oklahoma. Between 1933 and 1936 he trained as a musician at the Tuskagee Institute; although he later devoted most of his energies to writing, his interest in music, especially jazz, has continued throughout his life.

In 1952 he published *Invisible Man*, a novel he had been working on for five years. The book was instantly and widely acclaimed; it won the National Book Award, an honour rarely given to a first novel. He has also written many short stories, reviews and articles, a number of which are included in the collection *Shadow and Act* (1964). In recent years Ellison has lectured at several American universities.

Invisible Man has become a classic of modern American fiction because of its intrinsic merit: its author is a superb craftsman. But the book also interests readers for historical and sociological reasons, since Ellison represents one of many possible responses to being a black man, and in particular a black writer, in America today. Earlier black writers often hoped for complete assimilation between the races, and recent novelists like Leroi Jones advocate complete separation of the black and white man. Ellison has occupied a middle position, defining his cultural heritage as a combination of experiences peculiar to the black man and experiences common to all Americans; he argues that it is important for both to be preserved and respected. Similarly, while Ellison's predecessors frequently did not write about their race at all and Ellison's successors have tended to concentrate exclusively on the plight of blacks, Ellison himself is interested in relating his own dilemma to that of all Americans.

Invisible Man

SUMMARY The 'Invisible Man' (his name is never revealed) is living in a coal cellar illuminated by 1,369 bulbs; he is draining off the power from Monopolated Light & Power without paying for it. He has a fantasy, which includes hearing a sermon by a black preacher and talking about freedom with an old woman. He recounts the story of his life:

His grandfather, who had been subservient and respectful all his life, declares on his deathbed: 'our life is a war and I have been a traitor all my born days . . . I want you to overcome 'em with yeses.' The hero is disturbed and puzzled by the old man's words. He delivers a speech at his high school graduation ceremony and is invited to speak again at a smoker of the town's leading white citizens. A naked blonde dances at the occasion; the black boys who have been invited are threatened if they do look at her and threatened if they do not. The boys are blindfolded and commanded to box with each other. They are thrown coins as payment; but the carpet on which the coins lie is electrically wired, so that they receive shocks when picking up the money. Later the gold coins prove to be fake. The hero delivers his speech. Although he temporarily upsets his listeners by saying 'equality' when he had intended to say 'responsibility', the speech is considered a success, and at its conclusion he is given a scholarship to the local college for blacks.

The students at the college are passive and respectful; in particular, they worship the man who started the college, known as The Founder. The president of the college, Dr Bledsoe, acts equally respectfully to whites. The hero is chosen to escort a white benefactor, Mr Norton, during one of his visits to the campus. He takes him to a section of town where the poorest blacks live in dilapidated shacks; Mr Norton is appalled when he meets a man who has slept with his own daughter. They then go into a sleazy local bar, the Golden Day, where they encounter a group of lunatics, including one ('The Vet') who delivers incoherent but ominous pronouncements to Mr Norton and the hero.

Dr Bledsoe tells the hero he must withdraw temporarily from the college because he has upset Mr Norton by showing him the seamy side of black life; the college president gives the young man letters of recommendation which, he says, will help him to find a job. The invisible man leaves the college for New York; on the train he again encounters The Vet, who delivers more cryptic warnings and prophesies.

The hero cannot find a job in New York. Finally Mr Emerson, the son of a man to whom one of the letters was addressed, reveals that Dr Bledsoe has betrayed the invisible man: rather than recommending him for a job, the letters criticize him sharply and state that he will never be allowed to return to the college. He begins to work in a paint factory. His work is supervised by Lucius Brockway, who runs the furnaces; Brockway hates the union that is being formed and distrusts the young man because he fears he is a member of it. In fact, the invisible man stumbles into a union meeting by mistake but discovers that some of its members in turn distrust him because he works with Brockway. The invisible man is involved in a serious accident in the furnace room and loses consciousness. He is sent to the factory hospital, where he has a series of fantasies of being destroyed.

Friendless and ill, he meets Mary, a motherly woman who cares for him. He is stirred by seeing an eviction into delivering a speech; because of his eloquence, he is befriended by a Marxist group, the Brotherhood, and becomes a member of it. He studies ideology with Brother Hambro. The group is in conflict with Ras the Exhorter, a black nationalist. Internal tensions and jealousies also divide the Brotherhood; the hero is opposed to Brother Wrestrum. His assignment is changed from Harlem to another area of New York. He sleeps with a woman he meets at one of his lectures.

The invisible man sees Tod Clifton, a former member of the Brotherhood, selling puppets of comic black figures. Clifton resists arrest and is shot by the police. The hero mobilizes a protest in Harlem about the shooting; this action is, however, sharply criticized by the Brotherhood. Because he is a member of that group, he is threatened by followers of Ras. He puts on sunglasses and finds that in this disguise he is repeatedly mistaken for Rinehart, a black whose many roles include gambler, preacher, and lover. Disillusioned with the Brotherhood, he remains a member but begins to trick them; for example, he lies about the work he is organizing. Attempting to start an affair with Sybil, the wife of one of the party leaders, he finds that she has pathetic sexual fantasies about black men.

On the evening he is with Sybil, a riot starts in Harlem. He encounters Ras, and they again fight. To escape the chaos of the riot, the hero descends into a manhole; in order to see, he must burn the contents of his briefcase, which contains many mementoes of his past. His life in the cellar begins. On one of his excursions into the outside world, he encounters the white philanthropist Mr Norton, who does not recognize him.

CRITICAL COMMENTARY In the speech he delivered when accepting the National Book Award, Ralph Ellison explained: 'After the usual apprenticeship of imitation and seeking with delight to examine my experience through the discipline of the novel, I became gradually aware that the forms of so many of the works which impressed me were too restricted to convey the experience which I knew.' These words help us to understand the peculiar power of *Invisible Man*: the book reflects Ellison's experimentation with the techniques of modern fiction as well as his appreciation of the achievements of more conventional novels.

The most successful of his experiments are the passages of fantasy. The hero's surrealistic visions in the prologue and final chapter of the book and the sequence in the factory hospital are particularly moving. They are charged with the horror of nightmare.

The clearest sign of the influence of the traditional novel on Ellison's work is its central theme: like so many classic works in English and American literature it is a *Bildungs-roman*, the study of the development of a young man. Like other writers in this tradition, Ellison is interested in his hero's attempts to define his identity. While many modern novels are formless, Ellison relies on a careful structure: he himself describes the book as following a three-part division – the hero moves from purpose to passion to perception – and suggests that he planned further subdivisions in its structure as well. The novel is also unified by a number of parallel incidents, notably the speeches that its hero delivers at various points of his development.

Another sign of the author's craftsmanship is his carefully developed patterns of imagery. Throughout the novel Ellison plays off images of darkness and blindness on the one hand and light and vision on the other. For instance, at the beginning of the book its hero is blind to his own plight and the injustices around him; fittingly enough, he is literally blindfolded during the smoking room scene. The limited vision of his political allies is aptly symbolized by the fact that one of them has a glass eye. One sign of the insight he has achieved by the end of the book is that he is living in a room illuminated by 1,369 lights. A related series of images concern whiteness and blackness; for instance, it is no accident that the hero, a victim of a society that seeks to deny or destroy his identity, works in a factory that prides itself on producing sparkling white paint.

The central symbol, of course, is invisibility. Significantly, we are never told the hero's name. He is invisible in that both blacks and whites ignore his individuality, fitting him into their stereotypes. Later in the book, he consciously assumes and profits from his invisibility. He changes his identity several times; at one point, he trades on the fact that he is mistaken for Rinehart, a black man who himself changes rapidly from one identity to another. As the critic Ellin Horowitz observes, the hero's invisibility is like Hamlet's madness: it is both a plight and a device.

The symbols of the book are as complex and ambiguous as the events it describes. For example, at the end of the book the hero is living in a coal cellar, though one illuminated by all the bulbs. To some extent this is a sign of his defeat: he has literally sunk as low as he can go. Yet it also appears to be a sign of his victory. Is the cellar a fertile retreat, not unlike the pastoral world in so many American novels, from which the hero will emerge reborn? It is even possible to see the cellar in Freudian terms, as a womb, or in mythic terms, as a magical underground world. (Both the novel itself and Ellison's commentaries on it indicate his deep interest in myth.)

As all the images of light and blackness remind us, on one level *Invisible Man* is a book about the experience of being black in America and, indeed, it is one of the most powerful books yet written on this theme. Many of the people in the novel represent different identities that a black man can adopt, different identities that the hero considers – its characters range from passive blacks like the college students to the rabid black nationalist, Ras the Exhorter.

But, like *Herzog*, the novel transcends the local and ethnic and concentrates on problems shared by modern men of all races. The hero's coal cellar is an apt symbol of the isolation of the individual in an impersonal city. And his search for identity has broad implications; as Irvine Howe observes, Ellison is 'deeply concerned with the fate of freedom in a mass society'. In fact, the book ends on the query: 'Who knows but that, on the lower frequencies, I speak for you?'

Saul Bellow

Born in Canada of Russian Jewish parents, Saul Bellow (born 1915) spent most of his youth in Chicago – a city whose atmosphere permeates much of his fiction. After briefly enrolling at the University of Chicago Bellow became dissatisfied with its traditional syllabus, and went on to take a degree in sociology and anthropology at Northwestern University. Like many contemporary American writers, he has held a variety of academic posts.

In *Tradition and Dream* (1964) the critic Walter Allen suggests that Bellow's early fiction shows a marked dichotomy: he 'sometimes seems to be two writers, one introvert, the other extrovert.' *Dangling Man* (1944) and *The Victim* (1947) are both introverted novels; in a claustrophobic and sometimes surreal manner, they deal with the private anxieties of modern urban man. In the first novel the hero lives in limbo while awaiting induction into the Army, while in the second he is the victim of antisemitism. *Seize the Day* (1956) returns to this mode, but in *The Adventures of Augie March* (1953) and *Henderson the Rain King* (1959) Bellow reveals a new dimension to his talents. Both are loose and free-wheeling, abundant in movement and picaresque comedy; *Henderson*, in particular, moves into a realm of extravagant comic fantasy.

These works established Bellow as the most important of that generation of postwar Jewish novelists who were becoming increasingly prominent in the American literary scene. After the appearance of *Seize the Day* the influential critic Leslie Fiedler pronounced: 'Saul Bellow has become not merely a writer with whom it is possible to come to terms, but one with whom it is *necessary* to come to terms – perhaps of all our novelists the one we need most to understand, if we are to understand what the novel is doing at the moment.' This judgement was handsomely confirmed with the publication of *Herzog* in 1964. The novel was greeted with a hailstorm of superlatives from the reviewers; more than a decade later it still looks like one of the most substantial achievements of modern fiction.

The essence of Bellow's success lies in his reconciliation of his two earlier modes, the introverted and the extroverted. The story of Moses E. Herzog – the failed, confused, half-crazy academic – combines rich comic invention with a deep understanding of the dilemma of the modern intellectual. The result is a tragicomedy that lies close to the nerve-centre of modern anxieties. Taken by itself, it goes a long way towards justifying Tony Tanner's description of Bellow as 'perhaps, the most sheerly intelligent of post-war novelists'.

Bellow has subsequently published a collection of short stories: *Mosby's Memoirs* (1969), a work of non-fiction: *To Jerusalem and Back: A Personal Account* (1976), and two novels: *Mr Sammler's Planet* (1970) and *Humboldt's Gift* (1975). In 1976 he was awarded the Nobel Prize for Literature.

Herzog

SUMMARY Moses E. Herzog is a middle-aged Jewish intellectual, twice married with a child by each marriage, and with a distinguished academic career which he has recently abandoned. He now lives alone in a crumbling country house in Western Massachusetts, spending most of his time composing letters, which he never posts, to friends, relatives, enemies, dead philosophers and writers. He is fully aware that the world would think him mad, but in himself he feels curiously peaceful and happy.

Herzog's habit of compulsive letter-writing began the previous year just after his divorce from his second wife Madeleine, when he was working in New York as an adult education lecturer. His behaviour becomes progressively erratic, his teaching progressively absentminded, and it is soon obvious that he is near mental breakdown. He is having an affair with an ex-student, the sensual and charming Ramona Donsell, and she sympathetically suggests that he take a holiday with her to relax. But Herzog, scared that Ramona wants to trap him into marriage, decides instead to visit his friends Libbie and Arnold Sissler in Martha's Vineyard. After buying some fashionable summer clothes, Herzog sets out on the journey. As he travels he writes innumerable letters in his head and bitterly reviews his chaotic relationship with Madeleine. On their marriage, Madeleine, an aggressive but charming Radcliffe graduate, persuaded Herzog to abandon his teaching job in Chicago and buy the country house in Massachusetts; he planned to complete a new book while she finished her graduate degree. They soon became friendly with Valentine Gersbach, an extrovert intellectual and poet, and his wife Phoebe. It was a long time before Herzog realized that Madeleine and Valentine were having an affair: indeed, when the news was broken to him by his old friend Lucas Asphalter, it came as a complete shock. On his way to Martha's Vineyard Herzog composes eccentric and turbulent letters to his lawyers Simkin and Sandor Himmelstein and his psychiatrist Dr Edvig.

As soon as he arrives at Martha's Vineyard Herzog realizes that the visit is a mistake and returns to New York. Alone in his apartment he worries about his son Marco, by his first wife Daisy, and June, the daughter of his second marriage. He also affectionately remembers Sono, his mistress before his marriage to Madeleine. He finsd himself thinking of his childhood: his father was a Russian Jewish immigrant whose career in America was a failure. But most of all Herzog is obsessed by thoughts of Madeleine: he remembers her short-lived conversion to Catholicism and their unstable life together in Massachusetts.

Ramona telephones to invite him to dinner and Herzog accepts with some reluctance; on the way he is still writing letters to friends, public figures and philosophers, in his head. However, Ramona's voluptuous sexuality and kindness relax him. His depression returns the next day. He telephones his lawyer Simkin to inquire about the chances of obtaining custody of his daughter June. He visits a New York courthouse and is further depressed to witness a succession of petty and sordid criminal cases.

On impulse he decides to go to Chicago, where Madeleine and Valentine now live. He visits his stepmother Tante Taube and takes an old pistol belonging to his dead father – the very pistol with which Father Herzog once threatened to shoot his son. Herzog drives to Madeleine's house in a rented car, intending to murder her and Valentine. But as soon as he peeps at them through a window, his resolve fails him. He spends the night in Chicago with Asphalter. With Asphalter's help Herzog arranges to meet June the next day. The occasion begins well with a visit to the local aquarium but ends in disaster when Herzog is involved in a minor motor accident. The police discover his father's pistol and book him for carrying an unlicensed weapon. When she is summoned to the police station Madeleine attempts to blacken her ex-husband's character; but Herzog's brother Will, an estate agent, manages to secure bail. Will also insists that Herzog see a doctor, who recommends rest.

Herzog returns to the house in Western Massachusetts and lives surrounded by dirt and decay. His brother Will visits him to give a professional opinion on the property, which Herzog is thinking of selling, and tries unsuccessfully to persuade his brother to enter a psychiatric hospital. Ramona phones to invite herself to dinner. Herzog hires Mrs Tuttle, the wife of a local garage proprietor, to help clean the house and prepare the meal. As he listens to the sound of Mrs Tuttle at work, Herzog suddenly feels relaxed and at peace; he no longer has the urge to write letters to anybody.

CRITICAL COMMENTARY 'If I am out of my mind, it's all right with me, thought Moses Herzog.' From the opening sentence of *Herzog* Bellow establishes a distinctive tone of voice which blends wry sadness, sober contemplation and wild humour. He emerges as the master of an idiom which can snatch moments of comedy from the most tragic situations and discover what remains noble or moving beneath the slap-stick comedy. Although it is never a mere linguistic *tour de force*, the achievement of *Herzog* is based on a subtle and inventive use of language – what Leslie Fiedler (discussing *Seize the Day*) has called Bellow's 'rich, crazy poetry, a juxtaposition of high and low style, elegance and slang'. The author has clearly taken Joyce as his model; it is perhaps in oblique acknowledgement of his debt that he chose to name his hero after one of the minor characters in *Ulysses*.

Bellow called his first novel *Dangling Man*; *Herzog* could well have been called *Drowning Man*. As Herzog himself puts it with typical self-irony, he has risen from humble origins to being a complete disaster. In early middle age he can review a life whose keynote is messy failure. In religious

beyond his talents and powers, but this was the cruel difficulty
of a man who had strong impulses, even faith, but lacked clear
ideas. What if he failed? Did that really mean that there was no
faithfulness, no generosity, no sacred quality? Should he have
been a plain, unambitious Herzog? No.

Index